D0233474

821.914
PAD

52 WAYS OF LOOKING AT A POEM
Or How Reading Modern Poetry
Can Change Your Life

CANCELLED

By the same author

Poetry

Summer Snow
Angel
Fusewire
Rembrandt Would Have Loved You
Voodoo Shop

Non Fiction

In and Out of the Mind
Whom Gods Destroy
I'm a Man

RUTH PADEL

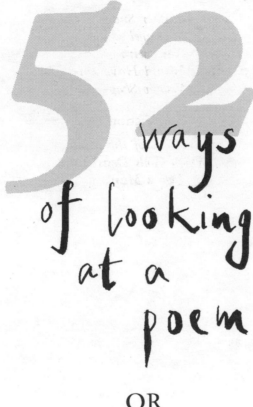

52 ways

of looking

at a

poem

OR

How Reading Modern Poetry
Can Change Your Life

Chatto & Windus
LONDON

Published by Chatto & Windus 2002

2 4 6 8 10 9 7 5 3 1

Copyright © Ruth Padel, 2002

Ruth Padel has asserted her right under the Copyright,
Designs and Patents Act 1988 to be identified as
the author of this work

This book is sold subject to the condition that it shall not,
by way of trade or otherwise, be lent, resold, hired out,
or otherwise circulated without the publisher's prior
consent in any form of binding or cover other than that
in which it is published and without a similar condition
including this condition being imposed on the
subsequent purchaser

First published in Great Britain in 2002 by
Chatto & Windus
Random House, 20 Vauxhaull Bridge Road,
London SW1V 2SA

Random House Australia (Pty) Limited
20 Alfred Street, Milsons Point, Sydney,
New South Wales 2061, Australia

Random House New Zealand Limited
18 Poland Road, Glenfield,
Auckland 10, New Zealand

Random House South Africa (Pty) Limited
Endulini, 5A Jubilee Road, Parktown 2193, South Africa

The Random House Group Limited Reg. No. 954009

A CIP catalogue record for this book
is available from the British Library

ISBN 0 7011 7318 1

Papers used by Random House are natural,
recyclable products made from wood grown in sustainable forests.
The manufacturing processes conform to the environmental
regulations of the country of origin.

Typeset by Deltatype, Birkenhead, Merseyside
Printed and bound in Great Britain by
Mackays of Chatham PLC

FALKIRK COUNCIL LIBRARIES

821.914 PAD GM

For Gwen at sixteen
with love and admiration

and huge thanks and love to Suzi, Maggie and Nicola

ACKNOWLEDGEMENTS

For criticism, comments and suggestions on various versions, passages of essay, and glossary, many thanks to Richard Askwith, Neil Astley, Gillian Beer, Suzi Feay, Elaine Feinstein, Lavinia Greenlaw, Blake Morrison, Andrew Motion, Sean O'Brien, Christopher Reid, Patsy Rodenburg, Jo Shapcott, George Schopflin, Matthew Sweeney and Boyd Tonkin. Idiocies remaining are entirely mine. For providing last-minute texts of poems, enormous gratitude to that unique, endlessly helpful resource, the Poetry Library on Level 5 of the Festival Hall in London's South Bank.

Many thanks also to readers of 'The Sunday Poem' who wrote to me or to the *Independent on Sunday*. After a while I could not answer all the letters but I was very grateful to get them. You are the people for whom this book is written. You showed me how poetry is needed and read. I couldn't include all the poems from the column; many poems you wrote in about are not here, I'm sorry. But I hope you enjoy meeting again those that are.

Thanks to Boyd Tonkin for suggesting the idea, and Suzi Feay who made it reality, helped the column develop, fought (I suspect) for it, and took a risk no one else would have taken. And heartfelt thanks to Maggie O'Farrell and Nicola Smyth, who worked on the proofs of each piece meticulously with so much patience, knowledge, tact and skill.

Many warm thanks to Alison Samuel for her enthusiasm and my editor Rebecca Carter for her insightful restructuring, encouragement, detailed editing and patience.

And thanks, above all, to the poets: those whose poems happen not to be in this selection (the names will always make me flinch) as well as those whose are. In 'The Sunday Poem' I was very lucky to explore the craft and depth of what they all made, and see the impact of it on readers. I'm grateful to them for making the garden; and glad to carry on with them in it under thunder, rain and the odd patch of sun.

CONTENTS

INTRODUCTION: THE BRITISH POETRY RENAISSANCE AND 'THE SUNDAY POEM'

Reader Power

We are in the middle of a large-scale renaissance of poetry in Britain today. It began in the late seventies and is still going strong. Never, even in the most glamorous eras of English poetry, like the Elizabethan or Victorian, have so many published poets been developing new ways of saying things to people in so many different parts of society. Supported by radio producers and arts administrators all over the country, poets are reaching out to new audiences. 'Poems on the Underground' has been slipping poems into advertising spaces on the London tube since 1986. The poems are much loved, and the idea has been copied on public transport around the world, from Dublin and Vienna to Helsinki, St Petersburg, Oslo and Moscow. Poetry festivals have burst out all over Britain, from Aldeburgh to King's Lynn, Ledbury to Huddersfield. Everywhere, poetry societies both feed and speak to a real appetite for poetry in Britain today, running workshops, competitions, readings. British poets are constantly travelling to read. Recently, I did readings in Peterborough, Poole, Suffolk, the New Forest and Cornwall within the space of ten days: not a tour, just where readings happened to come up. Poetry is active all the time, all over the country.

But poetry activity is localised around poetry societies dependent on local arts councils and the patronage and energy of local poetry lovers; the scale of public interest in poetry is not reflected in the British media. People who live outside poetry hotspots or do not know about them, but who want to find out what poetry can offer, may not know where to start. Poetry's very richness and variety, the number of books of poems in the bookshops, are a barrier. Faced with heaps of books, all carrying puffs on the back saying how great they are, how can you know which one is worth anything to *you*, if you don't know the names – of not just the authors, but the people who say they are so wonderful?

In 1998 the idea came to me of writing a newspaper column that would print a modern poem and add my own way of reading it. Would one poet sharing how she read another's work be a useful way to introduce people to the poems they were missing out on?

I asked Suzi Feay, books editor of the *Independent on Sunday*, if

1

she'd like a weekly article discussing a contemporary poem. She loved the idea and said yes at once. No other paper had anything like it. This was a big recommendation for her, but also meant she had no idea how readers would respond. What she did know is that she would first have to sell the idea to senior editorial colleagues, who were not exactly poetry lovers.

Every centimetre of a newspaper has to sell. Did readers really want to see such an unsexy thing as a poem undergoing that even unsexier thing: in-depth analysis? Advertisements fund the pages they appear in. How much advertising would extended literary analysis bring in?

We decided to do six pieces and see how they went. I would pick very short poems, by people whose names some readers would recognise. They had to be in print in Britain, so that readers could follow them up. I would use poems only by living poets, to make the point that poems are being written now, for readers living now. The point was the poem, not the poet: there would be no media hype of personalities. I was not grading poets and any 'premier league' mentality was out. This was purely about reading; suggesting ways into a poem so that readers could make their own relationship with it.

We began in January 1999 and the response took everyone by surprise. Letters cascaded in to me and the paper, saying 'Please do more. Please make them longer.' I made the discussions three, then four times longer. The editors allowed us space to do longer poems sometimes, too. By February, pure reader power had turned 'The Sunday Poem' into an institution. The books editor's gamble had paid off. The culture editor said he didn't know why the column worked but it did. If we missed a week, the paper's editor got angry or anxious phone calls and letters, asking where it was. The column ended two and a half years later, when a new overall editor arrived who did not fancy 'all that writing under the poem'.

I chose poems I liked, that I would enjoy writing about. They had to be shortish; newspapers are always pressed for space. The poem was not always typical of a poet's work: maybe the poet's best poems were too long for the column, or the subject I responded to was not characteristic of the poet's general output. But that did not matter. The point was reading: the poem, not the poet.

I was glad poets liked my readings of their poems, but what thrilled me was how much the column meant to the paper's readers. I got a bag of letters every week from men and women of all ages –

from pensioners in their eighties writing handwritten notes saying they had switched newspapers just for the poem, to A-level students (some of whom also fired off e-mails). Readers wrote in from Fife, Surbiton, Surrey, Leicester, Cleveland, Inverness, Chester, Suffolk, Derby, Dublin, Galway, Spain, Italy, Holland and even Israel.

The letters said loud and clear how hungry readers were to be introduced to modern poems. I realised how many people felt they had no access to new poetry, either physically, because they lived in a remote place, or intellectually, because they felt shut out by modern work. People wrote in to say how delighted they were to be introduced to poems and poets. Often the poetry they had met at school, and the ways they read it there, had been a barrier. (Anyone who has an inspiring teacher at school, from whom they learn to love poetry and approach it with confidence, has been given a gift for life; but such teachers seem to be rare. Or maybe people who had one didn't need to write to me.) Some of my correspondents learnt to love Shakespeare (or Wordsworth, or other pre-1900 poets), but were put off by anything later. Others found 'old poetry' remote and intimidating at school, hoped today's poets might talk about things that touched them more closely, but didn't know where to begin.

Some people wrote about my interpretation, adding supporting detail or arguing their own alternative version. I was thrilled when that happened, for the point was not convincing anyone that my way of reading a poem was right, but giving people tools to help them to read the poem for themselves. Hundreds of readers asked for back numbers missed, or replacements. They had cut out a poem, treasured it, and then lost it. Some had simply fallen in love with a poem and wanted to tell me so. Different readers responded passionately to different poems, saw things in them I hadn't. These poems were now part of their lives.

But many felt appallingly unconfident about reading contemporary poems. I began to realise that in the last fifty years the British reading public has lost confidence dramatically in its own poetry. Poetry is now said to be 'difficult'.

Some people say difficulty is part of the pleasure in a poem. The sound or music of the poem seduces the ear and lures in our imagination to make us work at understanding the meaning.

This may be true. But that word 'work' implies hard work, a chore. In fact, the sort of 'work' involved in reading a poem is exactly the pleasurable working-out-what's-happening that we all love doing in other arenas. In other genres – comedy, cartoon, film, ingenious TV ads – we are completely at home with work-outable difficulty and find the obvious boring. When we respond to a film, we don't feel intimidated. We are just enjoying ourselves, and don't notice how much subtlety goes into the way we work out what's happening. We go through the process automatically, as we perform the set of complex actions involved in changing gear in a car. That working-out, the penny-dropping understanding ('Oh, *I* get it'), is part of the pleasure of a good film. Many new films are no more 'difficult', and need no more sophisticated understanding, than new poems.

But most of us today begin learning the grammar and language of film before we read or hear our first poem, and we keep in constant practice. We keep developing our reading skills in film, keeping pace with the way film syntax changes.

For all art forms move forward, and many twenty-first-century films are far more 'difficult' than films of twenty years ago. They use more shorthand, move faster, imply more. They would have been incomprehensible in the twenties. We understand how they operate without realising how much work we are doing to understand, how much experience of film conventions, tricks of the trade, goes into our response. Most people have not evolved their ways of reading a poem in the same way, or kept pace with poetry as it developed.

That developing was exactly what people who wrote to me wanted. I wrote the essay that follows for them, to give them the background of today's poetry as I see it: technical things like rhythm and rhyme, but also poetry's relation to the media, the position of women in poetry, what has happened to British poetry since the eighties, and why.

Readers who would rather get straight to the poems should skip the essay, for as with film, the important thing is making your own relationship with the poem. No one understands everything in a poem all at once. What matters is being open to some hook in it, a thought, image, feeling, turn of phrase or rhythm which feels important. When something in a poem starts mattering to you, the poem is doing what it was made to do, and you are beginning to make it yours. If it's a worthwhile poem, there will always be more to see in it.

You can respond to a poem emotionally and imaginatively without being aware of the technical ways it gets its effects, and that's fine. The point is pleasure, after all. But poetry is a verbal art that asks you to notice the medium in which it is made. Being aware of its language is part of the pleasure. If you are someone for whom knowing a bit about camera work, or visual symbolism, or dramatic style, or colour, enhances your pleasure in films, theatre and art, then you will get more from a poem if you see how it works technically.

In the column I had to use some technical terms in discussing the poems. These are not jargon but a shorthand that has evolved over centuries – poetry is the oldest literary art, and people have been reflecting on the way it works for over two millennia – to refer to particular patterns and poetic effects. In the following discussions, therefore, words in SMALL CAPITALS are explained in the glossary.

Analysing is not dissecting. Dissection destroys a dead animal's body but analysing a poem is more like turning a spotlight on a living creature. With a live animal, studying its nerves, shape, movement, cells, skin, psychology and social being by touching or watching it, enhances your sympathy and pleasure in it as well as your knowledge. With poems, technical illumination increases your enjoyment in something that was, after all, made for you.

'British' Poetry is International

This book is primarily for readers living in Britain, but poetry is international. By a 'British' poetry renaissance I really mean a renaissance in the poetry *published* in Britain. Only half the poets who wrote these poems are English. Some were born in England, but others in India, Pakistan, the Caribbean or Germany; five were born in Northern Ireland. There are five from the Republic of Ireland, three from Scotland, one each from Australia, Canada and New Zealand; four from America. Several live in countries they weren't born in. Their work is available in British bookshops, but many do not have a British passport, or have another too.

Many British publishers have several North Americans on their poetry lists, but British and American tastes differ. Some British poets who are published and valued in America do not have that much of a following here, just as some American poets prized in America make little impact in Britain. I discussed many Americans in the newspaper; the four I have chosen here are some of those who currently matter a lot to poets and readers in Britain. But only two were born in America, and one of those lives mainly in Paris. The others were born in Serbia and the Caribbean.

So variety is the key to all the poets and their poems. It is also the key to their audience. In the thirties, most poets had the same kind of educational background and expected their readers to share it. But since the eighties, poets know their readers are as varied as they are themselves. Changes in education mean that people know different things; readers approach poems with wildly different mental baggage and experience. The variety of poetry available in Britain reflects the ethnic, educational and regional variety of the people writing it. The only thing they have in common is their craft.

A Range of Readings

There are fifty-two poems in this book: a year of Sundays. Writing the column week by week brought home to me how many fine poems there are around, and how varied. This book is not an anthology of important contemporary poems, nor a showcase for representative work by important poets. There is no star billing and the order they appear in is about the poems, not the poets. I chose them with the discussions I did in the paper, to bring out issues which I think matter in today's poetry. I wanted a varied range of poets and poems. Inevitably, I had to leave out many wonderful poems and poets. When you're dealing with a poetry renaissance, fifty-two is a very small number. It felt like having teeth pulled to leave out so many poets I admire, so many poems I love.

There is no single 'right reading' of any poem. Writing my column, I was delighted when readers suggested other ways of reading poems. All I do is offer my own version and show how, technically, the sound supports the sense. My readings only offer a way in. After that, it is over to you. You may completely disagree with my view of poetry, society and the media in the essay, and my interpretations of individual poems. But you can hate the tour guide and love the landscape. My readings are there to be argued against. For poetry slips away from rules and bossiness, is bigger than anything anyone can say about it, and is there for everyone. There is always more to find in it and the door is always open.

You will find poems here about experiences that touch us all today. About AIDS, multiple sclerosis, a legacy of parental abuse, fantasies of revenge on your husband's lover, or your own. About babies, children, buried rivers; a lost hat, broken window, wiped tattoo. About oral sex, sponsored concerts, a blind man making coffee, war. About being fat on the beach, or unable to pay the rent; about gutting a fish, dressing for sadomasochistic sex, listening to the last shipping forecast alone, sorting your dead mother's clothes. Poems to break your heart; but also to make you laugh, see things in a fresh perspective, put your heart together new.

Ruth Padel,
London,
December 2001

READING POETRY TODAY

1. 'I want to know about modern poetry, what are the rules?'

This question from a reader of the paper haunted me. I wrote back, but not in detail. Three years later, here is the best I can do by way of an answer.

Rules?

From leatherwork to Pacific Rim cuisine, all crafts have evolved their ways of making things. Jewellers have to make sure the earring's metal won't infect the ear. Bakers keep stones and pesticides out of their bread.

If you are looking for rules, that is the place to start: the materials, their practical requirements and essential courtesy to the consumer. No one will buy your earrings if the garnets fall out.

Then there are the conventions of your craft: the traditional shapes of a loaf, or ways of twisting silver. These are things you can play with. You can invent a new shape of baking tin, make earrings out of recycled Coca-Cola cans or cattle dung. If you make them well enough, people will buy the new things as well as the old.

Poets work along similar lines. There are general writing principles which apply particularly sharply to poetry because it is so concentrated, so small-scale. You have less room to manoeuvre than in prose, and every word has to count. (Ideally, of course, every word counts in prose, too, but poets feel prose writers can get away with things they cannot.) You must, for instance, have movement through your poem or there won't be any life in it. You must reveal or imply rather than spell out. (Workshop students know this as 'show, don't tell', and groan when you point out they have infringed it, as we all do, yet again.) You must be on guard against the great spellers-out – adjectives and (especially) adverbs. Be sparing with abstract nouns: they convey much less to readers than vivid, concrete language. And, at the end, frisk every word to make sure it's necessary, that it's pulling its weight.

But over and above these basic writing requirements, what is unique to poetry is gritty technical stuff, and that is all to do with pattern and sound. Line-length, line-ending, relation of vowel and consonant, arrangement of lines (or not) into 'stanzas' ('stanza' means 'room'; stanzas are 'rooms' in the house of a poem), the length and stress of each syllable in relation to all the others. Plus beat and rhythm; especially, but not only, metre.

These things are all-important: the instruments on the carpenter's bench which help you make a chair proportionate, stable, good to look at and sit in. They make a poem hang together musically, be aurally convincing. They have always been part of poetry, and still are. You can't work without them.

But they are tools, not rules. Not bye-laws to be obeyed but a ball to run with. Too conservative a technique does turn the tools into rules, but the more experienced the poet, the more eclectic and daring he or she can be with these instruments, picking them up, putting them down, using them in new ways.

Part of the art is making the way you use these tools as invisible as possible in the finished product. You don't see glue blobs or the tooth marks of the adze on a Chippendale chair. Many readers who feel alienated from today's poetry only see, as it were, the invisibility of these tools. The biggest alienating thing, the place where contemporary poetry seems to them to have broken with earlier poetry and therefore with what they feel poetry ought to be, is the role of rhyme.

Do You Use Rhyme?

Some people who wrote to me about my column felt strongly that only one thing makes a poem: rhyme. Poets are often asked, 'What sort of poetry do you write?' As they wonder how to answer that question yet again, another comes: 'Do you use rhyme?'

By this, people usually mean, 'Do your poems have a pattern of end-rhymes, a rhyming-scheme where the last word in the line rhymes with one or more other end-words?'

They feel, I think, that if they know your poems rhyme in this way, they'll have a handle on 'what sort' of poetry you write. Poetry that rhymes. That sort.

Rhyme in this sense, a repeated pattern of line-endings, has been a key element of English poetry since early medieval times, though English poetry has also always depended on stress and rhythm too. 'Rhyme' *was* 'poetry'. 'Thomas the Rhymer' was 'Thomas the Poet'. The desire to see rhyming 'rules' as the main thing bossing poetry about like a train timetable runs very deep.

In every language, poetry creates meaning and music by making

10

relationships between words. Traditionally, it has two basic ways of making this relationship: rhyme and rhythm.

Metre is the regular patterning of the alternation of long and short, stressed and unstressed syllables. It comes from the Greek word *metron*, measure. It is systematic; it involves, as music does, counting – and luckily the metres mainly used in English depend on patterns of only two or three syllables.

Metre is only one way among others, however, of generating rhythm in a poem. There is also what Robert Frost called 'the sound of sense', which derives from speech-patterns ticking away in your own aural imagination and memory, and in the talk you hear all round you. Frost argued that you have to 'break the sounds of sense, with their irregularity of accent, across the regular beat of the metre'. Other poets feel they do away with regular beat, i.e. metre, entirely, but still agree they pattern syllables more deliberately in a poem than they would in prose. Others feel that any regular patterning constitutes a metre, as long as the reader can respond to it as pattern.

These two things, rhyme and rhythm, are both about patterning and are equal partners in a poem. They are its basic ingredients, like fat and flour in making pastry. Rhythmical relationships may be less immediately obvious, but are just as important as the rhyming ones. You do feel an affinity, whether you are aware of it or not, between words and phrases that have the same rhythmic shape.

Languages like Greek, which inflect the endings of their nouns and verbs, have so many similar-sound endings that unimportant rhymes occur all over the place. In classical Greek and Latin poems, what mattered was metrical ways of relating words. Poets did use techniques similar to rhyme (like assonance and alliteration, the echo and repetition of vowels and consonants) to relate words to each other and bind a line together. But the principle, the basic way you related words and lines to each other, was metre. In stanzaic poems, Greek poets often mirrored the syllables exactly from stanza to stanza: the second stanza's new words had exactly the same rhythmic shape, syllable for syllable, as the words of the first.

Inflected languages are all different, and the importance of rhyme in each partly depends on where stress falls and how syllables lengthen or shorten as you change a verb into third person plural or a noun from the nominative to ablative case. Renaissance Italian swarms with rhyme. In the Russian tradition rhyme is so important that even modernists like Mayakovsky use it. They cannot imagine poetry without rhyme. Joseph Brodsky (who switched to English halfway through his writing life) was so committed to rhyme that he had a famously stormy public debate with Elaine Feinstein in the sixties, arguing that poetry was no good, even in English, if it did not rhyme. The names Shakespeare, Wordsworth and Milton – the great formative artists of English blank verse – could not shake him.

English is a non-inflected language, the most mongrel of them all. Its origins lie in different families of languages, Celtic, Norse and Latin (unlike, say, Italian, which derives purely from Latin), so it has more *kinds* of sound. There are excellent reasons for English-speakers to identify rhyme with poetry: to see it as essential. In a forest of different sounds, rhyme is what matches things up. Rhyme, said Oscar Wilde, 'is the one chord we have added to the Greek lyre'. It lords it over English sonic imagination, pounces out at us from nursery 'rhymes' and the jingle of mnemonic tags. 'Remember remember the fifth of November.' In English, rhyme is the strongest way to make words speak to each other. It can even make their relationship seem truer, more inevitable, than it really is. At its worst, rhyme can make the trashiest bromide suddenly, spuriously, important. Rhyme makes an idea feel like law.

But there is some impulse in poetry and the writing of it that keeps trying to get away from law to freedom, from the rigid and obvious to the oblique, new, surprising. This is true both of metre and of rhyme. Thomas Hardy, in the third-person autobiography supposedly written by his wife, wrote of his own poetry: 'He decided that too regular a beat was bad art . . . He knew that in architecture cunning irregularity is of enormous worth . . . He carried on into his verse, perhaps in part unconsciously, the Gothic art-principle in which he had been trained – the principle of spontaneity.' The critic Helen Vendler says that readers want words in a poem to 'spring towards each other in magnetic attraction', but get put off 'when the trick is done obviously'.

That is one reason why poets are always on the look out for subtle, fresh rhymes and startle away from the thumping, the banal. Rhyme is 'the spinal column' (as Sean O'Brien puts it) of poems by Paul Muldoon, one of the key figures in the British poetry renaissance. But Muldoon's rhymes are so inventive and surprising that they sometimes do the exact opposite of making a thought seem like law. Instead they make the reader question an idea, proverb or cliché. Once, after a reading, I heard someone in Muldoon's audience ask, 'Why don't you use rhyme?' For a moment, delight in having got away with the subtleties struggled in Muldoon's face with a touch of chagrin that all that dazzling technique had been overlooked. How he 'uses' rhyme is so original that this listener had missed it completely.

How A Poem Hangs Together: The Partnership of Sound and Sense

Asking a poet 'Do you use rhyme?' is like asking a painter if he or she uses white paint: the paint you mix with every colour. You may not see white on the canvas, but it is always there. Philip Sidney called rhyme 'the chief life' of verse. Today's poets 'use rhyme' all the time, but in many different ways, not always at the end of a line. End-rhyme is not the only sort. Internal rhyme has always been vital to English poetry and still is. It makes a poem hang together from within. There are plenty of end-rhymes in today's poems, and you will find a set pattern of end-rhyme in over a quarter of the poems here. But today's rhymes are not always in a set pattern.

In my newspaper discussions, I did not use many technical terms but talked mainly about echoes and sound-relationships. For that's where it's really at. What makes 'a poem' is not rhyme itself, but hanging together. Rhyme can make an idea feel like law, yes; but it is also an image for something even more basic, the one thing a poem has to have to be a poem: persuasive cohesion. The lines and words have to convince the reader that they belong together. Rhyme can get that hanging together brilliantly, but is not the only way.

The challenge for the poet is to relate particular sounds, and therefore the words and ideas that go with them, so strongly (but not obviously) that their closeness feels inevitable, and the sound-relationship becomes part of what is said. As the eighteenth-century poet Alexander Pope declared, 'The sound must seem an echo to the sense.'

An important way of creating that relationship of sound and sense is by the repetition of vowels and, sometimes, consonants. In Matthew Sweeney's poem, for example (No. 32), the sound of hat, the title word, chases through the first six lines in catch, perhaps, decapitate, statue, reflecting the way the hat blows through the square. The sound becomes the meaning while it expresses it. A good poem is a love affair of sound and sense.

Poetry 'Without Rhyme': Blank Verse, Free Verse and Iambic Pentameter

There is a long and shining history of poetry that does not rhyme. Homer did not rhyme, nor did classical Greek or Latin poetry. (Rhymed poetry in Greek or Latin is late classical and medieval.) In English, the two great examples of unrhymed poetry are blank verse and free verse.

People who equate English poetry with rhyme should remember that more than half the lines written by England's most famous poets do not rhyme. Most poetry in Shakespeare's plays is blank verse: in which a line's last word does not rhyme with the last word of any other line, except for a couplet at the end of a speech to seal it, to sign off.

But even in blank verse, rhyme is still an important principle in the lines' relationships with each other. The poet credited with bringing blank verse into English was Henry Howard, Earl of Surrey. Between 1530 and 1546 he translated two books of Virgil's *Aeneid* into this 'straunge metre'. To offset the lack of end-rhyme he drew on internal rhyme, making a honeycomb network of sound-patternings and vowel-echoes which other users of blank verse powerfully continued: especially Shakespeare, whose words and rhythms are in us all. In these lines from *The Merchant of Venice*, internal rhyme (*strained, rain*) and vowel-echoes (*quality, droppeth*) help make the lines hang together:

> The quality of mercy is not strained
> It droppeth as the gentle rain from heaven.

Milton wrote wonderful rhymed sonnets but he too helped to ensure the authority of blank verse, both in his dramas and in *Paradise Lost*. Rhyme, he said, acts on poets 'as a constraint to express many things otherwise, and for the most part worse, than else they would have exprest them'. Wordsworth also wrote some of the most authoritative and famous blank verse of all time.

Apart from rhyme, the crucial thing about blank verse is its metre, iambic pentameter, the magically flexible line which has dominated English aural imagination since the sixteenth century.

In an iambic pentameter, every line has five beats. When you count the number of beats you are counting the 'feet' of the line, and each foot is made up, like a musical 'bar', of a stressed syllable,

14

the beat, plus several others. The foot may be an 'iamb' (a unit of two syllables, the first short or unaccented, the second long or accented, as in *caress*; or, here, *it drop* – and then *eth as*). But it may, equally well, be the equivalent of an iamb: some rhythmic mixture of syllables which last an iamb's worth of musical time. By no means every beat is based on an iamb: you can have an iambic pentameter line with no iambs in it. And the last word may be a single long syllable (*strained*); or have an extra syllable or so left over (*heaven*).

Since the sixteenth century, the iambic pentameter has affected English speech-rhythms as well as verse. (Tony Harrison's *Mystery Plays* were based on English poetry that preceded the iambic pentameter, and did a brilliant job of forcing our ears back to a time before the pentameter came into its own: a beautiful shock return to metrical innocence.) I once met the poet John Wain exulting in a perfect iambic pentameter he'd heard a mother say on the bus to her son. 'Your face is dirty, don't you ever wash?'

All poets today have to be aware of their relation to the iambic pentameter. It is a natural and ancient resource of the language. And so, of course, it can trap you, can sound facile and banal.

Just before the First World War, four hundred-odd years after the blank verse iambic pentameter set its seal on English, free verse seized centre stage in poetry. In 'free' verse you are free, as blank verse is not, to shorten or lengthen the number of beats in a line. You do not need to be consistent. You can start with four beats and move on to seven or eight. You bind the lines together not by rhyme but other techniques like balance, stress and the way you use the end-word: whether it rests and breathes the line or sweeps on to the next.

Free verse was different in Britain and America; Britain received it basically from two poets (both American by birth): Ezra Pound and T.S. Eliot. They developed it brilliantly in counterpoint against an imagined iambic line; for freedom's first step was dislodging the hold of the pentameter. 'To break the pentameter: that was the first heave', writes Pound in *Canto* 81.

Free verse blew English-language poetry wide open. It was a technical way of being radical, of saying, 'Poetry doesn't have to do what people say, doesn't have to bow to old conventions.' It was a new point of exploration, freeing you to say new things in new ways.

Ever since the advent of free verse, free and formal methods have been at work side by side. You can use either or both; or mix them. There is immense rhyming variety now too. Increasingly, rhyme itself has a far wider general meaning than a simple *cat/mat* fit. 'How can <u>Inuit</u> and <u>defeat</u> be anything like a rhyme?' asked one reader's letter after my piece on Michael Hofmann (No. 46), but some of the most important rhymes today are near-rhymes which often involve words of more than one syllable. Or 'imperfect' rhymes (*dens/sirens, ring/striking*), 'unaccented' rhymes where the unaccented last syllable rhymes (*matter/lover*), and 'half-rhymes' where the accented syllable rhymes (*wily/piling, wilderness/building, cover/shovel*). There are vowel rhymes where consonants don't matter (*bite/strike/rhyme/tile*), and consonant rhymes where what matters is the consonant at the end of the last accented syllable (*design/maintain*).

These rhymes are not all that new. Emily Dickinson pioneered consonant rhymes in the 1850s: word-matches like *wind/God, plan/unknown, gate/mat, despair/more, one/stone*. Her technique was astonishingly ahead of its time. Looking back, we see her as a meticulously daring trailblazer, but only two of her poems were published during her lifetime and her friend Thomas Wentworth Higginson tried to 'correct' such rhymes in editing her poems. Like Muldoon's listener, he missed the scrupulous technical innovation. Her daring control of form and sound was as powerful as her poems' emotions.

Furthermore, poets since the sixties have been creating end-rhymes randomly, without a rhyme-scheme. Just as jazz brought syncopation, randomness and asymmetry into classical music, so since the advent of free verse poets may bind a poem together with rhymes that are not in a worked-out pattern. But random does not mean uncontrolled. Every effect has to have a purpose, a role in the poem. Jazz musicians get the effect of great freedom through enormous discipline, through carrying in their heads very complex structurings of bar and rhythm. Robert Lowell was a brilliant technician in metre and rhyme. After visiting the west coast of America in the fifties and hearing the Beat poets, he started building his own line with more freedom from rhyme and rhyme-scheme, more flexibility of metre, more rhythms of spoken speech. But as in jazz, powerful discipline and intricate knowledge of rhyme and

rhythm were still there in his head, and therefore in the words. As
Pope (again) said,

> True ease in writing comes from art, not chance,
> As those move easiest who have learned to dance.

Emily Dickinson pioneered consonantal rhymes a hundred and
fifty years ago very quietly on her own in small-town America.
Eighty years later, W.H. Auden – whom we see now as a formal
virtuoso, a guru of rhyme, metre and form – used similar rhymes in
poems that attacked British apathy in the face of fascism; and got up
the noses of the London literary establishment. Auden was not yet
thirty, but had published several volumes and young poets were
already looking to him as a leader. He meant to call his 1936
collection *On This Island*. It would explore themes of moral
stagnation and the collapse of civilisation in a politically uncertain
age, and that title would reflect its attack on the English
establishment. But he was away in Iceland when the book went to
proof and his editor, T.S. Eliot, titled it *Look, Stranger*.

The book was much praised, but some critics slapped him down
not for political content but sloppy form. 'He has no organisation,'
said F.R. Leavis in *Scrutiny*, and one reviewer, amazingly, attacked
his rhymes. In one poem within four lines Auden rhymed *dream/
come* and *dreams/arms*. Basil de Selincourt in the *Guardian*
pounced on the form (as defensive reviewers do when a book
threatens their own ideas) to scoff at the content, complaining of
'restless, impulsive, inconclusive' verse-forms, and 'new consonantal
rhymes'. Consonant rhymes were hardly new in 1936, but could
still feel like an affront to those who wanted to guard a *status quo*.
'New conventions have made such rhymes possible, but I should
prefer that the meaning, if there is one, had been conveyed in
prose,' sniffed de Selincourt. ' "The world is out of joint" seems to
be the basis of Mr Auden's inspiration; he has decided things are so
bad that poetry itself must change its nature.'

Yes, indeed. That is *exactly* what innovative poets want, from
Dickinson to Pound and on to Auden. To make poetry change its
nature. To test and challenge it, break new ground, find new ways
of doing things. No point in saying what's already been said. As
Glyn Maxwell's poem 'The Breakage' (No. 40) suggests, new
things come from breaking old ones. That is how a poetic tradition
moves forward: it risks itself to maintain itself.

One of poetry's jobs is to transform real life imaginatively so we understand our lives new-paintedly, more fully. To make familiar things look strange so you see them new. It does this through the ear, musically, and through the mind – both intellect and feeling – in relation to the world outside. In subject-matter, angle, ideas as well as in form, poets are turned on by inventiveness. 'Free' verse, when it arrived, changed things: meant freedom to look for new subjects as well as new ways of binding words together. Freedom to respond to new worlds, use old tools in new ways, make poems out of things that had not been poetry before. To get into what Derek Walcott has called 'unexplored, unuttered theatre'. De Selincourt spotted exactly what Auden was doing: making the challenge of form express the challenge of the message. He just refused the premise that change was crucial, in either politics or poetry.

But though poets want to say the unsaid, something that maybe seemed unsayable before the next new poem came along, they also go on tackling the fundamental human themes which poetry has made its own since it was first written. Which, in the West, means in the Greek islands of the seventh century BC. Sex, death, politics, power and injustice, parents, parenthood and children, ageing, illness, the social and physical landscape around us, religion, sorrow, loss and memory, jealousy, guilt, joy, desire, and every kind of love.

Philip Larkin said that a poem is a knife and fork partnership. The fork identifies an emotion: spears it, lands it on the poem's plate. The knife is analytical and technical, wants 'to sort out the emotion. Chop it up, arrange it and say either thank you or sod the universe for it.' The fork is what makes readers reach for poetry in a crisis. A poem can express deep, significant feeling and thought more concentratedly and lastingly than anything else. Poems move you – that's what they are for. Larkin also said poetry begins with emotion in the poet, ends with the same emotion in the reader, and the poem is the instrument that puts it there. Sex, death and the rest are not just subjects for poems. They matter to everyone. People who don't normally have much to do with poetry turn to it in the big transformative rituals and crises, the wedding, the funeral, the making and breaking of love.

Today's poets also use the story-shaped shared past of myth and history to reflect contemporary scenarios, personal, social, sexual and political: as all poets have done since the Greeks. Many Irish poets have turned to Greek myth, classical painting or history, to illuminate contemporary war in their own land (Nos 2, 3, 5, 6 and 7). In writing about women's dealings with modern men, poets invoke ancient or biblical heroines (Nos 33 and 34). Writing about black experience, poets have used Homer, or myths like El Dorado (Nos 22 and 50).

The concrete details, the texture of the now, have always been vital to poetry. From the seventh century BC, you hear the hot contemporary details of musical instruments, milk pails, footwear and brooches in archaic Lesbos or Sparta. The names of individuals dancing, fighting or running a race; how people light a fire or cut up meat. Like Paul Klee in Tom Paulin's poem, cutting his canvases from the fuselage of wrecked planes (No. 26), poets plunder the contemporary fabric of the world they live in, to think about themes poetry has always claimed.

Seamus Heaney once wrote a poem about a Presbyterian farmer standing in the yard at night, not going in to his Catholic neighbours until he heard them finish their alien prayers. 'Part of my pleasure,' said Heaney afterwards, 'was in thinking that the subject had not, so far as I knew, been treated in a poem.' Poetic newness comes both out of new ways of patterning words, and the new world we live in now. After my mother, a sceptical scientist, was dragged to her first poetry reading, she said, 'I see the point of poets now. They *notice* things.' A modern culture needs modern poems to reflect its changing self to itself freshly, through the tried tools of an ancient art but also through the evolving sounds of its own words.

2. History: A Changing Britain

'Look in thy heart and write,' said Philip Sidney; and we do. The emotions, relationships and experiences that hearts went through in Sidney's day may be roughly similar to ours. But hearts are also affected by external things, the clutter of a world which changes over time and makes today's hearts very different from those of the sixteenth century. Poems speak outside history, across the barriers of time and culture, but also belong to history: they come from and speak to a specific time and place. It is important to see the changes that happened in poetry in the eighties, and their effect on poems

19

today, in the context of social and cultural changes that happened in Britain through the eighties.

Poetry in the eighties was not a wiped slate or new beginning. Poetry never is: it uses the old as it looks to the new. Earlier twentieth-century poets, living and dead, continued (and continue) to give new poets new inspiration. Today's poets love and learn from all their predecessors, ancient and modern. They steal, rework and gesture to them. As Derek Walcott uses Homer (No. 22) and Paul Farley (No. 38) uses *Macbeth*, so Seamus Heaney's poem (No. 28) resonates with one by Robert Lowell and Armitage's (No. 20) with one by Ted Hughes. Important older poets who were working in Britain before the eighties are still working today, still influencing younger ones. Poetic tradition is an organic, living thing; you go on learning from each other all the time.

But some young poets who began publishing in the eighties gave a new edge to poetry's role in Britain to which other poets responded. Together, they generated an atmosphere that re-energised British poetry as a whole. These poets were individuals with their own gifts, but also a product of their time: a time of political and social change. Every poet would describe that time and its effect on poetry differently. I can only open my own door, share my way in to understanding how poets are writing now. In what follows, I have highlighted a few features of current voices and tones which I think were partly a consequence of the eighties historical context. I describe them simply as background to reading today's poems.

Regionalism, Thatcherism

In the sixties, poetry began to benefit enormously from the increasing value which the British media, especially radio, placed on different regional backgrounds. Two-thirds of the poets in this book are based in Britain, but few come from London. They come from Manchester, Newcastle, Yorkshire, Gloucestershire, Dorset, Wales, Scotland, Cornwall, Bristol. The rise of specialist poetry publishers like Carcanet (Manchester), Bloodaxe (Newcastle) and Seren Books (Bridgend, Wales) reflected the growing regional diversity of British poetry; especially in the north of England, home to two key British players who began publishing in the eighties and are now among Britain's most popular poets.

Carol Ann Duffy was born in Glasgow to Irish Catholic parents, grew up in Stafford, went to Liverpool University and lives in Manchester. Her first collections were published in 1985 and 1987. All her poems were sophisticatedly funny, feminist, wryly lyrical, but the specially startling and influential ones were dramatic monologues which tackled contemporary abuses of power.

This form was not new. The satiric monologue betraying the unpleasantness or helplessness of its speaker sparkled in the hands of Robert Browning, the Greek poet Cavafy, and more recently U.A. Fanthorpe. Or Philip Larkin, who said his poem 'Naturally the Foundation will Bear your Expenses' was both funny and serious. 'The speaker's a shit,' he said. 'That's always serious.'

But Duffy's eighties monologues, spoken by both abusers and abused (a murderous psychopath, a man beaten to make a false confession in a police cell), came over as witty, hard-hitting voicings of people who did not understand how mad, bad or badly off they were, in times we were living through, and became a poetic comment on that time.

Simon Armitage, born (1963) in Huddersfield, studied in Portsmouth and worked as a probation officer in Manchester. From his first collection (1989), he devastated British poetry with tough, polished work that combined enormous literary sophistication with laconic vernacular language, talking of hitchhikers, men helping East Riding police with their inquiries, or a probation officer holding 'the wobbly head of a boy / at the day centre': of people and places which had not appeared in poems before.

Building on the political critique of poets like Peter Reading, Ken Smith and Sean O'Brien, and utterly free from the Oxbridge–London circuit, these poets helped to create a new tough, confident, politically and socially sceptical atmosphere in poetry.

It is often said that bad politics make good art. The changes happening in British institutions everywhere in the mid-eighties, in hospitals, schools and public services, would have seemed immoral ten years before. Public ideology changed from the top down. Fashion commentators may look back at the eighties as a time when everyone made money and wore gold. Poets saw a different eighties. Unsalaried, travelling to underpaid readings in unfunded poetry societies, teaching in increasingly run-down schools with plastic buckets put out to catch leaks from the roof, poets saw in action, year by year, the giving up on the welfare state. As the divide between rich and poor was knowingly increased, poems increasingly spoke of the inner effects of Thatcherism: economic, educational and social oppression and depression, unemployment, miserable and underfunded care homes, corruption, pollution of the environment, extinction of animal species, and eventually a war played out on our own TV screens, which enabled us to exalt in the new technologies of mass killing while glazing over the gruesome details.

Compared to what goes on all the time in some countries, injustice in Britain was no big deal. But it was a sharp change, and poets saw its effect first-hand. With the suspension of the separation between the state and police during the miners' strike, the findings of the inquiry into the police handling of pickets at Orgreave, the denials of danger during the spread of BSE by a government that refused to fund research into an unknown disease 'because it would suggest to the population there might be a risk to them', the Thatcher era helped to establish a new political impotence in Britain, and expand possible ways of undermining civil rights.

Wit, Allusiveness, Adspeak: Screen and Street in the Age of the Image

Another aspect of the eighties was the way public tones changed. As a new generation of British became newly aware of being lied to, and ads became an image for the mismatch between public political promises and inner reality, poets began raiding the pacey wit, irony and allusiveness of ads and the increasingly dominant media. 'Do you fancy me, lady? Really?' asks the speaker of Carol Ann Duffy's poem 'Money Talks'. 'Don't let my oily manner bother you, Sir.' In increasingly varied textures, tones, voices and implications, poems spoke of lives with less and less money, increasingly powerless in an increasingly run-down urban landscape. The wit they did it with drew on the slick, ironic, allusive, throwaway style of those whose values they were attacking. Poetry always wants to explore the language it hears around it: both to use it and question it. Contemporary poetry ladles from all today's verbal puddles. Ironising and questioning political soundbites, headlines, media-speak, chat-up lines, it uses the tones of the age to show the age up.

By taking for granted the rainy pub, late-night curry, supermarket, tattooing parlour, old people's home, employment exchange (see Nos 12, 13, 36 and 46), poetry spotlights the surreally unfair, loonily fragile, alienating texture of ordinary life today. The humour, irony, deceptively casual shrug with which poetry began to do this in the eighties says more loudly than any direct attack that modern Britain is a place where it is easier and easier to abuse power. A generation later, Neil Rollinson wrote a poem in which the poet is thrown out of a supermarket because the manager tells him, bafflingly, he doesn't like 'the way you shop'.

Poets are also deeply influenced by the screen. 'Focus' is a visual metaphor (Simon Armitage's first collection was called *Zoom!*) and poetry depends on focus. It has learnt a lot in the last twenty years from visual techniques by which film and TV reveal a situation without explaining it. Armitage's poem 'Goalkeeper With a Cigarette' opens with TV's immediacy, and the quick images that follow reflect television's swift visual comparisons:

> That's him in the green, green cotton jersey,
> prince of the clean sheets – some upright insect
> boxed between the sticks, the horizontal
> and the pitch . . .

The twentieth century was the age of the image. Though the visual images of media and the image-spin of celebrity are very different from the imagery of poetry, these surface images, and the way media, politics and entertainment manipulate them, are part of the everyday currency on which poets draw (Nos 12 and 38) to satirise the values on which that process depends. Carol Ann Duffy wrote a poem, 'Weasel Words', in the voice of a Thatcher-like orator who carries out, mid-poem, the process which her own rhetoric is denying. 'Let me repeat that we Weasels mean no harm', says the speaker:

> You may have read that we are vicious hunters,
> but this is absolutely not the case. Pure bias
> on the part of your Natural History Book. *Hear, hear* . . .

> And as for eggs, here is a whole egg. It looks like an egg.
> It is an egg. *Slurp*. An egg. *Slurp*. A whole egg. *Slurp* . . . *Slurp* . . .

Poems also exploit the witty visual allusiveness of TV ads, which have turned us all into adept visual decoders. The technological revolution of the micro chip precipitated a range of new ways of focusing and presenting material. British poetry is increasingly influenced by the computer screen. The web has been an interesting new tool, image bank and meeting place for poetry. As we become a more visually than verbally literate society, poetry keeps watching out for visual techniques it can employ verbally: for ways you notice and reveal something, how you leave things implied rather than exposed.

The way that screen images change in a split second, flushing up and away like birds, underlies some of the transforming and juxtaposing of image and idiom which poetry goes in for today. In her prize-winning poem 'Phrase Book', Jo Shapcott used such techniques of juxtaposition to attack the Gulf War as seen on the TV which intersplices such shockingly different images. This poem has three ingredients: the Gulf War on TV and its euphemistic jargon; an antiquated foreign phrase book for English travellers, offering grammatical alternatives to what you want to say to other people; and (one assumes) the trauma of a broken relationship. It moves so swiftly between each of these that, just as with computer graphics where one image melts instantly into the next, you cannot tell where one begins and the other ends:

> I'm standing here inside my skin,
> which will do for a Human Remains Pouch
> for the moment. Look down there (up here).
> Quickly. Slowly. This is my own front room
>
> where I'm lost in the action, live from a war
> on screen. I am an Englishwoman, I don't understand you . . .
>
> TV is showing bliss as taught to pilots:
> Blend, Low silhouette, Irregular shape, Small,
> Secluded. (Please write it down. Please speak slowly.)
> Bliss is how it was in this very room
>
> when I raised my body to his mouth,
> when he even balanced me in the air,
> or at least I thought so and yes the pilots say
> yes they have caught it through the Side-Looking
>
> Airborne Radar, and through the J-Stars.

You could call this postmodernism; you could call it a reinvention of modernism. For at that period too, visual and verbal techniques moved forward rapidly together. As Picasso drew on the collage, colliding violently unrelated objects and images, so Ezra Pound and T.S. Eliot spliced fragments of street speech with foreign quotation, literary allusion, and alienated images of contemporary life.

Today's poets do something similar with contemporary technology and idiom, but in a different spirit from Pound and Eliot because cultural changes have meant they have a totally different relation to their readers. The only cultural knowledge they are sure to have in common with them is television and its realist counterpart, the street.

The Mother of Metaphor: Censorship and the Surrealities of Eastern Europe

In Thatcherism, British poets found in their own backyard a little of the surreal oppression, and grassroots despair in the face of menace denied by public lies, which they met in poems from the two places whose poetry was most deeply influencing theirs. One of those places was Eastern Europe.

During the sixties and seventies, new translations of major foreign poets became available, and a new atmosphere fostering poetry readings and festivals meant that British poets had opportunities to hear and meet these poets too. Some of the brightest stars in the biennial 'Poetry International' festival then set up in London were from Eastern Europe. British poets began reading translations of Zvigniev Herbert, Vasco Popa, the Polish Nobel Prize-winner Czeslaw Milosz, the Czech Miroslav Holub. And also translations of earlier Russians: Anna Akhmatova, Osip Mandelstam; or Marina Tsvetaeva of whom Elaine Feinstein, encouraged by Ted Hughes, did the trailblazing translation.

Poetry is often represented in Britain today as difficult, pretentious, boring or irrelevant. But where freedom of expression is forbidden, and the private becomes political, poetry is seen for what it is: a form of expression crucial to everyone. Because poetry is about the personal mattering, in public. On its own frail but stubborn level, it challenges controlling public perceptions merely by existing and being shared. A tiny David, backing small-scale private subtlety against a public violent Goliath. Dictatorships know it. In their moves against all freedoms of expression, repressive regimes target poetry fast.

Under Stalin, and in repressive Eastern European regimes, many poems circulated by means of *samizdat* (self-publishing). Poets traded typed carbons, memorised poems, got their families to memorise them ('learn it, then burn it'), wrote on bars of soap in prison – any way of recording poems so that they made their way in the outside world to readers hungry for profound articulation of their own suffering. For poets writing in Britain today, avoiding the obvious is an aesthetic need. For Russian and Eastern European poets, it was life and death.

They turned this need into poetic strength. All poems must, as Seamus Heaney puts it, 'make a thing' and also 'tell a truth'. Under Communist censorship, there was one big truth staring everybody in the face that no one could tell outright. Poems had to work implicitly: not spell things out but slide under the censor's eye, 'say the unsaid' to readers desperate to hear their truth, while pretending it hadn't been said. Through the sixties and seventies, various Eastern European poets found ways of doing this by giving a new, quasi-surreal status and transformative power to what has always lain at poetry's heart: the image. And not just image but the imagination to see things otherwise, for which that word 'image' stands.

'Imagery' comes from *imago*, the Latin for visual image. Poetry's deepest force is imag-ination, the power to visualise what does not exist. To 'see' (in a literal and metaphorical sense), the world otherwise, newly. The free, strange ways in which Zvigniev Herbert and Miroslav Holub put images before the reader suggested ways of getting new shifts and depths of tone in a poem, new air pockets of meaning, fresh, surprising ways of hinting, symbolising, parabolising. The work had a magical-realist quality which was grounded in an all too hard-edged reality. The Serbian-American poet Charles Simic described it as 'elemental surreality'. In this way, a repressive, mean-minded censorship – plus everything that underlay it, i.e. torture, assassination, prison, exile – became, as Jorge Luis Borges put it, 'the mother of metaphor'.

The most mundane little object takes on intense significance if you place it out there for other people to see against a background of surveillance and menace. The objects in poems – a bottle cap, a drainpipe, a pair of shoes – become something else as well as themselves. The very fact of putting them in a poem alchemises them into a powerfully subversive challenge. So, like a child's toy placed in the path of a tank, the objects in these poems became a statement about vulnerability and the power that threatened it. This Eastern European use of images to say what could not be said straight came over as the most naked pronouncement of poetry's power: the power of what is vulnerable, small-scale and personal, to point the finger at the horror of personality denied. At the impersonal, violent, unjust.

'History's a twisted root,' says Paul Muldoon,

art its small, translucent fruit.

Many Russian and Eastern European poets were persecuted, exiled, imprisoned, their poems banned and burnt, and several of the greatest died, because that 'small fruit' is also one of the most important and concentrated examples of being free in your thought. But in the eighties, British and Irish poets who did not share the same political situation began to borrow the effects of Eastern European poetry, especially this surreal power of concrete objects turned into images. You can see it at work in poems about personal as well as political situations, in poets as different as Jo Shapcott, Eilean Ní Chuilleanáin, Paul Muldoon, Selima Hill, John Hartley Williams, the fabulist Matthew Sweeney, Paul Durcan and Peter Redgrove (Nos 1, 3, 8, 11, 24, 32, 42 and 44).

But what about the twisted root, the history that produces poetry's translucent harvest, the oppressive situation itself? Auden said of Yeats that Ireland 'hurt' him 'into poetry'. Where was the hurt for British poets?

A weirdly unsayable feeling had grown up in the West in the sixties: an almost-envy of the Eastern European thing. Not of exile and torture and censorship in themselves, but of their importance and the intense creative pressure they generated. Apart from the Blitz, England had been uniquely privileged in being fairly safe, for most people. Unjust in many places, but free in living memory compared to the civil wars, occupations, purges and massacres that had scarred its European neighbours and Ireland. England hadn't even suffered McCarthyism and the Ku Klux Klan.

Thatcherism shook this security. One book that came out in 1985 purported to be by an imaginary woman poet in a country under a military regime (No. 10): maybe South Africa, Russia or somewhere in Eastern Europe. This book was by a poet who wrote his first collections under the influence of poetry which James Fenton had christened 'Martian', after Craig Raine's 1979 collection *A Martian Sends a Postcard Home*; poetry which wanted to see the world fresh through the metaphors of a shockingly innocent alien eye. Christopher Reid was five years younger than Raine and was taught by him. His way of moving on from Martianism was writing a whole book in the alien voice of a woman in an oppressive state.

But the year his book came out, the real poet Irina Ratushinskaya was still in a Russian prison, concussed and regularly beaten – for writing poems. (She was released in 1986, under international pressure.) Reid's project made several people very uneasy. Was it morally right to give your own poems poetic power by imitating other people's suffering; as safe white teenagers created sixties rock by imitating the anger and real pain of the blues?

Poetry has got to be free to explore other people's experience; as Carol Ann Duffy did, giving voice to a murderous psychopath, a man bombing a pub, or another beaten in a police cell. Reid was only taking one step further what everyone else was doing. Not just borrowing a technique, but borrowing the context which engendered it: a scenario in which one image could be so important it became a matter of life and death. He was doing it at a time when Britain itself was changing dramatically, and the ground under our feet was not the seemingly safe soil it had once been.

3. Fall-out from British Rule: The Common Wealth of 'English'

Meeting the British

British poetry of the last quarter-century was recharged most significantly, however, by poems written in English, but outside England. If you run your eye down the authors of the first ten poems in this book, it may look as if I have chosen mostly Irish poetry. In fact only a quarter of the poets here are Irish, but I put a lot at the beginning because British poetry, from the late seventies on, owes most to poems from Northern Ireland.

Like poems from Eastern Europe, these poems had violence at the back of them, and fear which was in everyone's mind but rarely mentioned openly. But unlike the horror behind Eastern European poems, this violence and its history directly implicated Britain.

The Troubles, and the history of British rule in Ireland that led to them, resonate from time to time in the work of nearly all Irish poets, and poets with Irish ancestry. To understand what British poets are doing now, in the new millennium, you have to reckon with the impact in Britain of a still-growing body of work which began in the mid-seventies and has been the major poetic influence and gold standard for all poets who have started publishing since.

The first generation of 'Belfast poets' was led by Seamus Heaney, Derek Mahon and Michael Longley, all about thirty when the Troubles began in 1969. Their response to the violence that followed the civil rights movement – the Catholic–Protestant conflict and its five-hundred-year resonance, the B Specials, the British army and *its* five-hundred-year resonance in Ireland, the bombs and guns of Republican and Loyalist paramilitaries – spearheaded one of the greatest achievements of twentieth-century poetry in English.

The individual gifts of these poets meant they would have been important anywhere, at any time. But under that pressure of time and place, what they wrote offered all English-language poets new ways of shaping thought and feeling about fundamental human things, and weighing up the value of any art, especially poetry, at a time when murder and military occupation were challenging friendship and justice in the street and home every day.

Heaney's first books came out in 1966 and 1969. His three seventies collections included the Bog poems that made him famous. They brilliantly balanced the way poetry 'tells a truth' and 'makes a thing'. They took the murderous present seriously, but also the pleasure of poetry. Like poems by Mahon and Longley (Nos 2 and 6), Heaney's poems often approached tragedy and violence at home by looking out and back to another era. In the poem for which he is perhaps best known, the parallel he chose was the prehistoric age of 'Tollund Man'.

That was one lesson. To look outside and be 'universal' through the grainily personal and historical. Don't make explicit the parallels your poem turns on, or else do it subtly. 'I lived there as a boy', says Mahon (No. 2) of backstreets in a seventeenth-century Dutch painting. Taken literally, that was mad. It was Mahon's way of making a parallel with backstreets of Northern Irish towns wide open to the 'maenads' of bombs and gunmen. Seventies Belfast poems came from a place where the best policy was, in Heaney's words, 'Whatever you say, say nothing'. As a working principle for British poets, this message cross-fertilised the lessons in surreal obliquity beaming in from Eastern Europe.

These poems from the North are in the hearts of all British poets under sixty. If there is a canon of modern poetry, they head the list. When I became a Poetry Book Society selector with a poet I hardly knew, what told us most about each other was which Heaney collection we liked best. Maybe that sounds precious. But Heaney *is* precious – in a good sense, the sense of necessary – to all poets. Not only as a wonderful poet, but as a great critic who has opened ground in talking generously about other people's work, the business of writing poetry, and the poet's role.

The second generation of Belfast poets included the first poet to win Britain's T.S. Eliot Prize, the brilliant Cieran Carson (alas, not included here), Paul Muldoon and Medbh McGuckian (Nos 8 and 9); the third generation includes Colette Bryce (No. 25). Influences are for reacting against. The talismanic warlord, or Puck-cum-Ariel of the eighties, came from the second generation: a poet from a roughly similar background to Heaney, whose work is in many ways a critique of Heaney's whole artistic stance. Muldoon, born in Armagh in 1951, is *the* postmodern master for his generation and beyond. He lives and teaches in America but is currently Professor of Poetry at Oxford and President of the British Poetry Society. Since his fourth collection, *Quoof*, in 1983, he has been accepted as one of the most important poets of our time, and one of the most influential on his contemporaries in Britain.

Why? His poems were innovative, both in their forms and in the way they angled up on their subject. With wonderful facility and inventiveness in rhyme and rhythm, they invigorated the sonnet. Their witty, intelligent, mischievous approach was serious but never solemn. They teased whatever they used, from verbal clichés and erudite historical references to the poet's perception of immediate tragic events; and teased themselves as they stalked their theme. They seemed to distrust 'public' poetry (here the critique of Heaney kicks in), yet took on large, tragic and public themes in their own way – implicitly; extra-obliquely. They were compassionate, but the compassion was sophisticated, casual, offbeat. One, ostensibly about the poet's sister confessing to a priest ('Father, a boy touched me once'), called 'Cuba', remembered the Cuban missile crisis as it affected the poet's family, raising with enormous economy all kinds of questions about Irishness, global dependence on America, and how we meet the political through the personal.

The conflicts of Ulster, the history of Ireland, run through all Muldoon's work – obliquely, tenderly, tragically:

30

> lie down with us now and wrap
> yourself in the soiled grey blanket of Irish rain
> that will, one day, bleach itself white.

For Irish poets, historical relations with Britain, and the ancient background to modern ambivalences in this relationship, underpin everything. (The best way to get known as an Irish writer is still, as in Swift's or Oscar Wilde's day, to be published in London.) Few poems published in Britain in the eighties talked directly of the British army in Ulster, barbed wire, hunger strikes, and Republican perceptions of the British. They didn't need to: those things were under the skin of every poem.

How did these poems affect English British poets?

The hardest thing to know about oneself, nationally or personally, is one's effect, or one's country's effect, on other people. Most Americans were shocked and surprised when international reaction to the terrorist attacks on New York on 11 September 2001 included resentment arising from American foreign policy of the previous thirty years. But in the eighties, younger British poets reacted profoundly to Muldoon's poetic strategies (the technical innovation, postmodern play with word and cliché) while not, most of them, really taking on board the fact that they themselves were implicated in it.

In *Meeting the British* (1983) Muldoon found the perfect way of questioning what 'British' was, and foregrounding everyone's problem in 'meeting' it. Thatcherism was making everyone question 'Britishness'; Muldoon, so enormously influential in his tone and style, encouraged British poets to question it through the persona and voice of their poems.

Meeting the British extended the ground of Muldoon's poems from Ireland to America, the traditional goal for Irish emigrants heading not for an anciently treacherous monarchy but a welcoming democracy. Since Tollund Man, Irish writers had found images for Ireland in many foreign countries with their own histories of civil conflict or foreign occupation. In the Irish Republic, Paul Durcan talked of 'Going Home to Russia' and Colm Tóibín's novel *The South* was set in Spain. The title poem of *Meeting the British* staged the treachery of Britain but also (typically, for Muldoon) undermined the 'land of the free' image behind the big alternative to Britain. It was spoken in the voice of Native Americans, cheated and supplanted by European occupiers (as, though the poem does not say so explicitly, native Irish were supplanted by British landlords). So the great democracy began with great injustice:

> We met the British in the dead of winter . . .
> They gave us six fishhooks
> And two blankets embroidered with smallpox.

Four years later, Carol Ann Duffy's title poem in *Selling Manhattan* (1987) concentrated on the same moment – in the buyer's as well as seller's voice:

> All yours, Injun, twenty-four bucks' worth of glass beads,
> gaudy cloth. I got myself a bargain. I brandish
> fire-arms and fire-water. Praise the Lord.
> Now get your red ass out of here.

Northern Irish poems put on the map, for all English-language poets, the project of questioning the meanings of the word 'British'. Challengingly, for English poets at a time when England was radically changing. More directly, for poets from other places with a history of British rule: Wales, Scotland (where Duffy was born), and Britain's former colonies.

Non-Standard English and Other Languages

In Muldoon, a key impulse (as in the Irish father of modernism, James Joyce) is the playful requestioning of everyone's common poetic tool, the English language. Muldoon opened up for British poets ways of playing with English, punning, inventing, waking up clichés or innate relations between words. Not that everyone started writing like Muldoon, but you see his influence in the wordplay, rhyme varieties and slippery, apparently casual personas of many poets (especially men) who began publishing in the eighties.

In Ireland, English is the language of the ex-ruler. Children in the Republic learn Irish. So do Catholic children in the North. The relation of Irish to 'English' is important throughout Muldoon's work:

> We kept a shop in Eglish . . .
> . . . Eglish was itself wedged between
> *ecclesia* and *église*.

32

Muldoon appears in this book with a poem of his own, but also with a translation of Ní Dhomhnaill's 'Ceist na Teangan' ('The Language Issue') (No. 7), which conjures yet another historical parallel for linguistically self-alienated Ireland: Moses in Egypt. Several Irish, Scots and Welsh poets today write only in Irish, Scots and Welsh. This is a political as well as aesthetic and cultural choice. It reminds the reader that one thing British rule did was erase and replace the indigenous language. British poets read Ní Dhomhnaill's poems in translations by other Irish poets, and the relation between the two languages is a reminder of the complex relations between two countries and cultures.

This interaction of language and history has now surfaced in poems everywhere. There is a rich and growing body of work not in Standard English by poets from ex-colonies and Scotland. These poets tread an intricate path between different aspects of their cultural and linguistic identity. Fred D'Aguiar and David Dabydeen (Nos 18 and 50) write both in Standard and Caribbean English. Many Scots poets write in both Scots and Standard English. Jackie Kay (No. 37) writes from a black as well as a Scottish sensibility. Jean 'Binta' Breeze lives half in Cambridge, half in Jamaica: her music belongs with Jamaican and Trinidadian rhythms but her voice ranges from Jamaican to Standard English. Lemn Sissay, poet-in-residence at Manchester's Contact Theatre, was born in 1967 to Ethiopian parents and grew up in Lancashire. His poems speak of British supermarkets, dreams of Africa, and getting picked up by the police for being black; they dance between different registers of English. So do those of John Agard from Guyana, much-loved resident poet at the BBC.

They and many others have opened up wonderfully the voices of 'English' poetry. So much so that, in several recent poetry competitions I know of, poems by white poets ventriloquising a 'black' voice have won prizes.

Poems in Non-Standard English echo with political as well as poetic history, plus a wish to speak to a wider language community. But this project has its problems. One function of modern poetry in Scots now, as W.N. Herbert sees it, is to edify. Through his own Scots poems he wants, he says, to make other work in written Scots, from the eighteenth century onwards, accessible to more people. But he does admit that, on the page, literary Scots is somewhat difficult to read, even for Scottish readers. After his readings, he says, some listeners come up and confess they can only really understand his poems when they hear them.

So it can be tough going, writing in a voice people are used to hearing, but not seeing written down. Still, novelists are doing it; and all these poems broaden the language base of modern British poetry. Apart from their value as poems in themselves, they sensitise everyone to the fact that Standard English is only one version among many. That whatever Standard English now is, to write in it is to make a deliberate choice of tradition, allegiance and voice.

Identity – and History's Twisted Root

I once told a Frenchwoman that some of the best English poetry was now written in Ireland, Australia, the Caribbean and America: the margins of former British rule.

'They have eaten your language!' she said, indignant.

No, I said, they have enriched it, and poetry, beyond all expectation.

'English' became the language spoken in many countries at the cost of terrible suffering in those countries. It seems unjust to have benefited poetically from countries Britain exploited. But in the end it was no thanks to Britain that English became the twentieth century's *lingua franca* and is the most widely written poetic language in the world. That was America's doing.

British poetry has had a complicated relationship with American poetry for over a century. The founding fathers of English modernism, Eliot and Pound, were both American-born. Pound came to Europe in 1907, Eliot came to Britain in 1917 and became a naturalised citizen in 1927. Forty years later, British poetry was influenced by the Californian Beat poets and Robert Lowell; more recently, Lowell's friend and contemporary Elizabeth Bishop has become increasingly read in Britain. Sylvia Plath came in the fifties and is a permanent influence. Also in the fifties and sixties, poets from Australia (pre-eminently Peter Porter) and New Zealand (Fleur Adcock, No. 19) settled here and became major presences on the British scene.

Poetry is international but uneconomical to export. For Americans or Australians to have an impact here, they have to be published in Britain. I have only included poets who are; whose work contributes to the way poetry written here develops (as do the great modern American classics like Wallace Stevens, William Carlos Williams, Emily Dickinson).

Eighties poems written from what were once 'the margins' have nourished and enlightened British poets not only through their language, tone, angles, but in the way they interrogate identity through history. In different ways, many contemporary British poems now make history their central concern (see Nos 4, 5, 26, 40 and 50).

Historical back-relations with British rule are part of the identity of Irish, Scottish and Welsh poets; but they do not have a monopoly on a history of suffering under imperial England. The origins of many British poets today lie in places that have what David Dabydeen (No. 50) has called a 'history of distress' in relation to Britain. Their poems often look to history to make emotional sense of Britain, and of living in it now. They bring into British poetry a sense of what Britain feels like when you or your family have come from somewhere else: Asia (No. 39), Africa, the Caribbean, any country where Britain has been savagely important. Or when you seem to be alien in Britain and yet it is 'your country' (No. 37). These poets have to find their own version of 'meeting the British', including 'the British' in themselves. Poets as different as Kathleen Jamie, David Dabydeen, Jackie Kay and Moniza Alvi interweave national and racial history with personal and family history, and relations with Britain; just as poems by Derek Walcott, Charles Simic and James Lasdun explore emigration to America.

By exploring roots, allegiance, family, origin, community, identity, these poets are voicing key questions of our age everywhere. Contemporary poems raise themes of alienation and self-transformation all the time at many levels (psychologically, for instance, in No. 15): questions like 'Who am I?', 'Where am I from?', 'What am I doing here?', 'What is "home" and my relation to it?'

Those questions have an ethnic as well as personal resonance in every Western society today and poems are a good place to ask them. But the questions have particular force in a context of post-colonial emigration or immigration; Dabydeen and D'Aguiar, for instance, set them in landscapes very different from Britain but historically related to it by slavery, empire and its aftermath. The famous phrase Heaney used for his relation to his homeland – Ireland, Northern Ireland – was 'inner emigré', and multiracial Britain is a whole world of inner emigrés: of many different kinds.

Some poets tackling these questions in their work are British and black, but readers should not expect them to address what that means all the time.

To go back to that question, 'What sort of poetry do you write?' Ideally, the poet would answer, 'A sort that keeps changing and growing.' But readers often want to typecast a poet after enjoying one poem or book, just as they typecast actors after enjoying them in one role. It's useful, faced with a variety of poets, to link each one with a particular theme; so readers often identify poets from particular ethnic or national backgrounds only with those backgrounds.

But it is reductive, and misses the point, to say of Kathleen Jamie that 'the sort of poetry she writes' is poetry about Scotland or being Scottish. That what Moniza Alvi 'writes about' is her Asian background (No. 39). All poets have a range of subjects and tones. If they are going forward, they are constantly hungry to extend them.

Audiences also ask, 'Where do your poems come from?' At one level, I honestly can't say. Your personality, experience, different aspects of your identity: all these shape your perceptions of the world. At a very deep level, I suppose they must decide your images, themes, rhythms, the way you connect words to each other, the way you choose words or get words to choose you.

But you do not write 'about' your own identity all the time. The most important place poems 'come from' is imagination, which takes you outside your own limited self. One poem by Alvi begins 'I would like to be a dot in a painting by Miró'. Her most recent collection is about pregnancy, and works by imagining the husband pregnant. Not much direct reference to immigration there. It is imagination – which alchemises personal perception and experience in (you hope) ever new ways – that is the poem's deepest provenance. In a sense, you might say Alvi's poems are 'about' imagination more than anything else.

In multiracial Britain, the flip side of having an origin different from the white English norm is that people expect you to have a particular agenda. To write 'about' being Scottish, black, or from Pakistan. It is the same for women or gay poets. You are always a woman, or gay, when you write, but you do not always write about it, directly. People do not expect straight men to address being a man, or heterosexual, in everything they write.

What you are, and your relation to the place you are in, is *in* the way you write. But you do not always write directly 'about' it.

4. Women

How Do Men Read? Think Technical, Think Male

I began 'The Sunday Poem' column with Carol Ann Duffy (No. 27) and discussed women and men alternately, as I do here. No one seemed to notice the alternation, but one reader wrote to say she was glad I discussed 'so many women'.

The fact that an utterly even half and half feels like 'so many women', even to a woman reader, shows the state of gender play in British poetry more clearly than anything. 'It's a boy's world still, out there,' said Angela Carter before she died, and this is true of poetry more than any other British literary scene. If you think of this book as a selection of poems, it is unusual in having equal numbers of poems by men and women.

Yes, some of the best poetry in English in the last twenty years has been written by the once-excluded; by poets on the margins of former British political power. That means not just Irish, Australian and Caribbean writers, but women, too. And yet, though the number of women poets has risen sharply (thanks to Bloodaxe Books), if you look at the way poetry is published in Britain and see who makes the decisions, you would not think Britain had ever heard of feminism.

With very few exceptions, most poems by women which appear in British pages, whether in books, newspapers or magazines, are published by men. To put it contentiously, most poems by women in print reflect how some man thinks women should sound. In some publishing houses the male poetry editor has a woman assistant who does a lot of the work but does not choose what to publish. There is currently only one woman commissioning books of adult poems in mainstream British publishing. This is the odder because the rest of publishing is full of high-powered women.

In 1997 the imbalance could have changed overnight. Labour came to power just as Faber (England's most powerful poetry publisher) was about to replace its poetry editor. The new government was about to appoint a new Poet Laureate. It was possible there might be, simultaneously, a woman Poet Laureate and a woman as Britain's most important poetry editor. But in each case the choice fell on a man. No complaint – these men are excellent at their jobs; and none of this is complaint. It is reportage. The imbalance may be coincidence, but I bet it is not. The decisions of these two male establishments reflected a cultural bias which for some reason is particularly strong in poetry. Poetry chat rooms on the web are dominated by men, too.

In any magazine or publishing house, the darker side of policy and taste – what outsiders might call prejudice – is also what makes the publication, or the list of authors, individual. But policy or prejudice, they all produce the same gender bias: not just more men, but an emphasis on male leadership. So do media profiles. Recently the male editor of a key poetry magazine wrote a series of profiles of leading contemporary poets. They were unsigned, therefore purportedly objective. In fact their unexamined (and I am sure unconscious) yardstick was masculine leadership. Male poets were glossed by prizes and superlatives ('master of tones', 'range of styles', 'most powerful voice of his generation'); women by one note or theme in their work, who they were 'influenced by', or what reviewers had said.

Among poets themselves, testosterone bias is often unconscious, but women poets are aware of it all the time. Often, the more formally strong or punctilious a male poet is in his work, the keener on controlling traditional patterns of rhyme and metre, the more damning he can be, in unguarded moments, of women's poems. Think technical, think male. I recently asked one such poet, who had just come back from reading in America, which US poets he'd met. 'Oh, several here and there,' he said. 'None of those awful women, of course.' I've heard another, a colleague I like and admire, say in his cups, 'There are no decent women poets except the lesbians.'

It is possible that deep in some men's minds the writing of poetry is so identified with their own sexuality that they cannot really open up to poems by women unless the women are clearly differentiated from their own sexual partners. I'd like to think that wasn't true. There are shining exceptions among male poets. But generally, in poetry as elsewhere, power and technique do become, profoundly and often defensively, associated with maleness in male minds.

Some male poets interestingly confront this part of themselves in their own poems. But off guard, many imply that being in charge of metre and music is like flying a Boeing 707. Women are okay with softer more whimsical stuff, the washing-up of poetry, but you've got to be a man to do the business. Only men can be authoritative, structurally reliable. Form is male uniform (armour, a power suit) and only looks good on a woman if she's in drag.

It is nobody's fault that form and technique still carry for many people an unspoken charge of masculine supremacy. It comes from poetry's history. Ever since eighth-century BC Greece, the muse has been feminine, the poet male. (Sappho, the main Greek exception, came in for a lot of male attack from scholars down the ages.) The first lines of those first, and very male poems, the *Iliad* and *Odyssey*, invoke her. Western poetry begins as male creation with invisible and unheard female help. Poems by men control images of women – think of Shakespeare's sonnet beginning,

> My mistress' eyes are nothing like the sun;
> Coral is far more red than her lips' red;
> If snow be white, why then her breasts are dun;
> If hairs be wires, black wires grow on her head.

In the past, this control reflected men's control of women in society; and so did conventions of rhyme and metre, by which a poet controls shape, sound and meaning. These strategies of handling words were (and still are) poetry's technical metaphor for all other types of control reflected and suggested in the poem.

In writing workshops, and in reviews, men sometimes criticise a rhyme for not being 'strict'. I have never heard a woman do that. That metaphor 'strict', applied to rhyme and metre, once reflected the 'strictness' by which men also maintained social, sexual or political conventions. As in de Selincourt's attack on Auden above (p. 17), criticism of formal elements often masks a critic's defence of other values which he feels are also, more profoundly, under threat in the poem.

Few male critics, however acute and experienced, really see why the starting point of women poets should be different. Many are mystified about where women poets are 'coming from', and are therefore put off the poems. Many of the strongest women in this book have had reviews in which men (not usually poets themselves) ticked them off as 'whimsical', 'formless', 'incomprehensible', 'loose'. Like de Selincourt in 1936, male reviewers who do not want to hear what women are saying attack the way they say it.

Sean O'Brien (No. 12) is a distinguished critic as well as poet. In his critical book *The Deregulated Muse* he was one of the first to tackle the question of why male readers bristle at some women's poems. Male reviewers of Selima Hill, for instance, complain of 'whimsy and triviality' because, O'Brien argues, her work is 'not mannerly, negotiated surrealism' and does not 'ask the reader to agree to the possible validity of her way of seeing things'. Representing the poet as voyager, or discoverer, O'Brien suggests that Hill's imagination 'has already landed on the new continent' before the reader is aware of it, or sees the point of a new image. Her imagination is 'already *there*, even if its whereabouts are not yet clear'. Male readers, 'disorientated and irritated, fall back on catch-all dismissals' like whimsicality.

When I discussed these ideas in his book with O'Brien he said, 'Maybe it is not a question of how women write, but how men read.' Male readers, he implies, prefer an orderly progression towards a poem's disclosures – like, for instance, the associations created by a new image. With Hill's poems they do not get this progression. Finding themselves dumped by her images in a world they never wanted to see, they 'turn back at the border'. As Emily Dickinson wrote to her first reader Thomas Wentworth Higginson, 'You may think my gait "spasmodic". I am in danger, Sir. You think me "uncontrolled". I have no tribunal . . .'

Feminism's Breaking Wave: Why the Starting Point Is Different

Women writers born before about 1945 sometimes say, 'I don't write as a woman', or 'I don't think you're aware of being a particular gender as you write.' Younger ones do not. Women born between 1945 and 1955 grew up into their craft in the seventies, as Britain assimilated feminism. They were British poetry's breaking wave of feminism and were crucial to the way poetry changed, gathered itself and sparkled in the eighties.

This breaking-wave generation grew up mainly unaware of women precursors. At school they read men's poetry and were told this was poetry. Anything else was minor, like the name Christina Rossetti at the bottom of 'Goblin Market' in a mainly male anthology. Nobody said anything about women from earlier centuries (though enlightened English teachers of the seventies did introduce Emily Dickinson): the Victorian or Renaissance women we know about now, thanks to feminist scholarship. Nobody pointed out that the great poems that went into everyone's memories were written by men, and that the formal 'rules', as well as the whole tradition, of English poetry were all man-made.

All this was true also of women poets born before 1945. But they made the discovery of male bias, and decided how to cope with it in their poetry, on their own, unsupported by the communal insights of feminism. The generation born between 1945 and 1955 found their voices enriched by feminism, which spread from politics to literature and opened up a multitude of radical new approaches, both analytical and creative.

These poets (future poets, as they were then) loved good poems, therefore loved past male poems. Feminism forced them to work out what the fact that they were written by men meant to them. In her memoir, *Object Lessons*, Eavan Boland describes how, as an apprentice poet in sixties Ireland, she was unaware of her own estrangement from the male tradition she was steeped in. Like young black writers in Africa or Asia in the same years, she only gradually realised that the writing she admired treated what she herself was as an object, alien to the writer. A writer was expected to be in their case white, in her case male.

For me, the crucial poets at school, whose work I learnt by heart, were Shakespeare, Tennyson, Keats, Donne, Gerard Manley Hopkins and T.S. Eliot. Then, out of school, came Louis MacNeice, Geoffrey Hill, Thomas Wyatt, Basil Bunting, Yeats, Auden. All became obsessingly important to me in turn. Only much later did I meet the work of Sylvia Plath, Elizabeth Bishop, Anna Akhmatova. It seems amazing now but I simply *did not notice*, just as I didn't when reading essential essays about poetry (by Auden, Eliot, Pound and later Heaney), that these writers were men, and were invisibly inoculating me (through no fault of their own, just by the maleness of the tradition they were part of) with unexamined male assumptions about masculine and feminine in poetry.

I was reading as if I were male, thinking male, when I was not. I believed that only words, and what they did together, counted; that you could handle words on their own without any luggage of attitude and belief. Male poets can still think that if they like. Since the seventies, women cannot. Feminism made them realise they couldn't.

Feminist insights are now clichés to all young women growing up and 'men's perceptions of women' are as integral to English GCSE as the poems of Carol Ann Duffy. But that does not mean everything is solved for young women poets today. One problem is that poets starting out need models – that is how they grow – and all poems are partly in dialogue with past poems by other people; and you can't change the fact that most of the great past poems are by men. Women poets' relation with these poems is always going to be different, in some degree, from men's. Eavan Boland will read Wordsworth's 'The Solitary Reaper' differently from Seamus Heaney.

For women, the conversation with the past that every responsible poet eventually takes on has to address its maleness. You can be teasing, passionate, challenging, antagonistic, indulgent or sceptical about it, as well as admiring. But you have to face it, and work out your own relation with it, in your work.

Poems by men through the ages tend to present women in two ways which women have to be aware of. They present women as objects of male attention. For women using them as models, this makes for a self-estrangement you may not notice at first, because you naturally identify with the poem's maker and the voice of the poem. Male poets also ventriloquise a woman's voice. (Think of the voices of Tennyson's abandoned women, Mariana, the Lady of Shalott, Oenone; or Ovid's women in the *Heroides*.) These voices are male versions of a woman saying 'I'. Ventriloquising women is a basic part of the Western male poetic kit. Homer describes not just how Helen of Troy looks, but what she says and feels. Men have made some of their best poetry (and opera, and popular songs) by imagining and expressing the feelings of women.

Until feminism questioned it, this body of work provided women's basic blueprint for how a woman sounds in words. As King Lear says of his daughter, 'Her voice was ever soft,/Gentle and low, an excellent thing in woman.' Inevitably, women poets in the past often wrote in voices precast for them by male poetry, ventriloquising back the voice ventriloquised for them by men.

All this means that for women now the starting point for writing poems has to be different from that of men. They have to be aware of and question both these things: woman as object, and the 'I' men have attributed to her. And then redo the whole thing, their way.

The solution of the breaking-wave generation (represented here especially by three very different poets, Carol Ann Duffy, Selima Hill and Jo Shapcott) was to make questioning the maleness of the tradition, and their own femaleness in relation to it, central to their work. Another reason why some male critics find that work rebarbative.

Questioning maleness sometimes involves questioning rules or conventions that male poetry developed. All poets have to question and test each bit of the tradition. If you also have to question the maleness of what's said, you may find you have to float free from man-made moorings in how you sound as well as in what you say: in architecture as well as thought.

Men who shrug off this problem should try picturing things the other way round. What if all the poems and songs they'd ever heard were by women? What if the male self-image and male voices in all the poems they knew and identified with were created by how women saw men, how women thought men should feel? Suppose a million female ideas of the male self-image had been at work in the imagination of Simon Armitage and Derek Walcott ever since they first understood words? If all the words they ever heard reinforced what women thought they, as men, should say, would they have written the poems they have?

Escaping the Ghetto: Persona, Tone and Talking Back

When feminism got going in Britain in the seventies it affected poetry instantly, but two elements tended to ghettoise women's poetry as a specialist subcategory. One was subject-matter. Seventies feminism claimed domesticity – domestic space, childcare, women's work, lives, fabrics, memories – as a valid subject for poetry along with the earth mother, earth goddess role for the poet. That was fine. It extended boundaries. But it also made it easier for male critics and poets to ignore 'women's poetry' as irrelevant, something they didn't need to read.

The other was emotion. Before feminism, it was a male cliché that women wrote more 'openly' about their feelings. Openly, therefore badly, was the unspoken corollary. Kingsley Amis wrote a poem set in a bookshop about the 'embarrassing' nakedness of women's verse, ending with the cosily patronising comment, 'Women are really much nicer than men. That's why we like them.'

No poet wants to limit his or her work to set topics, set ways of presenting emotion; especially not to ways men perceive as suitable for women. The generation of women who grew up into poetry through the seventies, and began publishing in the eighties, wanted to write *poetry*, not 'women's poetry'. They wanted, as Jo Shapcott said to me once, 'to work out of the main quarry', not chip away with pearl-handled penknives in a side-quarry marked 'women only'. They aimed to use the whole artillery, like blokes: the whole palette of vocabulary, registers, wit, politics. 'Open' emotion – yes, fine, when needed. But also a whole complex texture of tones, from witty to devious, mischievous, lyrical, tragical, pastoral. They wanted to experiment with everything that matters in a poem: form, structure, voice, surface lustre and vocabulary. Women's input into eighties poetry was powered almost more than anything else by new approaches to tone and persona: the voices of a poem.

Women's poems in the eighties and nineties increasingly spotlit the surrealities and oddities of man-made reality. They suggested new ways of seeing in many different ways: leaping sequences of images, dramatic monologues from politicised voices, surprising juxtapositions, rapid shifts of register and stance, through the strange perceptions of science, photography and painting, and the masks of different personas, either historical or invented.

Many fine women poets from all over the world – Britain, America, Australia and Russia – were writing important poems long before feminism came along. Several poets in this book were not affected by feminism in their formative years (see Nos 17, 19 and 21) and many looked outside Britain for their models. Feinstein, for instance, was deeply influenced by Russian women she translated, especially Marina Tsvetaeva. In the late fifties and sixties, just before feminism burst on the scene, there had been the American writers, Marianne Moore, Elizabeth Bishop, Anne Sexton, Sylvia Plath. Of these, the influential poets in the eighties increasingly became (especially but not only for women) Bishop and Plath.

They were very different. Plath is deep inside most British poets today, both women and men. Not because she is a feminist icon, but because of her poetic brilliance: extraordinary linguistic control, wit, imagery and risk; how her poems move, laughter in the face of despair. Bishop is becoming more and more read for her mix of subtle thought with deep feeling, humour, persona (her sequence of Robinson Crusoe poems, for instance), her sympathetic eye for the outside world that feeds straight back into the inner, her music, craft and strength. Both, in completely different ways, push at the boundaries of register. Within a single line they can shift the tone towards laughter and scepticism and interrogate what their own poem is doing, from inside it.

A development by British women poets of the eighties, in response to these models, to feminism, and the politics of the time, was a persona, a voice and a gaze that looked and talked back at the conventional (and usually male) observer. Poems by women began to talk sardonically, teasingly, sceptically, tenderly, back at male tradition and those who represent it.

The classic love poem made the women the object of man's feelings and gaze. So turn it round. In Duffy's book *The World's Wife*, women like Mrs Orpheus, Frau Freud and Elvis's Twin Sister look back at their men, just as Vicki Feaver's Judith (No. 33) watches Holofernes sleeping. Sometimes the looking back has a political or racial spin. One poem here looks back at a Scotswoman who asks the black Scottish poet where she comes 'from' (No. 37).

The looking back impulse can go both ways, and is fruitful now for men as well as women. James Lasdun (No. 34) parodies the way male poems objectify women, through the voice of a snake looking at, and being looked back at by, a woman; its voice is also that of the devil tempting Eve. Like Don Paterson (No. 30), Lasdun holds male narcissism up to the light; observes the man observing, or making love to, a woman. Both are post-feminist male poems by men who have learnt from the looking and talking back of women's poems and are taking it in their own direction.

Jo Shapcott's poems, in particular, are full of objects talking back to those who study them, denying the bossy reality constructed by other people. In one of her poems a 'quark' talks perkily back to the scientist observing it; in another series, the 'roses' of Rilke's French poems become female genitalia talking back to the male poet writing poems to them.

It is a risk to write in personas like that, and some male reviewers react to it as whimsical. Shapcott's 'Mad Cow' poems tease a male cliché – the words 'mad' (or neurotic) 'cow', applied to a woman men don't understand, are afraid of, do not want to think of as clever, unusual, strong, imaginative. (All the qualities which women are used to men feeling defensive about.) In 'The Mad Cow Talks Back', Shapcott's speaker explains how useful it is to have a mind full of holes, a spongiform brain. Her cow persona says,

> It's risky when
> you're good, so of course the legs go before,
> behind and to the side of the body from time
> to time, and then there's the general embarrassing

collapse, but when that happens it's glorious
because it's always when you're travelling
most furiously in your mind.

And she winds up saying, 'This is the way, this is the way to go.' For, despite problems of balance, it has been an enormous creative strength for women poets to work in forms created by men against some of the deepest assumptions and impulses inherent in those forms.

Yet it still sometimes feels – ask any poet who's a woman – like being under siege.

5. Readers: This is your Poetry

Why Has Poetry Lost Its Audience?

There is a paradox about poetry's role in Britain today. On the one hand there are poetry festivals, competitions and prizes up and down the country, resident poets in institutions from the Royal Mail to London Zoo, and poems commissioned every day by other institutions: town councils, hospitals, theatres, radio. Poems are bricked into pavements and written in glass on the windows of delicatessens. Poetry, it seems, has never been so popular. There are endless anthologies and collections for children, poems by living poets are key texts on exam curricula, poets teach creative writing in schools, and there are new creative writing courses in universities. Yet poetry has also never had such a low profile in the media and literary community, nor so few readers proportionate to the numbers who buy and read other serious books. Most poets feel they are existing in the cracks between the paving-stones; that what they write is not only unread but regarded by many people with wariness, indifference or hostility. Writing poetry, said Simon Armitage recently, is shouting down the toilet.

There are many sorts of poetry around. Oral poets, performance poets, charismatic storytellers and rappers have huge audiences. Experimental poetry, based mainly but not only in universities, is beginning to be more visible in poetry magazines. There is also a lot of importantly inventive work for children. Poetry is a spectrum: ideally, its different areas learn from and respect each other. Poems like the fifty-two here, available to the public in books, exist somewhere in the middle: you could call them mainstream. But would-be readers have no context to put them in.

In the past, the core audience of such 'mainstream' poetry was grown-ups who took an interest in other arts too: the middle classes, professional classes, people who had been to college. In Central Europe, such people still take an active interest in similarly mainstream poetry written and published for them, within their own society. But in Britain, these are the people outstandingly missing from poetry's readership.

If we look far back to, say, the early 1870s, we see British lawyers, bankers, doctors and their familes devouring 'The Idylls of the King' as their equivalents today queue for exhibitions at the Tate. Tennyson's reputation and popularity had by then been at their height for twenty years; the chattering classes read new collections of poems as they now read the Booker shortlist. By the 1880s–90s, poetry was becoming a little dangerous (Swinburne) or difficult (Meredith): William Morris and Oscar Wilde were all the rage, but in prose. Yet still, up to the 1920s or 1930s, the literate middle classes, especially people who dealt in words themselves – journalists, essayists, fiction writers – thought the poetry of their time was relevant and necessary to their lives. They knew who it was written for: them.

All that has gone. Most of today's professionals, even if they studied English at university, do not open a book of poems by a living author from one year's end to the next. Most people who read the Booker shortlist and the latest well-reviewed biography never buy a book of poems. Most college-educated people, and the wider literary community, see poetry today as élitist, irrelevant, obscure. Worthy perhaps (that backhanded compliment), but out of touch and marginal. Poetry does have an audience today, but the biggest and strangest slice of the population missing from it is that of the college-educated professionals.

How did this happen? How come the oldest, most passionate, concentrated literary form came to be seen by people it traditionally spoke to as marginal and difficult – especially when it isn't? When and how did the alienation set in?

I think you have to look for reasons in the changes which happened both within poetry and in its readers' working and leisure lives. These changes began roughly in the 1920s.

On poetry's side what did it, I think, was modernism. Many readers who felt comfortable with traditional forms were put off when modernism broke all these up, did away with familiar poetic furniture, and hauled into poetry language and objects they felt were 'unpoetic'. Poetry was suddenly both lower and higher than it had been. It was a collage of shockingly disparate colloquialisms and esoteric allusions.

As education widened and broadened, a lot of history and literature fell out of the curricula; people from the widening spectrum of the middle class no longer shared the same educational horizons, and erudite references in a poem made people who did not recognise them feel uncomfortable, resentful. Why should *that* knowledge (the literary quotations and foreign languages, for example, in T.S. Eliot's *The Waste Land* or Pound's *Cantos*) be privileged above theirs? And if poetry was into privileging knowledge like that, why read it? That was where the popular idea began that poetry is 'difficult', exclusive, and does not even expect the general reader to understand.

Modernism blew everything apart for poetry. It was exciting and innovative; it mixed everything up, beat down constricting fences, let in the jungle of modern life, brought vernacular speech back into poems – lines that were, as Sylvia Plath once put it in a letter, 'born out of the way words should be said'. But it was also where poetry lost its natural audience.

Many members of that audience wanted to rest in what they knew when they read a poem (as well as feeling uplifted, as they were by, for example, Tennyson). They also wanted to turn to poetry when they needed consolation.

Art should not 'console', said Iris Murdoch in a famous essay, but sometimes it is the only thing that can, and people often turn to poetry in a crisis. After the terrorist attacks of 11 September 2001, 'September 1st 1939', a poem on the beginning of the Second World War by W.H. Auden (which ruminates on Manhattan skyscrapers as an emblem of modern power and the isolation of American consumer culture, and says 'The unmentionable odour of death / Offends the September night') was read on US National Public Radio. Soon after, the Poetry Society of America (in alliance with ten of New York's literary organisations and writing programmes) held a reading in New York. Well-known American poets read poems by Ahkmatova, Yeats, Auden, Neruda, Dickinson, Bishop and others, and *twelve hundred people* came to listen. Poetry was suddenly needed.

At the same time Patsy Rodenburg, voice-trainer at London's

National Theatre, was teaching a Shakespeare-speaking course in New York. 'They were yearning for profound work,' she told me afterwards, 'because you can go to the great plays and not feel so lonely. I did *Richard III*, *Julius Caesar*, plays full of envy, grief, murder, horror; plays about what they were facing in their city and the world outside. They got the power of it – what's comforting is that it has happened before; that Shakespeare has structured the words and thoughts for us.'

Poetry helps us 'not feel so lonely'. The patterning of words, and the structure of thought, somehow echoes (and, if it doesn't heal, it validates and sets in a world context) your own feelings.

But when you turn to poetry for consolation like this, you want to be able to rely on it. When you fling yourself for comfort into an armchair, you are not looking for a bed of nails. Since modernism came, many people today, in Britain at least, no longer expect poetry to welcome, to be there for them.

On the readers' side, many changes in work, life and play since the twenties have meant a never-before pressure on everyone's time. We also have massive amounts of print to read daily; plus a multitude of other cultural artefacts competing with poetry for our attention.

You have to have time, and something like solitude, to go into and out of a poem, turn it over, think about it. That is part of the pleasure. 'Poems on the Underground' is a popular scheme partly because the crowded solitude of a tube ride among strangers is an oddly good place and time to be alone with a poem.

At work, most people now have an exhausting reading load. Even doctors have to spend longer reading patients' notes on screen than attending to the lesion those notes are about. I asked a fifty-year-old barrister, who'd had all of English literature at his fingertips when he was a student at Oxford, why he never read poetry now. 'Because of all the other stuff I have to read,' he said. 'Piles of papers – and hundreds and thousands of pounds hang on what I get out of them. The last thing I want to do after that is open a book, especially something you have to concentrate on.'

Compare early reviewing of poetry in late eighteenth- and nineteeth-century periodicals like the *Edinburgh Review*: many of those reviews were written by lawyers.

I think many people today feel they simply haven't got enough reading attention left over at the end of their working day to face a book of poems. With genre fiction – a thriller, romance, sex and shopping – you can throw your mind on the story, bob about on its surface, let its waves take you where they will. With a poem you have to check your own reactions, wonder what you think, or there's no point.

Then there is the cultural competition. 'I have backslid about poetry,' a writer on design and architecture told me. 'When I was at college I loved it. But I don't know what to read any more, and there are so many other things. It's not like the 1920s. They didn't have everything we have. To relax, I can go on the web, go to the movies, watch telly – there's no room for poetry.'

All these people – barristers, designers, doctors, whoever – *could* keep a book of poems by the bed and read just one before falling asleep. But they haven't the time and energy to sift the books and choose the one that will suit them. They are all read out.

And they are not helped, not given any context within which to choose a book they might like, by the mirror of our culture which also directs such choices: the media.

The Literary Community, the Media

Indifference to poetry is most startling in the literary community. With a few wonderful exceptions, most publishers, literary journalists and even books editors on newspapers do not read much modern poetry. I have heard a fiction reviewer say, 'Poetry lost its way in the twentieth century', and a top novelist declare, 'Poetry is an outmoded art form.' 'Do you read it?' I asked. No: but they had strong views about why they needn't, what was wrong with it, why it no longer mattered.

'Poetry is not an obligatory part of the territory,' one books editor told me. 'No one thinks you're slipping up if you run the books pages and haven't opened the latest Michael Donaghy. It isn't important.' Another books editor, on a Sunday paper, was shown by his predecessor how to decide (from the many bulging sacks, as big and weighty as body bags, lugged into the office every day) which books to review. 'You speed-read,' she told him. 'To know what a book's about, what the writing's like, skim the first sentence of each paragraph on the left-hand page to get the gist. But it doesn't work with poetry.'

Maybe that's one reason why, in a community which has to make fast public judgements about a huge range of books, poetry has been marginalised. Over a hundred thousand books are published every year. Even someone who did nothing else but read books would be pushed to manage more than, say, seven or eight hundred, and literary editors have a lot more to do besides reading books. They have to take short cuts by skimming, speed-reading; they have to form opinions by osmosis, hearsay and hunches. But poetry doesn't lend itself to short cuts in the same way. You either read it properly, or not at all. You cannot speed-read a poem.

Another reason is that publishing is now part of the entertainment business, glamour is an eye-catching way of writing about it, and poems, unless associated with scandal, do not give themselves easily to glamour. There is no shock; no story. Poets themselves are another matter – if, for example, they can be sold to the papers as 'Byronic'. But the media want the poet to be glamorous rather than the poems. The smouldering photo, not the critique or the craft.

Books editors, like the editors of all other sections of a newspaper, are constantly fighting for space on the page. Partly against the paper's designers and the impulse to make the pictures, even the wordless white margins, ever bigger. Which means fewer and shorter reviews.

But also, every books page you ever see in a paper is the result of a books editor's battle with two other things. One is with advertisements. Ads mean revenue. If the ad is for a book, the books editor has to take it, even at the last minute, and out goes a review to make room. 'When I was a books editor,' said Blake Morrison, a poet who is also an excellent journalist and has worked in papers as well as writing for them, 'what I resented was taking *house* ads just to use up "allocated" ad space. Sometimes I'd fight these off and get a couple of extra reviews in as a result.'

The books editor's other battle is against other pages of the paper, which most people at that paper (and most editors higher up) believe to be more important, i.e. more popular, than books. Papers vary in their attitudes and resources: how much money they allot to, for example, their books pages. Any book review space can be seen by higher powers in the paper as being out of proportion to the interests of most potential buyers; and poetry is seen as a more glaringly minority interest still.

This view of the situation may be writerly paranoia on my part. 'I don't think books and poetry fare worse in this respect than politics, say, or fishing,' one features editor said to me, 'and I don't think advertisers or editors have anything particular against poetry as opposed to prose. Everyone fights for space for their own section.'

And yet right across the board of the broadsheet newspapers, most books of poems these days are now not reviewed at all. Wordsworth's *Lyrical Ballads* was given an average of six to eight pages' coverage in the reviewing weeklies of the day. Today a book of poems by even a well-known poet is lucky to get a few lines in a five-hundred-word 'poetry round-up', as if poetry collections roam untended on the prairie, rarely sighted in the civilised corral of a bookshop. Many collections in which the poems in this book first appeared were not reviewed in the national press at all, and you may have to order them in bookshops, which increasingly return books to the publisher's warehouse after three weeks of 'shelf life'. The public never knew they had come out.

Books editors tell poets that editors higher up the paper don't like poetry reviews (and this tends to be true), but they themselves may also feel that poetry reviews just don't make interesting reading. There isn't a story to tell, as with fiction or biography; quoting from poems produces awkward line breaks, off-putting on the page; and poets reviewing poetry sometimes talk in an insiderish way which makes other readers feel left out. The poet-reviewer probably knows the author (the poetry world is very small), so personal feelings may be lurking in the judgement too.

All this, quite reasonably, makes books editors uneasy. Poetry is not like other sorts of book.

Radio gives space to poetry: poetry programmes are very popular. TV does not: it is hard to fit into current TV ideology and schedules, though if an imaginative producer dreamed up a five-minute slot for a daily poem and twisted the programmers' arms to make them run it, this would, I suspect, become very popular too. In newspapers, the traditional conduit through which the media bring poetry before the public, the recent disappearance of poetry reviews is very marked. 'When I was at the *Observer* between 1981 and 1989,' Blake Morrison told me, 'Peter Porter did a monthly round-up, so forty or fifty new collections got at least a mention every year. Other people did the same at the *Guardian* and the *Sunday Times*. Where is that coverage now?'

Yet newspapers print more actual poems than they used to do. The *Independent* has a daily poem, the *Guardian* prints one or more each Saturday, there is a poetry series in the *Mirror*. So here is another paradox: more poems in papers, but fewer reviews.

Without the reviews, readers who have little contact with poetry get less and less of a context within which to read any poems they come across. Suppose you only saw one TV programme a week, an untypically short programme (poems in newspapers have to be extremely short) chosen for you by someone who probably does not watch a lot of TV themselves. With no TV reviews either, and no mention of TV activity in the news, would you get a fair idea of what's available, how TV is developing, what it can offer?

Poetry has had a complicated relationship with journalism ever since newspapers began. The term journalism covers a wide spectrum of voices and quality, from some of the best writing of our time to celebrity gossip. But nearly all journalism loves the line that Bob Dylan is better than Keats and Eminem is the new Browning. Many non-literary journalists seem to assume the poetry they do not read is less 'relevant' to the modern psyche than pop lyrics. 'Poetry – it's all about daffodils and dead men, right?' asked the 'Hot News' slot in a recent issue of *Elle*. 'Wrong. Not with Robbie Williams and J from Five about to bare their souls with collections of poems.'

Indifference and suspicion sometimes slide into hostility. When the current Poet Laureate publishes a new poem, other poets are rung up from news (not books) desks and asked what they think of it. This is not a neutral question: the journalists are looking for comments to underpin a headline like, 'Poets Knock Laureate's Poem'.

On one of these occasions I refused to look at the poem but said the Laureate was a great ambassador for poetry. That was not quoted in the piece which, when it came out, was so gratuitously negative that the paper's editor wrote to the Laureate to apologise. Meanwhile the news desk of another Sunday paper asked the books editor of its sister daily paper to write an account of the same poem. He wrote the piece, saying enthusiastic and critical things about the poem. The news desk did not think he was negative enough. They rewrote the piece as reportage: an objective-sounding description of the poem which quoted only the negative comments from his original article. That is how accounts of the Laureate's work – and professional reactions to it – reach the public.

This situation hangs on something much wider than a single poet's profile. It is not only poetry stories that news editors sensationalise or formula-ise. 'Ultimately,' a features editor told me sadly, 'all journalists end up as creatures who make snap judgements of everything.' But the snap-judgement poetry formula in use by news desks today does seem, at least to poets, strangely combative.

News journalists seem to attribute to poets the negative reaction and hostility to all new poems which they themselves assume. The stories they look for are about infighting or disagreement between poets. That's the angle. They do not ring up other cooks for negative comments on a recipe from a celebrity chef. It is as if news journalists suspect poets of setting themselves up as 'better' in some way, and have to keep bringing poetry down a peg; laugh at it for pettiness; make it know its place.

Maybe behind the uneasy relationship poetry has with written journalism is a divergence in attitude over the thing the two have in common: writing. One comment editor on a national broadsheet told a friend of mine he would never commission a comment piece from a poet because, he said, 'I hate poets. They never say things straight.'

For a while I used to choose the best of fifty unpublished poetry collections every quarter with another poet far senior to me, for the Poetry Book Society, which offers its members discounts on these books. It took a long time to read the collections and agree on 'the best': decisions like that matter a lot in the small world of poetry, and profoundly affect the fortunes (and sales) of a book. Our fee was £100 each. We needed the money, but one quarter the cheques got lost in the post. My colleague was worried; I happened to mention our lost cheques to a journalist friend. He was in the middle of writing a magazine profile, for a fee of £800, of a play he had not seen. I sat beside him while he phoned someone who had, to get the material. Then he reacted to my story.

'That man,' he said, about my poet colleague, 'is *famous*. Surely he doesn't have to worry about *a hundred pounds*?' He knew writing poems was an uneconomic activity but could not imagine a 'famous' writer needing desperately what was to him so lightly earned.

Such discrepancy of work, pay and responsibility inevitably creates other differences. Ezra Pound called poetry 'news that stays news'. 'If he's right,' said Blake Morrison to me, 'maybe that's why some journalists feel touchy or inferior, and aren't comfortable with poetry. Poetry reminds them of their own evanescence, of the place today's newspaper will have tomorrow – wrapping fish and chips or lining the cat litter. Maybe poetry will always sit oddly in newspapers because (at best) it's deeper and more lasting than daily ephemera.'

The minority interest argument is a self-fulfilling prophecy. If you

54

treat something as a 'minority interest' and hardly mention it, the interest is likely to become more minority still. Once something is marginalised, it becomes more marginalised. And because most people, including journalists, don't meet much poetry first-hand, they start to think of poetry as a closed world in which small cliques promote one another's work and exclude outsiders: another media story that appears about poets from time to time. It is easy for journalists to perceive poetry as an exclusive little world of its own, to perceive themselves as outsiders to it, and imagine that an axis of personalities has carved up the realm of public poetry. In fact the same names appear all the time because the media itself demands recognisable names when reporting any subject.

It is a pity that the people most likely to feel 'touchy and inferior' to poetry, for whatever reasons, are the ones with the most power to bring it – or not – to public attention. For in the end it is the public, whom newspapers supposedly serve, who lose out on something they need at least as much as they need politics or fishing.

It's Not that Difficult, Not Elitist, Obscure or Irrelevant: and It's Written for You

Poets today back off from the word 'poetic'. They associate it with facile waffle, impressionistic imprecision. So did Shakespeare. 'I took great pains to study it,' wails Viola, forbidden to recite her master's love speech to Olivia in *Twelfth Night*, 'and 'tis poetical.' 'It is the more like to be feigned,' replies Olivia.

Shakespeare is laughing at 'poetical'. In his day, as in ours, good poets, like good journalists, would far rather be called accurate. The 'difficulty' of poems lies in their compactness, the way they fold many connections into a small space; not in any obscurity. Their so-called difficulties are anyway, as I've argued, not that different from complexities we really enjoy sorting out when we watch a film.

But many people do not expect poems to operate in a modern elliptical way like smart TV ads or film. They are encouraged to feel that poetry belongs to the past. I was recently asked to comment for a TV news programme on a CD by a performance poet. 'Can you talk about how this is the modern poetry?' said the producer. 'Instead of the old-fashioned stuff?' 'What do you mean by old-fashioned stuff?' I asked. She wasn't sure. 'Do you mean, "Poetry in books?"' Yes, that was it exactly. Poetry in books. Old-fashioned.

Led by the media, many people tend to feel that 'poetry in books' is also élitist: that word redolent of the British obsession with class that underlies many cultural judgements.

Whatever 'élitist' is, the poets in this book are not it. Not all went to college, few went to Oxbridge, none (not even the Nobel Prize-winners) are rich. Less than half, I'd say, came from middle-class homes. In their work, they aim (and I think succeed) to be the exact opposite of superior, obscure or irrelevant.

The subjects of the poems that follow are things that matter to all of us: memory, childhood, embarrassment; war, illness, death, love; dreams, art, jealousy, betrayal, loss. They are about cooking, rain at the bus stop, parents, defloration; about being unable to drive, shitting in the woods, being misunderstood. About cruelty, self-transformation through sexuality, male chauvinism; about identity, origin, landscape, home and hope, mourning, inequality and immigration; ambition, incest, and failure, slavery and exile. About not being able to handle the world, and yourself, as you'd like.

The writers tackle their subjects with fun and expertise; they want to give readers pleasure through the way they put together their vision of the upsetting but interesting reality they share with them. The hardest, longest stage of writing a poem is equivalent to the film director's experience on the cutting-room floor. You have most of the material. The problem is how to arrange it, what tiny additions might bring out a connection between one bit and the next, and what (above all) to cut. Hard work, discipline, concentration and tricky decisions are common to both enterprises. But no one calls the director of *Bridget Jones* élitist.

Poets do not want to be 'obscure', either. They would rather be clear than 'poetic'. They meet audiences all the time at readings. Poetry's rejuvenation in the eighties followed the rise of poetry readings in the sixties, and poets know how poems go over, what clarity means for a modern audience. A crucial feature of today's poetry is its desire to be clear to readers without giving up on complexity.

The poems here are carefully crafted and structured, but not all of the ways they get their effects will have been put there consciously by the poet. Some will have been, some won't. How conscious they were does not matter, and the same goes for the reader. Technical effects hold the poem together and make it effective, but you don't need to know about them consciously to feel them at work as you read. When you admire the lines of a

56

bridge, you don't have to understand the principles of structural engineering. When you catch your breath at gorgeous mosaics in a church, you do not need to know rules of design, religious symbolism and technique of fixing tesserae, nor see the hidden bits round the tops of the arches, to have a satisfying emotional and aesthetic response to the whole thing.

Responding is what matters: the reader's unconscious as well as conscious mind is at work in reacting to the poem, just as the poet's conscious and unconscious thoughts worked together to make it. Poems by Simon Armitage, for instance, are hugely popular but work with deeply literary subtlety. Very sophisticatedly, they use the whole box of literary tricks that poetry has developed over the centuries, side by side with a modern grammar of implication which audiences take in their stride in other media. Somehow, readers have just not been told that they can enjoy in poems all the wit, irony, comedy, imagination and obliquity they take for granted in a film.

I'm not pitching a line about the poetry renaissance. This *is* a good, interesting time for poetry: strong, rich, original poems are being written. But only readers can make this a good time for reading it. Borges said a poem is completed by the reader: it does not exist till it is read.

So it's over to you. The poems that follow were made for you from all the textures of life around you, from what we all see in newspapers and the home, on TV, on the street. There are a lot of acute, lively and non-élitist minds out there making poems from the world we live in: from styles of thought and phrase, jokes, events and experiences we all share. If you pass them by, aren't you missing out on an important part of modern life, and modern pleasure?

THE POEMS

1. Jo Shapcott

MRS NOAH: TAKEN AFTER THE FLOOD

I can't sit still these days. The ocean
is only memory, and my memory as fluttery
as a lost dove. Now the real sea beats
inside me, here, where I'd press fur and feathers
if I could. I'm middle-aged and plump.
Back on dry land I shouldn't think these things:
big paws which idly turn to bat the air,
my face by his ribs and the purr which ripples
through the boards of the afterdeck,
the roar – even at a distance – ringing in my bones,
the rough tongue, the claws, the little bites,
the crude taste of his mane. If you touched my lips
with salt water I would tell you such words,
words to crack the sky and launch the ark again.

(1998)

Shapcott was born in London in 1953, grew up in the Forest of Dean, and studied in Ireland and America. She has worked in arts administration, often with musicians, and been influenced by poets as diverse as the American Elizabeth Bishop and the Elizabethan Philip Sidney. Her poems use playful, feminist, often surreal postmodern wit, quick changes of tone pivoting on a single adjective, to explore sexual politics, loss, longing, identity, language and myth. They sometimes approach their subjects through sensual things poetry often leaves unmentioned: smells, tastes, detritus in the crannies of the house or human body. Inside all that is a persona howling in a multitude of poetic disguises which range from Greek goddesses to roses and mad cows.

This poem is about memories of passion voiced afterwards by a woman now back on dry land, middle-aged and plump. The word taken in the title has several resonances: each implies a different sort of flood. Most obviously, a woman taken sexually, and a flood of overwhelming feeling in remembering a 'voyage' of animal sexuality; but also physical liquids. Taken also suggests a photograph, as if the whole poem is a snap taken on Ararat after Mrs Noah's cruise. And it resonates further with lines from *Julius Caesar*:

> There is a tide in the affairs of men,
> Which, taken at the flood, leads on to fortune . . .
> On such a full sea are we now afloat . . .

These resonances in the title sustain the poem as it moves to its final image: something is about to be 'launched' again. On a 'full sea', no doubt, as in the Shakespeare.

The last lines compound the poem's turbulent Shakespearian feel. Before King Lear goes mad, his speech (beginning 'O, reason not the need') ends in unspecific threats: 'I will do such things – / What they are yet I know not – but they shall be / The terrors of the earth.' In his next scene he cries, 'Blow, winds, and crack your cheeks!' Shapcott is steeped in Shakespeare. From I would tell you such words to crack the sky, echoes of tragic need, madness and unbearable memory surface at the end to explain the opening, I can't sit still.

The music works through close vowel-echoes. Some in close pairs (suggesting the ark's animal pairs, perhaps) or triplets: sit still, memory/fluttery, real sea beats, hear/fur, rough tongue, taste/mane, crude/you, and salt water (followed by launch). Others ripple (like that purr) through the poem in waves, underpinning the feel of that fluttery ocean, a sea that beats inside both the woman and her words (the one repeated word).

I, the key word, is echoed in my (in a stressed position in the second line), inside, I'd, I, I'm, dry, I, idly, my, my, bites, I, sky. The vowel on which the poem first pauses, days, is echoed in middle-aged, face, taste, and the last two pause-places: mane, and again, the word on which the whole poem rests, as it prepares to get up and go (because – as it says at the beginning – it can't sit still). The vowel of the poem's second pause word, dove, is echoed in plump, the first word that ends a sentence at a line-end; then in rough tongue, touched, such. Fur (which begins to elide human and animal) rises out of here, where (picked up in air), then ricochets through turn, purr, words, words, widening en route to boards, roar, claws.

There are technical points here about form and rhythm that will come up in other poems, so it is worth unpacking them now.

This poem is a SONNET. There are six others coming later (Nos 3, 6, 8, 16, 27 and 35). SONNETS traditionally have fourteen lines with a shift or TURN of emotional direction after eight lines. If they are divided into STANZAS, the division is normally either four QUATRAINS (four-liners) with a COUPLET at the end, or (the shape which tends to dominate how you feel about SONNETS) an OCTET (eight lines) followed by a SESTET (six). 'A sonnet', says Seamus Heaney in an essay, 'is about movement in a form. It is about eight and six, a waist and a middle.'

The SONNET's asymmetrical proportion has sometimes been compared to the 'Golden Section', the mathematical ratio of roughly 8:5 which appears all over the place in nature, classical architecture and painting. People have argued that because of this 'eight and six' proportion the SONNET is a 'natural' unit of human thought.

Greek and Roman poets seem to have given this bit of 'natural thought' a miss; but it has certainly become natural (whatever natural is) for poets in the European tradition ever since the Renaissance, when the SONNET was invented.

Nearly all English-language poets write SONNETS at some point. Modern poets do a lot of them. The poems may be in BLOCK FORM like this one, with no STANZA divisions, but they normally keep some feel of emotional or imaginative TURN, an intellectual change of direction or focus, after roughly eight lines. The TURN here, though, comes after six lines, at things: when the physical things which the woman remembers about her lover's body start 'flooding' back.

The twentieth century diversified the SONNET's form, sometimes changing the number of lines from fourteen and taking the metre away from the IAMBIC PENTAMETER of the Renaissance, changing line-length (see No. 8) and rhyme-pattern. Unrhymed SONNETS (like this) have been popular since the fifties. So there is a lot of formal choice now in writing a SONNET, and as with any poem the poet chooses a shape that will underline what the poem is deeply about.

Such a choice is not necessarily conscious. When you decide a poem's shape, you go for what 'feels right', never mind why. (Poets often say things like 'the poem decides the form': they feel led to a form by the material as it unfolds.) But relation of form to meaning, the way form serves meaning, is always behind that 'feeling right'.

Here, the BLOCK FORM reflects the speaker's desire to make everything stick together: fur and feathers, woman and lion, ark and ocean, paired vowel-sounds. 'No separateness' is the motto for a poem upset by distance, whose vehicle, the ark, was the target of that archetypal animal two-by-two.

Then there's rhythm.

English poetry, like other modern European languages, feels rhythm through stress and beat. The decisive thing is which syllable you stress in a word when you say it normally. In this poem, for instance, we would stress the first syllable of memory and ripples, the last syllable of again. But when these words with their given stresses are worked into metre and rhythm, the terms we use to describe the patterns they make come from ancient analyses of GREEK VERSE, which worked in a very different way: not syllable-stress but syllable-length. Ancient Greeks would analyse this poem's rhythm in terms of long and short syllables. Three 'shorts' for memory, the short I of ripples made long for metrical purposes by a double consonant after it; and the 'short long' of again.

So we have taken over words for metrical units that differentiated syllables in terms of length, and applied them to our system of analysing word-shapes by stress. This means there is a paradox, and potential ambiguity, about the ways we feel and talk about these metrical units in English.

For of course syllable-length does matter in English as well as stress. If you look at the two-syllable words in this poem (ocean, inside, feathers, idly, ripples, distance, ringing, little, water, again), the differences between them are created not only by where the stress falls (again and inside are the only words stressed on the last syllable), but also by each syllable's length. A composer setting them to music would take into account the length of time it takes to pronounce the NS of inside, which slightly lengthens that first syllable; whereas the first A of again is unimpededly short. Though the other two-syllable words are all accented on the first syllable, the last syllable of ringing and distance are lengthened by the consonants that follow, and feel longer than the end-syllables of idly and ocean.

So though stress is the main factor in analysing rhythmic patterns via metrical units in English, syllable-length is important too. We feel this in terms of time, how long it takes to pronounce a syllable, to honour the weight that particular word needs.

How ancient Greeks felt about their long syllables, we cannot know. But GREEK VERSE was sung, or accompanied by a musical instrument; and a lot of it by dancing too. The dancers' movements mirrored the syllable-patterns very precisely. So musical time must, in some sense, have played a part in the way they felt, too, about syllable-length.

The main metrical units in English verse are five. First, the DACTYL (*long short short*, or stressed syllable followed by two unstressed). Memory and fluttery here are each three short syllables, but English hears them as DACTYLS.

The DACTYL's mirror image is the ANAPAEST (*short short long*, or two unstressed syllables followed by a stressed one). Because they are opposites, DACTYL and ANAPAEST belong together and often melt into each other in an English line (see No. 12). They bond together to make a rhythmic, and therefore an emotional, world of their own. This is often humorous (like the limerick), but poets also use ANAPAESTS for excited emotion and swift narrative, as in Byron's 'The Assyrian came down like the wolf on the fold'.

The SPONDEE in GREEK VERSE is two long syllables. In English, it is basically two syllables that are equally stressed, but the effect is a dragging feel which suggests length, as well as an emphatic weight which suggests the pressure of the stresses. So here, in a line of SPONDEES, words with short vowels (lost dove) count the same as other SPONDEES (sea beats). The syllables are, as it were, lengthened simply by the stress they bear.

64

A SPONDEE obviously has no mirror image, but the last two units, and their mutually mirroring relationship, are at the heart of English verse.

A TROCHEE, *long short*, or stressed followed by an unstressed syllable (as, in this poem, ocean, water, ripples), is the backwards version of our most important metrical unit, the IAMB, *short long*, or unstressed syllable followed by stressed. The IAMB is the basic metrical ingredient of English poetry. The IAMBIC PENTAMETER, a five-beat line, is made of five IAMBS or their temporal equivalent.

Each of these metrical units makes a FOOT, which corresponds to a musical bar. When you count the number of FEET in a line, you are also counting its number of beats. Clustering round the stress in the beat word are other syllables, of course, but there is only one beat in each FOOT. And just as a four-crotchet bar may have no actual crotchets in it, so an IAMBIC FOOT can be made up of other units than IAMBS. Here, Back on dry land I shouldn't think these things is an IAMBIC PENTAMETER with no IAMBS, just an ANAPAEST (back on dry), and three SPONDEES: land I; shouldn't think (a SPONDEE with a hiccough in the middle); these things.

English SONNETS are traditionally in a regular RHYME-SCHEME, and in IAMBIC PENTAMETER. But since the 1950s many poets have changed the beat and line-length (even, sometimes, the number of lines in the whole poem), and chosen not to rhyme. Poets writing SONNETS now have far more choice in their lines and shapes than a hundred years ago. And the more choice you have, the more alert you have to be to how your rhythm can make an emotional point and serve the meaning.

This SONNET establishes a four-beat line, unsettles this rhythm with excited rocking DACTYLS (memory, fluttery), and in the third line heavy SPONDEES stop this fluttery stuff short. So the first three lines insist on a rhythmic instability. You can analyse this in metrical terms, but the point of it is emotional. Instability becomes the poem's keynote, and suggests two things: the movement of ocean, plus the turbulent feeling of being unable to sit still, for which the rocking sea is an image.

As in music, the beat (the essential feature of any line of poetry) translates into feeling. Poetry 'moves' you by beat, by feel. All the technical stuff, the metrical units and their combinations, is there very precisely for the emotion these patterns engender; for how the sound illustrates and furthers what the words, when they get together, mean.

*

In the fourth line of 'Mrs Noah', after the rhythm has established a feeling of unestablishedness and upset, we settle down to IAMBIC PENTAMETER as we reach the centre of the speaker's attention: what's inside me, here. But we expect upset now, and the four-beat choppy rhythms return for my face by his ribs, rough tongue and little bites. The rhythmic changes reflect the powerfully rocky changing memories and emotions which the poem is about.

This poem is about aftermath; about facing the feelings that come after the voyage of passion is over. The title changes Shakespeare's 'taken at the flood' to after (picked up by afterdeck, suggesting both 'aft' and sexual 'afterglow'). It talks of female sensuality so strong it could launch its own ark, which nevertheless needs contact from outside (if you touched). It is about the 'after'-effect on a woman of a man whose 'roughness' and roar are both those of ocean (with its taste of salt water), and the lion whose purr ripples through the deck; whose mane (which brands him animal more than human) resonates with 'main', that archaic word for sea which proverbially goes with 'might' or 'strength'.

This poem in a woman's voice is partly *about* woman's voice: the voice of a woman remembering the male 'main', or power. Language, beat and rhythm all suggest that she, the first woman 'after the flood', is upset and disarrayed by the memory of man's crude, rough power (tongue, claws, bites); but she also longs for it. All that power, and the power of her own longing, go into her words – which will themselves have power to crack the sky and launch the ark again.

2. Derek Mahon

COURTYARDS IN DELFT
(*Pieter de Hooch, 1659*)

Oblique light on the trite, on brick and tile –
Immaculate masonry, and everywhere that
Water tap, that broom and wooden pail
To keep it so. House-proud, the wives
Of artisans pursue their thrifty lives
Among scrubbed yards, modest but adequate.
Foliage is sparse, and clings. No breeze
Ruffles the trim composure of those trees.

No spinet-playing emblematic of
The harmonies and disharmonies of love;
No lewd fish, no fruit, no wide-eyed bird
About to fly its cage while a virgin
Listens to her seducer, mars the chaste
Precision of the thing and the thing made.
Nothing is random, nothing goes to waste:
We miss the dirty dog, the fiery gin.

That girl with her back to us who waits
For her man to come home for his tea
Will wait till the paint disintegrates
And ruined dykes admit the esurient sea;
Yet this is life too, and the cracked
Out-house door a verifiable fact
As vividly mnemonic as the sunlit
Railings that front the houses opposite.

I lived there as a boy and know the coal
Glittering in its shed, late-afternoon
Lambency informing the deal table,
The ceiling cradled in a radiant spoon.
I must be lying low in a room there,
A strange child with a taste for verse,

While my hard-nosed companions dream of war
On parched veldt and fields of rain-swept gorse;

For the pale light of that provincial town
Will spread itself, like ink or oil,
Over the not yet accurate linen
Map of the world which occupies one wall,
And punish nature in the name of God.
If only, now, the Maenads, as of right,
Came smashing crockery, with fire and sword,
We could sleep easier in our beds at night.

(1981)

Mahon is a legendary stylist, terse, concentrated and lyrical with a profound sense of history, art, irony and pain. He was born in Belfast in 1939, like Seamus Heaney, and was a student in Trinity College, Dublin, with Michael Longley. These three were in their mid- to late twenties in 1969, when the Troubles began in Northern Ireland, and their work led the Belfast poets' response to that conflict: one of the most important bodies of poetry in English in the twentieth-century.

This much-loved, much-revered classic begins by talking about an art which represents with chaste precision the mess and chaos of ordinary human living. The poem's own structure, eight-line STANZAS of four rhymes each, reflects that precision, but in a changing RHYME SEQUENCE (ABACCBDD, AABCDBDC, etc).

Many rhymes (tile/pail, coal/table, town/linen, oil/wall) are, like the painter's light, oblique – the poem's first word. This is art talking consciously about art, and its complex relation to life. It moves towards the dirt and violence which Dutch art of this genre (like house-proud wives with their scrubbed yards) traditionally keeps at bay. No dirty dogs (canine or human), drink or sex. And yet the poem suggests that dirt and decay are as much a part of life (is life too) as the things designed to protect us: like those railings, which may be <u>sunlit</u> in the picture but are actually only a frail <u>front</u> for the mortal <u>houses opposite</u>. <u>Dykes</u> get <u>ruined</u>, sea invades, doors crack; and paint, art's medium, <u>disintegrates</u>, as human lives do in time of war. If this kind of Dutch art celebrates the everyday but neatens it, eliminates the mess of it, Mahon's poem goes beyond that vision. Though, paradoxically, it does so through its own neatness and formality.

In the fourth STANZA, the poem turns personal. <u>I lived there as a boy</u>. These Dutch courtyards 'are' the poet's childhood home. <u>I must be lying low in a room there</u>, dreaming poetry (another art which tries to create <u>precision</u> from human chaos), while his contemporaries (future <u>IRA</u> leaders, also <u>lying low</u>) dream <u>war</u>.

The poem is working towards the sense that if you do not acknowledge dirt or misbehaviour (or injustice, which led to the sixties' human rights marches and the Troubles), you open the floodgates (<u>dykes</u>, <u>doors</u>) to backlash violence. We have to accept lust, drink, dirt, disorder, the breeze that <u>ruffles the trim composure of those trees</u>, both in the world and in ourselves.

In Greek myth, the 'maenads', or 'maddened women', were followers of Dionysus, god of drink and violence. Here, their <u>fire</u> echoes <u>fiery gin</u>; they rush in like <u>esurient</u> ('greedy') <u>sea</u>, heaving on to the scene all the <u>random</u> violence which a Dutch interior conventionally, almost sinisterly, leaves out. <u>Broom</u> and <u>pail</u> convey a clean morality, designed to keep life <u>immaculate</u>.

In a Catholic context, <u>immaculate</u> is a loaded word. The poem's contrast between trimness and chaotic violence has a special charge in a city trigger-sensitive to Protestant versus Catholic. One idea here is, perhaps, that if we accept things like smelly dogs and drunkenness in our <u>courtyards</u>, maybe we won't be so vulnerable to worse things coming into them, and into us, from outside.

The title contains a pun. 'Delft' is Irish-English for crockery, the most breakable thing in the kitchen. Comparing twentieth-century Belfast to seventeenth-century Holland, Mahon underlines the message that domestic vulnerability to violence is universal. Like paint on canvas and china, words (his medium for representing human vulnerability) are the stuff of both art and everyday life. They too gesture to other spaces, other times. <u>Veldt</u> half-rhymes with <u>delft</u> and is as Dutch as Delft, or as the Boers whose war was fought in the <u>veldt</u>. <u>War</u> too is universal. As Delft landscapes are painted on smashable <u>crockery</u>, so war paints destruction on every

69

landscape. And religious wars (which the conflict in the North nominally is) punish nature in the name of God.

But Mahon's parallel is not all that oblique. In the sixteenth century, the Protestant northern part of the Netherlands, led by William the Silent, broke away from areas ruled by Spain to become Holland, while the Catholic south stayed under Spanish rule. Ulster's division comes similarly from sixteenth- and seventeenth-century European religious wars. Its icon on the Protestant side is another Protestant, Dutch William. A year after this painting was made, Cromwell's grip relaxed in Ireland, Parliament was restored in Dublin, and the English had a Catholic king. Thirty years later, Catholic James was fighting William of Orange, in Ireland.

Just as its sound spreads through the poem (to trite, light, right, night via echoes in immaculate, adequate, waits, disintegrates, sunlit, opposite), the light of dirt-denying art (pale as Death's horse in the Apocalypse) will spread over this not yet accurate . . . map of 1659. Both map and painting omit crucial areas of the world, and crucial aspects of life.

This poem suggests a particular and passionate view of art, as something which explores large, universal ideas through small details: 'courtyards in delft', which you can interpret as protected domestic interiors in one small Dutch town, as little landscapes painted on china, or as everyone's modest but adequate individual attempts at living their human lives. Art tackles important issues through the trite: through trivial everyday artefacts like spoons whose heads cradle the ceiling, or coal / Glittering in its shed. But art also has the responsibility, which the Belfast poets took on superbly, of dealing (both head-on and in oblique light like this poem, which is ostensibly about a five-hundred-year-old painting) with the random . . . waste and contemporary smashing of such modest, individual lives.

3. Eiléan Ní Chuilleanáin

SWINEHERD

When all this is over, said the swineherd,
I mean to retire, where
Nobody will have heard about my special skills
And conversation is mainly about the weather.

I intend to learn how to make coffee, at least as well
As the Portuguese lay-sister in the kitchen
And polish the brass fenders every day.
I want to lie awake at night
Listening to cream crawling to the top of the jug
And the water lying soft in the cistern.

I want to see an orchard where the trees grow in straight lines
And the yellow fox finds shelter between the navy-blue trunks,
Where it gets dark early in summer
And the apple-blossom is allowed to wither on the bough.

(1986)

Ní Chuilleanáin was born in Cork in 1942, and lectures in Dublin. Her haunting poems elide the legendary and the modern in sharp-lit detail; their surprisingness is both musical and visual. The more you look at the picture she gives, the more surreal it becomes. In a series of poems about Odysseus, for instance, she imagines the hero staring down at 'the ruffled foreheads of the waves / Crocodiling and mincing past', and thinking, 'If there was a single / Streak of decency in these waves now, they'd be ridged / Pocked and dented with the battering they've had'.

In No. 2, Derek Mahon approaches the Troubles through the parallel of Dutch art; many Irish poets also approach them via Homer. The Trojan War and its aftermath offer a more familiar parallel for the years of conflict and their after-effects. The last nine books of Homer's *Odyssey* are about having to go through more conflict on your own home ground, in Ithaca, just as you've got back from a ten-year voyage from hell and, before that, ten other years of war. If you looked at this poem 'Swineherd' without Ní Chuilleanáin's other Odysseus poems, the title and all this in the first line would not absolutely have to speak to Odysseus's home island in the *Odyssey*. But modern life is not overstocked with swineherds, and literature has only two famous ones I know of: the Prodigal Son and Odysseus's servant.

In Homer, the swineherd is the first human being Odysseus talks to, back on his own island. The swineherd tells his king (whom he thinks is a stranger) what has been going on here in the last twenty years. The palace has been completely taken over by the greedy bad-mouthed suitors of Odysseus's queen. He himself has stayed loyal to his king, and now gives him, unknowingly, a bed in his hut. Later he will show him the loutish squatters occupying the palace, and help Odysseus plan their assassination.

If this swineherd is that swineherd, then the speaker is the archetypal unsung, humble hero who plays a key role in a violent and secret campaign to recover a kingdom and see years of wrong righted. The parallels with Northern Ireland are all the stronger for being unspoken.

But Ní Chuilleanáin's imagination also leaps away from both Homer and Ireland to dole out Umberto Eco-like clues to a completely strange situation whose details are unknowable. What are these special skills? Bomb-making, garrotting or pig-care? Who is this Portuguese lay-sister? Are we are in a monastery? And what brass fenders? Are they gleaming in the monastery kitchen, is he planning to retire to a villa with log fires, or are we talking vintage cars?

The point is, we cannot know. The poet is unloosening us from any original setting, kicking the ladder away to let our own imagination get to work. Once she's established this, she gives us the impossible: the sound of cream crawling to the top of the jug, of water lying soft in the cistern. But then the surprisingness goes wrong. The last STANZA seems a pastoral idyll, but everything is the wrong way round. Happy orchards are not in straight lines, a decent summer does not get dark early, and the final wish for an orchard paradise lands us among serried ranks of militarisable navy-blue trees. You wonder again about those special skills. Who is this speaker with his surreal desires? Why does his blue-skies-over-the-white-cliffs-of-Dover vision of peace following a war end with blossom withering on the bough?

The emotional effect is a delicate seesaw. On one hand, when all this is over offers the optative dream of a soldier doing his job, longing for domestic peace: coffee-making, polishing, cream. On the other hand, you get the increasingly disturbing details: cream crawling, straight lines, dark early in summer, withering. As if the fantasy is for a peace that will not happen, or will happen wrong.

The climax of longing comes with the word allowed in the last line. Whatever his special skills he wants nobody to know them; wants not to have to talk about whatever campaign this is; wants shelter (even for foxes), and a withering. He wants everything, including himself, to be allowed to stop. He wants, in some sense, a negative.

This is a strange, unknowable situation, described by an unreliable, increasingly disturbing voice. The first really clear thing we understand as we read is the wish to be out of all this. And yet the rhythm, sound-patterns and structure are deceptively clear. Two STANZAS of four lines, flanking one of six, make this a broken-apart SONNET: the SESTET nestling inside the OCTET. The rhythm is dominated by the TROCHEE (the shape of the first key words over and swineherd). In this strangely clear-edged vision of an unattainable world, the key TROCHAIC things are mostly concrete: nouns (weather, coffee, kitchen, fenders, water, cistern, orchard, shelter, summer, blossom), or activities (crawling, wither).

A few vowel-harmonies hold each STANZA together (over/weather, swineherd/heard; make/awake, lay-sister/day/cistern; see/trees, lines/finds, allowed/bough) but this poet works by surprise all through. She gets a songlike clarity by juxtaposing apparently unrelated sounds as well as concrete details. That syncopated break nearly at the end of the second line between the two long syllables (retire, where) marks musically the conceptual switch from real life (all this) to the longed-for future.

Though we do not know where we are, who this is, or what the issues are, the movement of thought has a nervy clarity. Structurally, the first seven lines hang on I mean, I intend: the voice begins in considering, planning mode. But the last half hangs on I want, I want: the voice has a mounting urgency, wanting the impossible, now. It refers to that yellow fox and those navy-blue trunks as if we ought to know them, creating in us some weird complicity, an assumption of shared knowledge which leaves us with sympathy for something we know nothing about; for a speaker simultaneously confidential and secretive, surrounded by eeriness, whose vision of a longed-for future is visually clear as crystal but context-wise utterly dark. It could be Ireland imagined after the IRA disbands; or Oz when the Wizard has departed.

This poem made such a deep impression on one reader of my column, who cut it out, treasured it, then lost it, that he was desolate without it and wrote to ask how he could find it. He had forgotten the author's name, but remembered the crawling cream. To him, it was a poem about the retirement of a civil servant. And maybe that is its essence. A poem about an intense, possibly unfulfillable, longing to retire from service and give up the special skills that service required.

4. Charles Simic

TWO DOGS

An old dog afraid of his own shadow
In some Southern town.
The story told me by a woman going blind,
One fine summer evening
As shadows were creeping
Out of the New Hampshire woods,
A long street with just a worried dog
And a couple of dusty chickens,
And all that sun beating down
In that nameless Southern town.

It made me remember the Germans marching
Past our house in 1944.
The way everybody stood on the sidewalk
Watching them out of the corner of the eye,
The earth trembling, death going by . . .
A little white dog ran into the street
And got entangled with the soldiers' feet.
A kick made him fly as if he had wings.
That's what I keep seeing!
Night coming down. A dog with wings.

(1988)

Simic, one of America's foremost poets, was born in Yugoslavia in 1938, lived through the German occupation, and left when he was eight. After that he was educated in America, went to New York University, and has since won innumerable American poetry prizes.

He writes, of course, in English, and his hallmark is a combination of spare, unpretentious words and a mysterious childlike clarity. The poems often seem to elide downtown America with an anonymous Eastern European city whose rules are completely unknowable. 'Kafka in Manhattan', he has been called. The sinister, surreal details have a silent-screen realism in the midst of bareness, but also convey a wide-angle, unspelt-out compassion. His poems are tiny steely fables of strangeness, often set in an urban landscape where meaning is just out of sight around the corner.

This poem is about our vulnerability to darkness, cruelty, death and the blows of fate (shadow . . . creeping, going blind, sun beating down). The second STANZA ties all this to a specific historical horror: the German invasion of the poet's home town in 1944 (marching, death going by).

Another poet might have called it 'War', 'Shadows', or 'Death Going By'. By homing in on the different dogs, in film-like METONYMY (the process which takes one small detail to stand for a larger whole), Simic gives his theme a precise, very small-scale focus, and binds different moments in time together into a sequence.

We are given three scenes: a woman going blind, telling a story on a summer evening in New Hampshire; the story she tells, which is set in a Southern town, about a dog afraid of his own shadow; and the poet's own trembling, left-behind home.

The dogs carry the emotion. The first STANZA is full of anxious intimations of mortality: old dog, going blind, shadows . . . creeping out of the . . . woods. Never mind the New of New Hampshire: woods are the old proverbial European place of danger, where you meet witches; where wolves and outlaws live and (as in *Peter and the Wolf*) creep out of, to harm you at home.

Fear comes at the outset: afraid, shadow, worried. The frightened dog foreshadows (since shadows are an important vehicle of fear here) the real terror in the second STANZA: a street with soldiers in it, earth trembling, death, and another dog: which is white (image of purity, against the dark shadows, woods, blindness) and little (therefore vulnerable). The kick from soldiers' feet stands for everything these soldiers, coming down on this town like the night (or like the Assyrian and 'the wolf on the fold' in Byron's 'The Destruction of Sennacherib'), will do to this country.

As though seen through a child's eyes, the image of the kicked entangled dog leads on to fantasy: as if he had wings. And this, in turn, leads to the surreality of the last line which suggests one of Chagall's images of animals and people flying over a threatened European town, at night.

This last line is the only one with a strong CAESURA, or 'break', in the middle. One earlier line, earth trembling, death going by, followed by sinister dots which indicate the death and carnage to come, has a light pause in it. But this one has a full stop, and the break at the full stop turns round the way the reader who has been following the poem begins to see everything it has mentioned retrospectively in a new way. Everything – blindness, shadows, worry, sun, soldiers and Night – has been coming down on us all the way through. That down, with the stop after it, is the climax of the darkness and terror. Now here is a winged dog, going up.

This is a scene of an end. (Many Yugoslav villages were razed to the ground during the German occupation and resistance to it.) But the end becomes a beginning, too. The last half-line is a vision of take-off. The first line had a fearful dog; the last has a dog with wings, image of victory, escape and imagination that triumphs over disaster and fear.

The street/feet couplet marks the one action shot in all this fear, and has a trotting four-beat nursery-rhyme rhythm which matches both the child's clarity of vision and the Germans marching. Around it is a web of vowel-echoes. Old has echoes in shadow, told, shadows. Town is answered by down and town, the first STANZA's last couplet; blind has fine, street has beating, Southern has summer and sun. Wings, repeated at the end, concentrates the ING sound which has run through the poem in present participles (evening, creeping, chickens, marching, watching, trembling, going, seeing).

It is as if the participles, denoting the continuous present, the thing-that-is-going-on-happening, incarnate the human condition (creeping, trembling, going blind, death going by). Then this sound, distilled in wings, soars up above the threat they all represent.

As for consonants: the movement of D through the poem carries a lot of the emotional movement. In the first STANZA, D appears in a static scene: old dog afraid, shadow, told, blind, shadows, woods, worried dog, down. It reappears in the second, again in a static context: the watching villagers, what they feel (everybody stood . . . death). But D is active too now: from made me remember to the new dog who triggers the action and is made to fly. D is left behind as Night comes down and the dog escapes on wings.

This dog has taken on the poem's movement, and is now taking it out of the poem, out of its tension between action and standing still. This tension has been gathering in the tug of war between all those present participles and the short finite verbs (told, made, stood, ran, got, made). It is resolved in the final compound, which brings finite verb and participle together: I keep seeing.

These long stressed syllables, after the patter rhythm of the kick line (keep echoes the street/feet jingle), prepare for the turnaround of feeling in that final phrase. I has been surprisingly absent in this poem about remembering a major historical and personal trauma. As the poet becomes the subject rather than the object (told me, made me) of his own verb, I picks up the vowel-sound running through the second STANZA (eye, by, fly). From eye to fly: the effect of I keep seeing . . . a dog with wings is of something saved, a new vision, active and valued. Something positive, like the poem itself, has come, or been made, from a dark, cruel time.

5. Maura Dooley

1847

Ma's face is black with hair
her hands are paws.
She does not know me anymore.

Nights toss us cruelly.
Afraid I'll no more wake
I sit stony.

What knots my belly now's
not hunger. Anger.

In Liverpool ships gob us up.
We rot, we scatter.
The quays are maggoty with us.
We do not matter.

(1993)

Dooley is a Celt twice over, born in Cornwall in 1957 but of Irish descent. Her work is delicate, detailed, intense, rising lyrically out of landscape and memory as if memory itself is landscape, ranging through love, history, family, and the political undercurrents of ordinary life.

The background to this poem is the Irish Famine, 'The Great Hunger' of 1846 and 1847, and the emigrations, especially to America. Its pared-down images, short lines and lean STANZAS – getting out of kilter at the third so symmetry is lost – incarnate the subject of the poem. Famine, starvation, deformity; focused shrunkenness. The voice is that of a child whose mother is dying of starvation on the boat from Ireland to Liverpool, where boats gob . . . up the starving refugees until the quays of the docks are crawling with them (maggoty).

One of the first things poets teaching creative-writing students do is try and stop them using abstract nouns, and go for vivid concrete detail instead; get them to make the poem 'show' things rather than 'tell' them, so the words lose that didactic note that abstracts always carry. So the words reveal the scene or situation, without explaining.

But abstracts work fine when there's a point to them. Those two words hunger and anger give us the intellectual point of the poem, the poet's historical awareness of the national results of that emotional move (which the poem enacts) from suffering to fury. 'Great Hunger' became great anger: a whole century of violence to come is lying in wait. These abstract nouns also lie at the centre of a web of concrete personal detail (from face, paws, does not know me anymore, to Liverpool). The poet uses abstracts not to explain the poem's emotion but to pinpoint the movement that turns the knot in the belly from physiology to passion, victimhood to fury.

Yet the personal identification in my belly works on another level too. It is also, implicitly, the voice of the poet; her comment on her own imaginative and emotional identification with the emigrés. The Famine has increasingly become a focus of retrospective Irish anger against the British government of the time, and has been compared to the Holocaust. Consciousness of this political investment of historical feeling surfaces in the poem at the point where its symmetry and formality break down: that stop between hunger and anger.

Within its tiny verbal scope, the poem packs a whole city of correspondences between words, lines and STANZAS, creating a net

80

of verbal relationships which, like a prism focusing light, make a concentrated statement of pain and anger.

There are vowel echoes everywhere. Most words have an echo relationship with more than one other. You get them within single lines: Ma, hair; afraid, wake; know, anymore; hunger, anger (the climactic echo, underlining the causal relation between the two); between lines (paws, anymore; cruelly, stony, belly; gob, rot, maggoty, not; scatter, maggoty, matter); and between STANZAS (black, wake; not, toss, knots; know me, stony; paws, now's; sit, ships; quays, we; know, anymore, no more).

The poem begins at sea, with child and mother, those particular terribly altered hands, these nights, this specific fear (afraid I'll no more wake). In the second STANZA, as the poem moves from sea to port, so the voice moves on from I to us. After the hunger/anger break, the poem radiates out from this particular family to the whole family of Ireland, which cannot eat and instead is getting eaten up and spat out (gob us up) by impersonal, exploitative ships.

The literary critic Terry Eagleton has related the Irish Famine and emigrations to Emily Brontë's novel *Wuthering Heights*. Heathcliff, the alien, black-haired, wild-eyed child, carried home out of pity on the father's saddle, ends up filled with violence, devastating an English home. He must (says Eagleton) have been an orphan Irish boy picked up in Liverpool where starving Irish children rot and scatter. The anger and wildness to come, that violence imported (like Heathcliff in the novel) into Britain whence the violence of injustice originally came, knocks through this last STANZA in the barking of gob/rot/scatter/maggoty/not/matter.

As words, they evoke the disgust with which the impoverished Irish are regarded by the British. But the sounds they make express an answering contempt and anger, which British contempt rouses in the speaker then and the poet now. They represent a knock-on effect: a sonic warning, as it were, of the effects of this anger, felt on such a scale. And also offer a lesson in writing a political poem: that less is more, that concrete detail packs more of a punch than explanation.

6. Michael Longley

CEASEFIRE

I

Put in mind of his own father and moved to tears
Achilles took him by the hand and pushed the old king
Gently away, but Priam curled up at his feet and
Wept with him until their sadness filled the building.

II

Taking Hector's corpse into his own hands Achilles
Made sure it was washed and, for the old king's sake,
Laid out in uniform, ready for Priam to carry
Wrapped like a present home to Troy at daybreak.

III

When they had eaten together, it pleased them both
To stare at each other's beauty as lovers might,
Achilles built like a god, Priam good-looking still
And full of conversation, who earlier had sighed:

IV

'I get down on my knees and do what must be done
And kiss Achilles' hand, the killer of my son.'

(1994)

An exact contemporary of Seamus Heaney, born in Belfast in 1939, Longley has fantastic lyric grace, and is a wonderful classical nature poet, love poet and war poet, with a gift for making moments from the ancient world, or ancient literature, come tremblingly alive in the modern. He edited Louis MacNeice's *Selected Poems* and, like MacNeice, studied Classics at college. Whether he writes about the Troubles, mating swans, or Jews in a Polish ghetto, his feathery, precise, fine-crafted poems are always driven by pity, beauty and tenderness: formality melting into intimacy.

I remember this poem appearing in the *Irish Times* in August 1994, that miraculous summer when the IRA announced their ceasefire and it seemed everything was over. Today, with the peace process which evolved from that moment still appallingly far from completion, the poem is a wonderful example of the way Longley uses the classical world, without any didactic posturing or élitism, to make a passionate contribution to the marking, and respecting, of contemporary tragedy.

Towards the end of Homer's *Iliad* (set during the Greek siege of Troy) the Greek hero Achilles kills Hector, son of the Trojan king, Priam. Early in the epic we see Hector strutting his stuff, glamorous and armed, laughing with his wife when their baby is scared by his helmet, taking off the helmet to kiss the little boy. When Achilles kills Hector he strips off all that armour. To pay Hector back for killing his own friend Patroclus, he also drags Hector's corpse behind his chariot in the dust. Braving the Greek lines, the old king Priam comes to Achilles secretly and alone, at night, to try and buy back his son's corpse. Achilles is nearly sparked into murderous rage again, but then thinks of his own father and relents. This is the *Iliad*'s climactic moment of reciprocal compassion. The audience knows what will happen afterwards. (After the *Iliad* itself is over, in fact.) Achilles will die, Troy will be sacked, Priam will be killed by Achilles' son. But for this moment, in a huge poem full of male fury and killing, this is a breath of shared pity: of two men for each other, and the poet's for all human beings in their loss and grief.

Longley creates a quiet, lyric encapsulation of that whole passage, giving it a dragged out, peaceful rhythm suitable to a moment of 'ceasing fire'. Many of the lines have six beats in them (like Homer's line, which was a HEXAMETER built from DACTYLS), rather than five. The dragged line has the slow motion of post-violence or post-sex (see as lovers might), which offers itself (both in its title and in subtle modernising changes, like Hector dressed in uniform rather than Homeric armour) as a poem about hope now. Hope for a post-violence chance for peace, for doing what <u>must be done</u>: accepting and burying the past, sharing the mourning between Protestant and Catholic in Northern Ireland.

In its architecture, this is a SONNET of three QUATRAINS (four-line STANZAS) with a rhyming COUPLET at the end. The RHYMING-SCHEME is XAXA XBXB XCXC DD, but the rhymes loosen up: in the third QUATRAIN we get the vowel-rhyme <u>might/sighed</u>, not the stricter rhymes of <u>old king/building</u>, <u>sake/daybreak</u>.

Around that form, the lapped vowel harmonies are as resonant and balanced as a Romanesque chapel. <u>Achilles</u>, the key name, appears in every STANZA. Its central syllable is repeated in the first STANZA (<u>until</u>, <u>filled</u>, <u>building</u>, with a sideways echo in <u>curled</u>, a startlingly vulnerable action to ascribe to the king of Troy, suggesting a child or pet), reappears in the second, resonates in the third with <u>built</u> and <u>still</u> (plus an echo in <u>full</u>), and reaches a climax in <u>killer</u>: bringing out the fact that <u>Achilles</u> has the sound of that word 'kill' in his name.

The word <u>own</u> in the first line is the first strongly accented word, and the starting point for the poem's basic movement from self to reciprocity. It reappears in the first line of the second verse and is mirrored in <u>home</u> at the end of that. The move is towards sharing grief for what is yours: your <u>own</u>, your <u>home</u>. The third STANZA replaces that sound with the flicker of <u>together</u>, <u>other's</u>, <u>lovers</u>, stressing the fact that <u>own</u>-ness, valuing only what is yours, must give way to valuing <u>each other</u>. Hector's body is <u>wrapped like a present</u> for Priam.

But reciprocity comes at a price. In the last STANZA the <u>own</u> sound mutates to the sound we end on: first <u>down</u>, then <u>done</u> and (the emotional climax, the point of the action) <u>son</u>. <u>Hands</u> have been important all through. Reconciliation begins in the <u>mind</u> and is shown in the <u>hand</u>; the sound of <u>mind</u> mutates to <u>hand</u> in the first STANZA. <u>Priam</u> is the vulnerable one, the one we identify with. His name resounds with 'I am', containing both the I of <u>mind</u> and the A of <u>hand</u> – which is backed up by <u>and</u> at the end of the third line.

It is always risky to end a line, a poem's basic unit, with <u>and</u>. You have to have good reason to do it. The point here is partly musical: <u>and</u> rings back to <u>mind</u>, <u>Priam</u> (the name carried through three STANZAS, balancing that of <u>Achilles</u>) and <u>hand</u> – the word which will be crucial in the last STANZA. But this positioning also stresses <u>and</u>, and spotlights the slow-motion, sculpted quality of the actions suggested both in the rhythm, and in the Roman numerals above each STANZA as if this were a memorial inscription or frieze.

There is a Greek rhetorical term *parataxis*, which means 'arranging things beside things'. When you apply the term to style and syntax, it means joining words by lots of 'ands', rather than making one subordinate to another. The structure of these first stanzas is all 'paratactic'. Achilles is put in mind and moved: he took and pushed, Priam curled and wept. In the second STANZA there is more taking on Achilles' part (took harmonises with pushed in the first verse, taking is followed up by sake and daybreak in the second). All these momentous actions are revealed gently, side by side, as if we were seeing them in carved relief. The body is washed and, . . . laid out. This and is accentuated by the comma, and by the explanation (for the old king's sake).

The side-by-sideness of these acts, placed together by and, reflects a human situation in which subordination cannot be the issue. This poem is in a sense about and; about putting two people side by side who have not stood side by side before. Both have lost people they loved and are equal in grief.

Or not quite. Achilles appears in all STANZAS but Priam disappears in the last. To be reconciled, you may have to give up, maybe even kill, some central thing in your own identity. Priam was taken by the hand in the first verse. Now, in the last, he pays the last farthing of that cost of reciprocity: he kisses the hand that killed his son.

7. Nuala Ní Dhomhnaill

CEIST NA TEANGAN
(THE LANGUAGE ISSUE, translated by Paul Muldoon)

I place my hope on the water
in this little boat
of the language, the way a body might put
an infant

in a basket of intertwined
iris leaves,
its underside proofed
with bitumen and pitch,

then set the whole thing down amidst
the sedge
and bulrushes by the edge
of a river

only to have it borne hither and thither,
not knowing where it might end up;
in the lap, perhaps,
of some Pharaoh's daughter.

(1996)

Nuala Ní Dhomhnaill was born in Lancashire in 1952 but grew up in Kerry (her mother was originally an Irish-only speaker) and started by writing poems in English. One day she switched to Irish in the middle of a poem, the work satisfied her better, she won a competition for poetry in Irish, and has written poetry in Irish ever since. She says it is the language her soul speaks; that writing in Irish is the oldest continuous literary activity in Western Europe.

But why include in this book, which is basically about the relation between a poem's sound and its meaning in English, a poem originally written in another language?

I have put several Irish poems here at the beginning of this book to emphasise the debt that contemporary British poetry owes to Ireland. British poets have learnt from these poets: not only their technique, but the way they worked awareness of a major, tragic political situation implicitly into concrete everyday detail. But just as Irish poets writing in English stand behind British poets writing in the same language today, behind them, in turn, is the Irish language, and other Irish contemporaries writing in that language: a language that was given up as a result of the same political situation, Britain's historical presence in and impact on Ireland, and retrieved as a result of independence from that presence.

Ní Dhomhnaill is one of the most influential Irish language poets. She has been translated by many Irish poets who write in English, including Paul Muldoon, Seamus Heaney, Michael Long-ley, Derek Mahon, Eilean Ní Chuilleanáin, Cieran Carson and Medbh McGuckian. She was once writing (in English) an essay for the *New York Times,* and her mother asked, 'What is it about?' 'Writing poetry in Irish,' she said. 'Well I hope you told them it's mad,' said her mother. But her poems press upon political, historical and cultural tensions underlying the very idea of that thing which so enriched twentieth-century British poetry: Irish poetry in English. They rattle the bars of the relationship between two grammars, syntaxes and word-root systems, but also the political power relationship implied in that linguistic relationship. As if poetry in Irish is an echo chamber, a mirror, and a challenge, to Irish poems in English.

This poem is her ultimate answer to why she writes in Irish. Its main theme is hope of survival: literary, cultural and linguistic survival. The baby's fate among the bulrushes is the fate of the Irish language. Just as Mahon, Longley and Ní Chuilleanáin looked for parallels for violence in Northern Ireland in the human chaos implied in a Dutch painting or described in Homeric wars, Ní Dhomhnaill finds a parallel for both the Irish diaspora (Irish people out of their country, in exile) and the domination of the Irish by the English (Irish people whose language and culture was repressed) in another ancient story: the Jews enslaved in ancient Egypt. Moses' Jewish mother could either give her baby to the Egyptians to be killed, or send him downriver to the crocodiles. She entrusted him to a little boat, a frail basket: and the result was Exodus.

This is where relation to the dictating power and ruling language, Egyptian or English, comes in. Pharaoh's daughter, child of this ruling power, will nurture the helpless infant: a word which means 'not-speaking' (from Latin *infans*). She will save him for his God-given destiny, until (as Moses did) he becomes adviser to the Pharaoh himself. Writing in English rescued Irish poetry, gave Irish poets new power; and subsequently Irish poetry in English has influenced English poems written in English.

When you write a poem (in any language) you have to let it go where it will after it leaves you. You don't know what it will come to mean to other people. If it will reach them, what it will say to them. Since this poem draws on a Bible story, its language draws on biblical language. The first line here echoes with a famous image of trust, casting your bread on the water, and maybe also the trust which the psalmist places in the hills he lifts his eyes to, where help comes from.

This act of faith is partly the mad faith you have to place in language, meaning and music when you write any poem. Tony Harrison said once that you discover what you feel in and through writing the poem. Here, thought and feeling get borne hither and thither. You put yourself in the vulnerable position of not knowing where it might end up, but hope it'll be okay.

'The language issue', the poem's title in Irish, followed by its translation into English, refers to a political and cultural issue in Ireland, the role of the Irish language. But the poem's use of the Moses myth gives the phrase far wider meaning, and radiates it out to the fate and role of any small naked communication that has been entrusted to the frail but pliable, interwined construction of language, i.e. a poem, which is made from something that has grown organically over the years in an individual psyche but within a larger cultural context. And then the whole thing is shot out into the public arena, on to a public river, in the hope that someone else will read it and care about it, place it at the centre of their own selves: their lap.

This is not just what an Irish poem wants, but any poem. Iris is a pun on 'Irish' (whether this is the poet's pun or the translator's, a non-Irish-speaking reader cannot know), but also reminds us that Iris, in Greek mythology, is the rainbow, the messenger, communication between earth and heaven. Here, the source of communication is not above us in the sky, like the rainbow. The IN and UN of infant, in, intertwined, underside suggest it is inside us, underneath what we say, and maybe unconscious.

One thing the reader of a poem needs to feel is a working relationship between the movement of thought and the movement of sounds. If we treat this as an English poem, this relationship has been created, or recreated, by the translator. People sometimes describe translation as the threads on the underside of a poem's tapestry, and here all the arrangement of these threads, the pattern of word-sound and implication, has been made by the translator, Muldoon.

Musically, Muldoon has intertwined the poem's sounds to match the image of the containing basket: this little boat. He has made it into a little boat itself, and ringed it with the first-line-last-line rhyme of water/daughter. From the long O of hope he moves to boat; then language (from the title) begins a running-stitch connection to the next STANZA's pitch, which links on to amidst, sedge, edge. Bitumen is shadowed in the whole thing; river in hither and thither.

He uses this ring-composition to underline the enterprise of trust the poem enacts, and in the last STANZA brings back the two elements of the key word, the point of the action, hope. That word is made of long O and soft P. The long O comes in only, knowing, Pharaoh's; the P in up, lap and perhaps. So the stressed word from the first line breathes through a poem whose whole theme is risking trust.

8. Paul Muldoon

QUOOF

How often have I carried our family word
for the hot water bottle
to a strange bed,
as my father would juggle a red-hot half-brick
in an old sock
to his childhood settle.
I have taken it into so many lovely heads
or laid it between us like a sword.

An hotel room in New York City
with a girl who spoke hardly any English,
my hand on her breast
like the smouldering one-off spoor of the yeti
or some other shy beast
that has yet to enter the language.

(1983)

Muldoon, born in 1951 in Armagh, is the quintessential post-modern master, a Catholic from Armagh who started out working as a broadcaster in Belfast and has since made his life in America. Currently, he is also President of the British Poetry Society and Professor of Poetry at Oxford. His work is a major influence on nearly all British poets under fifty.

His poems combine deep lyricism with complex comment on history, politics, identity and art, brilliant wordplay, and virtuoso technique. He can fish up the most peculiar-looking words from the deep sea bed of language and link them by a rhyme no one else would have thought of; or place his rhymes miles away from each other as the first and last lines not just of a poem but an entire book.

The range of reference is extraordinary. It sometimes seems abstruse, but the learning and the technique always have a point. They enjoy themselves, but they are never just show: they are there to serve the poem's meaning. And you hear a deep lyric tenderness for what Virgil called 'the pity of things', *lacrimae rerum*, running through all his work.

He has also revolutionised the contemporary SONNET, and the lines of his SONNETS usually vary in length. Here, the EIGHT AND SIX appear in a RHYME-SCHEME of interlocking concentric rings: ABCDDCA ABCACB. Muldoon has also opened up the scope of poetry today (see essay, pp. 12–13) by expanding away from obvious rhymes towards near-rhyme, imperfect rhyme, unaccented rhyme, half-rhyme, vowel rhyme, consonant rhyme.

These rhymes are word/sword, bottle/settle, brick/sock, bed/heads, city/yeti, breast/beast, English/language. None, not even even bed/heads, are straight rhymes. This is not only technical playfulness. The way rhyme is used in a poem has to serve its implications and meaning, and rhyme is essentially about identity and difference. The likeness of the rhyming syllables, consonants or vowels, points up their difference, in both their sound (their beginnings are different, their endings are somehow the same) and their meaning. Part of the point of rhyme is to provoke the listener to respond to that play-off between identity and difference. In Muldoon, it is as if his whole project, the way he deploys rhyme, is to show how everything – words, things, worlds – is vitally related but also vitally different. In this poem, the two things that are rhymed and related, 'the same but different', are male sexuality and language.

Male sexuality is as private as quoof, which is a doubly private word: it is (says the poem) a private family word for a private source of heat, in bed.

But poetry makes the private public, and in a Catholic childhood male sexuality can be a red-hot, hot water, issue. Something which your father used to juggle on his childhood settle, becomes a thing which you as an adult man 'carry' into a strange bed, 'take' into women, or wield (a word, a sword) to keep them at bay. Echoes of that other Irish English poet Oscar Wilde come in here: 'Yet each man kills the thing he loves . . . The coward does it with a kiss, the brave man with a sword.'

With girls you cannot talk to, when you have no words in common, this sexuality becomes a shy beast, a word which has not entered some language which the lovers cannot speak. Its meta-phors (sword and spoor) echo each other's vowel. One is a weapon; the other, the footprint of something which may not exist, over which the word 'abominable' hangs, and which smoulders like your father's original red-hot half-brick.

Yeti is also a 'snow man'. Strange beds may be exotic, the heads may be lovely, and yet (or and yeti) you may be cold as snow in them. Everything here is about cold and hot. But who is cold, hot, or shy? Who (and what) is one-off? Language and sexuality are both forms of communication but both can also be intimately alienating, abominable. They may turn out to be a not-yeti, which has yet to appear; as quoof has yet to enter English and the breast-touching poet has yet to enter the girl. This is verbal virtuosity exploring and mastering tentativeness, play, and any ambivalence about the power of the equipment, sexual or linguistic, you 'carry' or 'take' with you on your journey.

The relation of OCTET to SESTET describes the movement of that journey. The OCTET starts I on his outward move away from a comfortingly shared family experience where juggle (with its blend of tentativeness and physical play) is answered by settle (with its security and calming down); where red-hot (with its dangers) is married to old sock (suggesting trusted, comfortable continuity). In the family home, sexuality has been earthed and tamed, by (literally) familiarity. But in the OCTET's last line, the idea that this same thing can be not cosily comforting at all, but laid . . . between people as a weapon, makes the journey suddenly dangerous. Sexual adventur-ing begins ambivalently, jugglingly, in the family, and meets danger as it grows awkwardly from it. What warms also burns; language communicates and separates. Sword rings back to word: language and the aggressive armour of male sexuality belong together.

In the SESTET, the poet has crossed the white space between the STANZAS, and also the Atlantic. He is now in a New World, with its new dangers and excitements.

America has been a sexual image in English poetry at least since Donne's line, 'O my America, my new-found land', which breathes the discovering thrill of male sexual conquest. (No. 30 does the same thing through the image of imperial Japan.) In this poem, the New World breeds uncertainty. The punctilious N before 'hotel' contrasts with the unpunctilious follow-up (that one-off hand suggests 'one-night stand' – one night, and he's off), suggests that sexuality is now a shy, possibly non-existent creature, like the title word, quoof. What exactly is so strange and shy round here: the poet, the word, or the bed?

The two last lines of each chunk of the SONNET bring the parallel between language and sexuality home to the rhymes themselves. Sex and rhyme are both about partnering. At the OCTET's end, though each end-word partners another (heads to bed, sword to word) they also form a near-rhyme themselves. The end-words of the SESTET's last two lines have an assonant relationship of their own: beast (which partners breast) and language (partner to English).

So the whole poem is about relating. Relating words to words, words to objects, private to public, male to female (from the male point of view). And when these words suddenly seem to have different rhyming partners from the ones you thought they had, you start understanding the poem's whole system of relating differently, with new eyes, new ears.

9. Medbh McGuckian

THE BUTTERFLY FARM

The film of a butterfly ensures that it is dead:
Its silence like the green cocoon of the car-wash,
Its passion for water to uncloud.

In the Japanese tea house they believe
In making the most of the bright nights:
That the front of a leaf is male, the back female.

There are grass stains on their white stockings;
In artificial sun even the sound are disposable;
The mosaic of their wings is spun from blood.

Cyanide in the killing jar relaxes the Indian moon moth,
The pearl-bordered beauty, the clouded yellow,
The painted lady, the silver-washed blue.

(1982)

Born in Belfast in 1950, McGuckian was the key woman in the Northern Irish poets of the early eighties. She is famous for her electric metaphorical language which seems to some male readers provocatively 'feminine' because it seems to work by association, by a gauzy, apparently inconsequential irrationality, rather than logic: qualities which male society tends to attribute to women.

But under the shimmer, the thought is sharp, socially critical, impatiently intelligent. This poem, with so much surface beauty of its own, is about violence underneath surface beauty, about the savagery involved in overvaluing the exquisite in female beauty at the expense of the person inside it.

McGuckian's poems move and make their point through METAPHOR, and most definitions of METAPHOR point to the idea of uniting one world (or thing) with another. Aristotle's definition of it in *The Poetics* is itself a METAPHOR: 'a carrying across of something from home to foreign'. The Spanish poet Federico Garcia Lorca called METAPHOR, 'the equestrian leap that unites two worlds'. In this poem, the two worlds united by METAPHOR both prize surface exquisiteness: a butterfly farm which kills what it farms, and a Japanese tea house which exploits division between male and female. These blend into one image for what the poem is talking about beneath its own exquisite METAPHORS: relations between men and women in the modern car-wash world.

The poem suggests that these relations too are artificial, in that they are culturally created by human belief (see they believe). The biological difference between men and women may be as natural as the front and back of a leaf, but institutions (like a Japanese tea house) based on seeing male and female as absolute opposites enclose and exploit the one for the other's delight.

The anger is aimed at the explanatory voice from which the poem dryly borrows (see the pompous stiffness of ensures that it is dead and disposable), and the destructive cultivation of artificial beauty. (See mosaic spun from blood; cyanide, relaxes, pearl-bordered, painted lady and silver-washed.)

The individuals who sport wings and white stockings, whose names appear at the end without the capital letters that would identify them as insect species, are both butterflies and geisha-like women. By prizing surface beauty, butterfly farms kill their butterflies and society destroys its women.

But from the moment the butterfly's silence is compared to the green cocoon of the car-wash, METAPHOR is at work in the poem more radically still. Why compare those brushes that roar round your Honda in the car wash to something as protective as cocoons? How can they illustrate silence?

McGuckian's METAPHORS often 'unite two worlds' by connecting not the words themselves, musically, but the ideas associated with them. In relation to silence, cocoon suggests both an enveloping smothering death and a butterfly's life cycle, its pre-existence. So that phrase the green cocoon of the car-wash is doing a lot of work. It suggests the poem is thinking in terms of today's Western world even though its METAPHORS draw on oriental ceremony. It reminds you that 'wrapping' is involved in both death and birth: swaddling and pupa, yes, but also a shroud. It also reverberates with Andrew Marvell's image of paradise as a private garden: 'Annihilating all that's made / To a green thought in a green shade'; slyly drawing, perhaps, on the violence of Marvell's word 'annihilating', which means 'bringing to nothing'.

Like cocoons, farms and tea houses should nourish; their role is providing food. But these ones suffocate.

At first glance, the exoticising METAPHORS are surface gloss upon this poem which is itself about deadly surface gloss. The first noun film (which tells you about death) is an image for the surface METAPHORS of this poem so full of patina (front, back, artificial sun, mosaic, bordered, clouded, painted, washed). After you hear tea house, film suggests white lead face-paint, or ceremonies that mask deep cruelty in human relations. The butterfly's passion is for water to uncloud, but these butterflies are landed with cloudiness themselves (see clouded yellow). A wash may clean (see car-wash) or paint over something (silver-washed blue). In a geisha context, surface film implies secret sex (so do making the most of the bright nights and relaxes), which leads on to grass stains, blood and cyanide. In the butterfly context, these words suggest moths fatally drawn to brightness at night: a mothy female annihilation (Indian moth, led up to by blood and moon) and the killing jar.

METAPHOR in a good poem is not just decoration, but structurally integral to its poem. McGuckian's metaphors sometimes seem to critics (mostly male) as arbitrary patina, a webby juxtaposing of random things. But this poem's glamour (Japanese tea house, pearl-bordered, artificial sun) is not just superficial film on its surface. From first to last, the poem moves from death to death (from dead in the first STANZA to killing in the last) by making deep connections

between ideas rather than words. METAPHOR is both how it moves
and its principle of sexual-political revelation.

10. Christopher Reid

TIN LILY

A salvo of blurred words
from the oracular tin lily
on top of the olive-green van.

Just one of those anomalous things
that city-dwellers are no longer surprised by
at certain seasons of the year.

I mean – not the seasons of nature,
but those speedier human phases
that run athwart them.

It was often tricky
to separate the words from the razzmatazz,
and the sentiments could be difficult.

But the way the driver kept his van moving
at a regular walking pace –
anyone could admire that.

Only in eyes here and there
I might see something like resentment,
or terror, or disdain.

Picture an olive-green van
and its four-ways-facing lily
strafing the boulevards.

This is no surrealism,
but an image of the new reality,
a counterblast to Copernicus.

(1985)

Reid was born in Hong Kong in 1949, and at college was influenced by Craig Raine, who taught him at Oxford and then preceded Reid as Faber's poetry editor. Raine's own 1979 collection, *A Martian Sends a Postcard Home*, established him as standard-bearer of what James Fenton christened 'Martianism' (after that book): a poetry that saw the world fresh via the metaphors of an eye so shockingly innocent of what it was looking at that it had to be imagined as alien. The title poem of Raine's collection conjured a vision of ordinary Western life, with its lavatories, books and telephones ('a haunted apparatus . . . that snores when you pick it up'), through the startled gaze of an alien. Reid, in his first two collections, also became known as a 'Martian' poet. But in his third collection, *Katerina Brac* (from which this poem comes), Reid explored a different way of making the ordinary seem alien: by making the estranged onlooker, the fictitious persona voicing the poems, not an alien species but an imaginary woman poet living in a persecutory regime like those of Eastern Europe under Communism. Her name, Katerina Brac, was also the title of the collection. The book also, playfully, presented her as its author.

This collection developed Reid's voice, and his gift for quasi-surreal imagery, beyond the clever whimsicality of Martianism into the direction it took later. These days, his voice blends self-deprecating English reticence with artful playfulness, and his scenarios are both surreal and domestic: funny, touching, but also somehow lost in space with its elegant (see *tin lily* here) but teasing images.

For Reid's development of his voice, the *Katerina Brac* collection helped him to find this note of Kafkaesque, arm's-length danger: gesturing at violence but keeping it at bay. As if making surreal images were a policy statement: play it light, in the face of the existential threat which is the human condition. But the enterprise also raised more widely, in an extreme form, various moral issues behind impersonating: writing a poem in the voice of another person. The imaginary context, political terror and repression, gives the poem's vernacular lyricism a weight and shadow it might not otherwise have. But just as in algebra you transform the value of X + Y by placing a bracket round them and a Z in front, real-life terror and repression change the value of everything, in or out of poems.

Western poets of the sixties to the nineties were transformatively influenced by reading the work of the great Russians who had written under Stalin, like Mandelstam, and by Eastern Europeans, like Holub. The Z behind the Russian and Eastern European poets was terror, surveillance, imprisonment, torture; it was also a passport to Western attention. (It is said that the minute the Berlin Wall came down, Russian poets stopped being fashionable in the US.) As in Belfast in the seventies, the individuals would have been gifted poets anyway. But what they produced under the pressure of political tragedy, all that wonderful surrealising imagery, brilliant obliquity, passionate reticent lyric, became a witness to the suffering. 'A source of truth', as Mandelstam's widow put it in her memoir *Hope Against Hope.*

Northern Irish poets (and, you could argue, women poets) have their own Z, a lived social context of estrangement. But most Western poets had only the X + Y. Reid was imitating persecution and menace by inventing a Z.

Katerina Brac was published in 1985 when, as it happened, the real woman poet Irina Ratushinskaya had for two years been imprisoned (where she was beaten and often concussed) for writing poems. (She was released in 1986 under international pressure.) No one would imprison Reid for writing a poem. Did he have the right to imitate terror, injustice and persecution that was really going on at the time?

Invented and borrowed voices, both of victims and of aggressors, have been a vital part of modern poetry's imaginative freedom. Their justification is the poem itself. If it convinces you, it works. You could say that Reid, by imitating Z, the situation of terror and censorship, just took further what everyone was doing, borrowing (X + Y) from Eastern European poets: the externals, poetic tricks and tones, the literary consequences of Z. What matters is whether the poems work in their own terms.

Imagistically, this poem focuses on the paradox of a *tin lily*: hard blossom, fragile purity which is the sinister mouthpiece of threat and power. But it convinces through its sound-patterning and emotional movement. It sets up a basic three-beat line in self-contained STANZAS (suggesting it is dangerous to hang loose), each held together by a dominant sound. Vowels for the first three: short stressed A (salvo, oracular, van) plus UR (blurred words); short stressed O (one, anomalous, longer); EE (mean, seasons, speedier); then consonants (often, difficult; separate, sentiments, razzmatazz). Vowels for the next three (way, pace; driver, admire, eyes, might, like; here, there; ways, facing, strafing), and consonants for the last:

counterblast, Copernicus. An aura of tricky euphemism runs through it, from blurred and oracular (the Delphic oracle was famously unclear) to certain seasons and ambiguous abstracts (phases, sentiments). Emotions come in eyes, not words.

From salvo to strafing, the poem moves towards the violence hidden inside that olive-green van, the violence of the regime which the van and its lily represent; and also towards the speaker's increasingly clear response to that violence. From I mean to I might see to a partly self-referential statement (this is no surrealism) which ends with a reference to one of the most famously suppressed truths of history. Copernicus (another Eastern European) finished *De Revolutionibus*, which proved that the Earth moved round the Sun, in 1530. A hundred years later, in the 1630s, Galileo was tried and imprisoned for supporting it. This triffid-like, four-ways-facing rhetoric, this new reality, is athwart nature. It is a counterblast to objectively agreed truth.

So in this poem about the fire power and the blurring possibilities of words, the speaker witnesses to a belief in the truth of the human situation. But obliquely, through a discipline that has nothing (on the surface) to do with the ethics of writing poetry: science.

11. Selima Hill

THE WORLD'S ENTIRE WASP POPULATION

This feeling I can't get rid of,
this feeling that someone's been reading
my secret diary
that I kept in our bedroom
because I thought nobody else but us
would want to go in there,
except it's not my diary,
it's my husband,
I'd like you to smear this feeling
all over and into her naked body like jam
and invite the world's entire wasp population,
the sick, the halt, the fuzzy,
to enjoy her.

(1997)

Hill, born in London in 1945, writes extraordinary poems; they are constantly taking new risks, but all carry her fingerprint of erotic, anxious, funny, deliberately ungrand feeling, driving through wildly original images, narratives and seemingly wayward juxtapositions. Her poems marry shockingly naked directness, saying upfront emotional things no one else has said, with far-out similes that pour through the poems like loose change. Her poems are mostly free form rather than patterned into STANZAS. There is lots of IAMBIC PENTAMETER running through the lines, yet the words fall free in apparently spontaneous speech like honey from the spoon.

This poem is a single sentence about the helpless, furious horror of knowing that your husband's girlfriend knows your intimate secrets, growing from repetition like a prayer or curse to end in the sweetness (see jam) of imagined revenge. The first six lines are a close-meshed, private world. The way they hang together is a sonic image of that space the poem can't bear to feel has been invaded: the close, secret, marital bedroom; her own bedroom. They are bonded by Rs and Ds – rid, reading, secret, diary, bedroom, nobody, would. Small key words are enclosed in some of the big ones: us in husband, I in diary (and see the relation of go to nobody). Rhythmic units mirror each other (the strong accent on the second syllable in rid of and bedroom), the long EEs of feeling, feeling, been reading, secret, hold things together, then make way for the long OR sound in because, thought, want.

The first comma introduces a new thought, which unpacks the image of the diary, pivoting on except which echoes what she has, till now, done with that 'diary': kept it. Her husband, this place she thought no one else . . . / would want to go in, is not a kept secret any more.

The follow-up commas show the working of thought, as in algebra. They mark off the steps away from impotent pain towards imagined revenge. The third comma in line eight, after the key word husband, marks what, if this were a SONNET, would be the TURN of focus and attention. I'd like you, says the poem, addressing someone outside its own frame of reference. Maybe the reader, or maybe (remembering the liturgical repetitions at the beginning) God. What does the poem require of this you? To smear.

This startling verb is part of a rising wave of 'ear/air' sounds, moving from there to that stressed word entire in the climax line. It speaks (maybe with resonances of cervical smears, smear campaigns) to the sense of taint and spoil: secret pages smeared, a marriage stained. But it also prepares for the next startling image. This initial feeling, like a bedroom's dirty linen exposed to a hostile gaze, solidifies into jam. So we get to her, the rival, the centre of jealousy; and her naked body which the poem wants to smear that jam all over.

The stressed long syllables, all over and into, make this the poem's only HEXAMETER. The next line, though it looks longer, has only five beats: this has six, and is all about beat. The sounds are really making the vengefulness stick.

Their glee explodes with the repeated 'in, in, in' of the last three lines: invite, entire, enjoy, but the jammy revenge of the final image is counterbalanced by a change of register, the kind of vocabulary in which it is described. Entire . . . population: this formal, rather clichéd, impersonal, grandifying abstract phrase suddenly deployed on wasps is both funny and menacing. You suddenly see the point of smear, jam; and of naked body, which – you now realise – has entered the poem not only as the flashpoint of jealousy, but to get very hurt indeed.

As we arrive at the wasps themselves, the poem summons back both the prayer-like repetitions of the beginning, and the unexplained you required to aid the poet. We are in the curse area of prayer. Any God addressed is not just jealous Himself, but expected to act on the side of revenge. Sick and halt (that biblical word for 'lame'): these are not happy wasps. They are suffering: like the poet, or like beggars waiting to be healed by Christ. But the only healing that happens here comes through imagining the 'enjoyment' taken by those wasps (as distinct from my husband) in that naked body. After the formal language comes biblical language, and then another change of register in the surprising, childish, uniquely Hill-like word fuzzy, evoking pubic fuzz or fluffy toys. Fuzzy triumphantly links the early bedroom intimacy to the final buzzing, accompanying those stings we'll never see.

Discussing Hill among other women poets in his book of essays on post-war poetry, *The Deregulated Muse*, Sean O'Brien (see No. 12) brings up the disorientating effect some women poets' imagery has on some male readers, who react to it as uncontrolled metaphorical spillage: as 'whimsy', not 'mannerly, negotiated surrealism'. Women's poems sometimes offend male readers, he says, by failing to 'ask the reader to agree to the validity' of their vision. But he argues that Hill's similes destabilise metaphor. That she uses images to track feeling, to pattern or control in language something which is not controllable in life – our shifting mental states.

When I rang O'Brien to discuss this gender division and the way male critics often feel that making imagery the structuring principle in a poem is a 'feminine' and suspect procedure, he said, interestingly, that maybe all this comes not from the way women write, but how men currently read.

For structuring a poem's movement round outlandish images whose associative links are not immediately obvious is in fact one of the oldest games in the lyric business. Aeschylus was brilliant at it in the 470s BC. The bizarrely shifting, ambiguous images of the first chorus in his play *Agamemnon* are as kaleidoscopically surreal as anything the twentieth century came up with. Hill read Moral Sciences at Cambridge. Disciplined intelligence and sophisticated understanding of traditional forms structure her rhythms, sequence of association, and the movement of feeling and thought through her poems. But as with McGuckian (No. 9), the way the poems highlight imagery as a principle of organisation, and the very images themselves, can seem, to a reader ready to be hostile, as if they are chosen by random association rather than transparent logic.

You have to make up your own mind. Either the poem persuades you or it doesn't. But first you have to go with, and try and understand, the flow and movement of its images.

12. Sean O'Brien

RAIN

At ten pm it starts. We can hear from the bar
As if somebody humourless fills in the dots,
All the dots on the window, the gaps in between.
It is raining. It rained and has always been raining.
If there were conditionals they too would rain.
The future tense is partly underwater. We must leave.
There's a road where the bus stop is too far away
In the dark between streetlights. The shelter's stove in
And a swill of old tickets awaits us.
Transitional, that's what we're saying,
But we're metaphysical animals:
We know a watery grave when we see it
And how the bald facts of brute nature
Are always entailed by mere human opinion,
So this is a metaphor. Someone's to blame
If your coat is dissolving, if rain is all round us
And feels like the threats-cum-advice of your family
Who know I am up and have come and will go to no good.
They cannot be tempted to alter their views
In the light of that sizzling bulb. There it goes.
Here we are: a black street without taxis or buses.
An ankle-high wave is advancing
To ruin your shoes and my temper. My darling,
I know you believe for the moment the rain is my doing.
Tonight we will lie in the dark with damp hair.
I too am looking for someone to blame. O send me
A metro inspector, a stony-faced barmaid.
The library is flooding and we have not read it,
The cellar is flooding and we shall be thirsty,
Trevor McDonald has drowned as the studio shorts
And the weather-girl goes floating past
Like Esther Williams with her clothes on,
Mouthing the obvious: raining.

There's no need to labour the obvious, dearest, you say,
As you wring out your nylons and shoot me.

(1995)

Born in London in 1952 but deeply identified with the north of England (he lives in Newcastle), a perceptive and original critic as well as poet, O'Brien mixes hard-hitting political and social comment, urban landscape, drink, humour, history, and male-related subjects like trains and football with (increasingly, in his new work) a heady under-tugging lyricism, and beautifully controlled rhythms.

This mix of ANAPAESTS and DACTYLS drives a swift-paced poem which, if it were a cartoon, would be captioned, BLOKE LEAVING PUB IN RAIN FAILS TO HUMOUR FURIOUS GIRLFRIEND BY WRITING POEM ON WET WALK HOME. It illustrates O'Brien's characteristic mix of literary and metrical sophistication, humour, and conviction that poetry should address every detail of our rebarbative vernacular world from metro inspectors to freezing wet bus stops.

English has often used DACTYLS for light verse. ANAPAESTS appeared mainly in popular verse until the beginning of the eighteenth century, when they came into serious poems. In the nineteenth century, for instance, Robert Browning used them for 'How They Brought the Good News', a poem which evokes the sound of a galloping horse. But like the DACTYLS whose mirror image they are, ANAPAESTS too are good at humour: in limericks, for instance. This poem is dominated by DACTYLS and ANAPAESTS, which here evoke not a galloping horse but the background drumming of relentless rain. They start (of course) after the word starts in the first line and run on, equally relentlessly, to the end.

The poem is in seven five-line sections. The first ends on that title word rain, which dances through the poem and chimes with blame at the end of the third section. This sound-bond between rain and blame is one relationship driving this poem about a relationship:

another sonic relationship underlies the play between tense and 'tension'. The notion of grammatical tense begins at it is raining. It rained and has always been raining, and is followed up in future tense, transitionals, and then illustrated in the mock-apocalyptic fourth section, we have not ... shall be. The poem is charting mounting 'tension' in the speaker's relationship with you up to the climax: shoot me.

For this is also a disguised love poem, reminding her that the rain is not his fault, that it's universal to blame others for the mess we're in. It combines mock self-denigration with a swipe at her family and submerged sexual puns (I am up and have come). The rueful humour (trying to raise a smile from her, at least) gets wilder as celebs go down in the deluge. The poem transforms the wetness into an out-of-place metaphysical meditation on the human condition as a road where the bus stop is too far away; where we are always in transit, and depend on transport whose shelter's stove in/ And a swill of old tickets awaits us. This is the human situation: we face an underwater future, and lie in the dark, looking for someone to blame. The poem mocks itself in trying to transform this meditation further into an affectionate apologia.

These transformations depend on a finely calculated tension between eight tones: formality (expressed in the capitals beginning each line), demotic blokeishness (intellectualising references to grammar and metaphysics), dry academic precision (they too would rain, entailed by mere human opinion), mock-high-flown poeticism (see O send me / A metro inspector and the classic ZEUGMA – that 'yoking' process which 'joins' two completely different things – ruin your shoes and my temper), jokiness (we know a watery grave when we see it), dry wit (mouthing the obvious: raining), sarcasm (dearest, you say), and despairing (but patronising) maleness faced with female accusation (my darling, / I know you believe . . .).

Acoustically, it is dominated by the AY of rain/blame: raining, rained, raining, rain, away, awaits, saying, grave, nature, entailed, blame, rain, wave, rain, blame, faced, raining, labour, say. The OO of the climax (shoots) is prepared for by too, too, brute, views, shoes, you, doing, too, you, and you: a list which blends the possibility that the world is too much for the poet, with the emerging fact that you are, too.

Although English has associated DACTYLS with humour, they are also the standard line in Homeric epic. Here they become mock epic. We move from leaving the boozer to missing the bus, getting

108

home through an ankle-high wave to the fall of civilisation (as in epic Troy, or Rome). The library is flooding and we have not read it, / The cellar is flooding and we shall be thirsty, has an archaic, prophetic ring. We think of the lost library of Alexandria, but the image is pinned to our own day by electricity (that sizzling bulb; the studio shorts), and TV: weather-girl, Trevor McDonald, Esther Williams.

In the centre of the poem, though, is the relationship. When things outside (the bald facts of brute nature) look black, you tend to think blackly inside too (we're metaphysical animals). The poet is getting hell from her for this hell of a night, so in the two central lines of the central section come the threats-cum-advice of your family, and the no good they know of the poet. Introduced tangentially as metaphor (feels like), this family grievance is at the heart of the poem and its allegory of wet collapse. The end of civilisation becomes the poet's demise, as his partner disposes of everything she so dislikes: the rain in her nylons, and him.

Yet from tonight we will lie we are (as in the sixth line) in the future tense. The shooting is fantasy, a conditional with 'would' left out. (If there were conditionals they too would rain: but there aren't and they don't.) This is a metaphor – both the rain (standing for the paranoid human condition, surrounded by adversity) and the poem's self-mocking, fantasising attempt at repairing this relationship.

13. Rita Ann Higgins

SOME PEOPLE

Some people know what it is like,

to be called a cunt in front of their children
to be short for the rent
to be short for the light
to be short for school books
to wait in Community Welfare waiting rooms full of smoke
to wait two years to have a tooth looked at
to wait another two years to have a tooth out (the same tooth)
to be half strangled by your varicose veins, but you're 198th on the
    list
to talk into a banana on a jobsearch scheme
to talk into a banana on a jobsearch dream
to be out of work
to be out of money
to be out of fashion
to be out of friend
to be in for the Vincent de Paul man
to be in space for the milk man
(sorry, mammy isn't in today she's gone to Mars for the weekend)
to be in Puerto Rico for the blanket man
to be dead for the coal man
(sorry, mammy passed away in her sleep, overdose of coal in the
    teapot)
to be in hospital unconscious for the rent man (St Jude's ward 4th
    floor)
to be second hand
to be second class
to be no class
to be looked down on

to be pissed on
to be shat on

and other people don't.

(1988)

Higgins is a Galway poet, and so popular in Ireland that long TV programmes are made about her. Her poems, in dramatic and often very funny monologues with wonderful speech rhythms, create a witty, spiky, surreal mix of the erotic and political, swinging colourfully from the mundane to the surreal and back again to make an often savagely bitter political point.

This one makes its bitterness bearable, and makes you meet the shock of what it is saying head-on, through laughs: through fantasy, wit, and surreality, which make sure you do not flinch away; which delight and intrigue you while rubbing your face in injustice. Both the fantasy and reality are contained within a single frame like a steel strip: the unemphatic observation some people know what it is like . . ./and other people don't.

By the second line, the shock of the language, cunt, announces the level of political ferocity you are going to meet. This is not the poem's word: it is spoken by the unjust. It is not the poem's fault the world is like this and speaks like this. But the poem underlines the shock of it by echoing the word, first in front then obliquely in rent.

The first four lines have an implacable forward rhythm, with short words (everything is short in this bit) carried by consonants that shift from a softening N (cunt, front, children, rent) to the harder T (short, short, light, short), and then on to hard K in school books, the crunch phrase of these first four lines.

You've got to have those books. The children must get out of this, education is the only way: everything is endured for those children in front of whom she is insulted.

The next four lines lengthen for the longueur of the waiting

111

rooms of Welfare which are (self-refutingly) full of smoke. We move from to be short to to wait. This is the first active verb (we are about to plunge into another passive, be half strangled) but it has as much impotence about it as the first verb, be called. The only active thing you can do is wait – even with a four-year toothache – and be half strangled by your varicose veins.

We move from the first desperation, about money for the kids, to the woman's own health. But the same hostility, same system, stonewalls her at every turn: from rent to school, from the ironically titled Community Welfare to the list. The people who operate this system, who call her names, look at teeth, put her on lists, do not appear: it is all implacably impersonal.

She now gets more active. In the next couplet, there is talk, but no one to talk to. All the talk ends in dream. In real life, bananas are used to train jobseekers in using the phone: so talking into a banana surrealises reality, makes you see how unreal this reality is. Then jobsearch scheme becomes jobsearch dream. Dream is there partly (impudently) because it rhymes with scheme, but also because you won't ever find a job. Again, the madness and weirdness is in the real life around you, not in your delusions and dreams. She puts this reality in terms almost of the *The Wizard of Oz*, pitching us over the rainbow from real-life black-and-white poverty and the grey unemployment office to unexpected colour, a world of talking bananas. This is not the speaker's joke: it is the world's. The bananas suggest it is all mad, and gets you nowhere.

The next four lines, the out of sequence, make this the third spittingly short word ending in T you have faced. Be short, to wait, be out.

Work, the first thing you are out of, leads straight on from the no-job dream. The second, money, follows from that. The third and fourth are more personal. Out of fashion has two meanings: this woman needs clothes and friends as well as basics for her family and health. But, as Bessie Smith sings, nobody knows you when you're down and out. You are out of fashion among your friends. The jokily singular friend sums all that up. When the last penny disappeared, so did the last friend.

At this thought, the poem begins to sprout people. The first is welcome – the Vincent de Paul man from the Irish Catholic charity. But the rest want money. You move from being out to being in, but the things you are in get madder and more painful, and the person who describes them, the only voice with direct speech in the poem, who has to cover for you with despairingly jokey (but bracketed) excuses, is your child. First you are in; then you are suddenly in space, i.e. out, away from home. Then you're in Puerto Rico.

Why there? Apart from the harmonies (week with Rico, the bunching of its K inside blanket and coal) I guess it gestures to *West Side Story*. Puerto Rico reminds you poverty is everywhere. It is where the Sharks and their struggling families came from. 'I Like to Be in America' (where even poverty is dreamed to be better) sums up the everlasting immigrant dream, as strong in Ireland as Puerto Rico. 'Puerto Rico, my heart's devotion, let it sink back in the ocean.' Being there is not going to do mammy much good.

Now you move into a blend of speedy tragedy and surreal wit – dead for the coal man, and overdose of coal in the teapot – and back to pathos. You are in hospital unconscious (St Jude's ward – patron saint of hopeless cases, who often turns up in Catholic humour) for the man who wants the first thing you were short of. The rent has come back to haunt you.

The next three lines move to the climax, and make explicit the mounting anger. Each is chain-linked to a word from the line before. From 'second hand' to 'second class'; from 'second class' to 'no class' (which, among many ambiguities, flicks back to school books).

The last four lines, with their climax of short angry words, end in ON. Lists are an ancient and popular poetic tool. Formally, this one is set up in rhythmic bunches of lines mostly related to each other by one short word: for, into, out of, in and finally on.

As in many of Paul Durcan's poems (see No. 42), the incantatory repetition (every line beginning to be, as Durcan's poem repeats its pattern of forty-five years . . . / And you say) plugs into the Catholic Mass, into the feel of repeated prayer. The repetition turns this poem into a litany of anger and despair. The Vincent de Paul man does arrive, but so do all the hostile demands which you can only escape by being, or pretending to be, in hospital unconscious. The last line, completing the grammar of the first, turns the commonplace observation which contains the poem to a furious shrug, which the title itself could also be read as laughing at. Some people!

14. C.K. Williams

HARM

With his shopping cart, his bags of booty and his wine, I'd
  always found him inoffensive.
Every neighbourhood has one or two these days; ours never
  rants at you at least or begs.

He just forages the trash all day, drinks and sings and
  shadowboxes, then at nightfall
finds a doorway to make camp, set out his battered little radio
  and slab of rotting foam.

The other day, though, as I was going by, he stepped abruptly
  out between parked cars,
undid his pants, and, not even bothering to squat, sputtered out
  a noxious, almost liquid stream.

There was that, and that his bony shanks and buttocks were
  already stained beyond redemption,
that his scarlet testicles were blown up bigger than a bull's with
  some sorrowful disease,

and that a slender adolescent girl from down the block
  happened by right then, and looked,
and looked away, and looked at me, and looked away again,
  and made me want to say to her,

because I imagined what she must have felt, It's not like this
  really, it's not this,
but she was gone, so I could think, But isn't it like this, isn't
  this just what it is?

(1992)

114

Williams is an American, born in New Jersey in 1936, who lives mainly in Paris, teaches part-time in the US, and is very popular in the UK. Over the years he has honed the characteristic long line of his poems into cadences that brilliantly reflect the movements made by an exploratory, self-doubting and self-correcting mind as it examines its own feelings and insights. The poems shift and flinch between action and reflection, the physical and metaphysical. They start from social watchfulness – scenes between people, parent and child, lovers, and street scenes like this one – to mental watchfulness (of both his own mind and, as in this poem, the imagined mental processes of someone else), and move towards abstract, moral issues. With their always surprising, energetic verbs (see here shadowboxes, sputtered) and Williams's keen visual eye, his poems work constantly deeper into some restless to and fro between what goes on in your head and the outside world of relationships and street. 'Tar', for example, is a brilliant political poem about the Three Mile Island nuclear accident, but approaches its subject through details of builders retarring a roof.

You could take the abstract question on which this particular poem ends – isn't this just what it is? – both morally and existentially. It implies social and ethical comment, but also the species shame of feeling responsible, in front of a child, for the degradation and injustice all around us in society. This moral self-questioning rises purely out of the vivid street scene, which is described with no word of subjective emotion except sorrowful. And that is itself transferred from human feeling on to the unknown disease.

We start with details, things collected by the tramp (shopping cart, bags of booty, wine) and how he behaves (forages the trash, drinks, sings, shadowboxes). Then we move to the particular episode, the almost liquid stream of shit, the scarlet testicles. From there, via changes of grammar and rhythm, we move to the moral issue, and the mind.

In its long lines, this is a poem of six COUPLETS, with a break halfway through. The second half moves from that – as if the poem is waving its hand at something it sees, but is detached from – to this. Where, in the last lines, the poem accepts its own involvement in humanity's 'harm'.

In the fourth STANZA the repeated that changes its grammatical function mid-sentence. It stops being an ordinary 'demonstrative' word, as in there was that (i.e. that scene). Instead, it begins to introduce indirect speech (that his . . . shanks were . . . stained, that his . . . testicles were blown up, that a . . . girl . . . happened by). These changes are matched by a rhythmic reversal. The poem starts with an ANAPAEST, echoed later in little runs of short syllables (as in forages). But halfway through (after there was that), and that his introduces the DACTYLS (ANAPAESTS reversed), on which the poem ends: asking, in a cascade of DACTYLS, isn't it like this, isn't this just what it is?.

These shifts in grammar and rhythm mark the poem's shift from the scene itself to the human gaze and its moral implications. '*Ecce Homo*' – 'Look at the man' – is what Pilate says to the crowd in St John's gospel, when Jesus is brought out to them in His crown of thorns. Painters, sculptors and poets have explored the wider meaning of those words. 'Look – this is what humanity is.'

The *Ecce Homo* scene depends on a triangle: the presenter, suffering humanity (or Christ) and a spectator. Here, the poet watches a slender adolescent girl – our society's ideal image of beautiful, on-the-threshold human joy and hope entering the adult world – confronted by a vision of humanity that is stained, both physically and maybe morally, beyond redemption. The repeated looked, in the sequence of looked, / and looked away, and looked at me, and looked away again, forces (see made) the poet to want to repudiate this vision on her behalf.

But the spectator vanishes (she was gone). And so the poem moves on to the final stage: the poet, confronting his own admission, turns the reader, too, into a spectator. Makes us 'look' and see that, this is what it is. You cannot, like the girl, 'look away' from what human society contains (every neighbourhood has one or two these days). You have to share the poem's witnessing of what society does, both to its underdogs, physically and emotionally, but also to itself, morally. That insight is the poem's title: harm.

116

15. Kathleen Jamie

SKEINS O GEESE

Skeins o geese write a word
across the sky. A word
struck lik a gong
afore I wis born.
The sky moves like cattle, lowin.

I'm as empty as stane, as fields
ploo'd but not sown, naked
as blin as a stane. Blin
tae the word, blin
tae a' soon but geese ca'ing.

Wire twists lik archaic script
roon a gate. The barbs
sign tae the wind as though
it was deef. The word whustles
ower high for ma senses. Awa.

No lik the past which lies
strewn aroun. Nor sudden death.
No lik a lover we'll ken
an connect wi forever.
The hem of its goin drags across the sky.

Whit dae birds write on the dusk?
A word niver spoken or read.
The skeins turn hame,
on the wind's dumb moan, a soun,
maybe human, bereft.

(1994)

Jamie is a Scottish poet, born in 1962. Her precisely observed, funny, mysterious, exuberant, imaginative poems, in both Standard English and Scots, blend all kinds of subjects (landscape, nationhood, politics, sex, poverty, motherhood) into Scottish history, economy, identity, but also radiate out to universal, existential themes. 'Mr and Mrs Scotland, here is the hand you were dealt', says one poem, sifting knitting patterns, photos and fridges festering on a 'civic amenity landfill site' to show us both the detritus of a particular society and the small details through which all human lives are lived.

This poem is the last one of its collection, and projects a feeling of bereftness on to an evening scene where high-flying geese leave a sound on the wind, a mark on the sky. Who or what is bereft, and why? The first two STANZAS set up a soft nasal moan that runs through the poem like wind towards the poem's last word: skein, gong, born, lowin, stane, sown, blin, ca'ing. Against harder sounds (twists, script, gate), this moan dies away in the central STANZA, present only in the whole poem's central line, sign tae the wind. Then it returns, in strewn aroun, skeins, hame, dumb moan, soun. It is the vowel of bereftness, backed up by the alphabet's softest consonant (contained in some of those words) which also blows through the poem: the W of word, wis, lowin, sown, word, wire, wind, word, whistles, awa, we'll ken, connect wi, whit and finally, aptly, wind. That word bereft is prepared for both by deef (deaf, in English) and death.

The Latin word 'omen' meant a sign in augury, which used to read destiny in birds' flight and calls. In this poem about omens, the vowels and consonants are signs we decipher to read its meanings. Barbed wire is archaic script, signing to the wind; the sky word is a gong / afore I wis born (like an ancient sign at a birth). But we are really talking about how impossible divination is. The poet, blin / tae a' soon but geese ca'ing, will never read the word they write. It is not spoken or read. Both literally and metaphorically it is over our heads, ower high for ma senses.

Deciphering the sky's pattern and sound is an art that is both ancient and impossible. It is a hope, that's all. At the end of Shakespeare's *The Merchant of Venice*, Lorenzo talks about the music of spheres. 'Look, how the floor of heaven / Is thick inlaid with patines of bright gold,' he begins, and explains that these stars sing a song we cannot hear. 'Whilst this muddy vesture of decay / Doth grossly close it in, we cannot hear it.' Jamie's poem is about not being able to read what is up above us in the sky: not the stars, not this heavenly field of lowing cattle, not any of the scripts that lie aroun in the world and would tell us the future – if we could read them.

What we know is different (no lik). We may live surrounded by omens, but what they say is ower high for our senses. Instead, history, death and love connect us – to each other and to meaning – through our senses. Whatever reason the poet has for feeling barren, empty as stane, ploo'd but not sown, she is still rooted in human connection. What we'll ken / an connect wi forever is a lover, in a human forever. It is not us but the heavenly world, with its illegible words, that goes awa.

Like a curtain, heavenly meanings have a hem, a bottom line that drags across the sky as they leave: and this line, the one PENTAMETER among all these three-beat lines, itself 'drags' out its syllables in an AG sound foreign to the rest of the poem.

You speak of skeins of fabric and fate, as well as geese. The sky in this poem has now become an alternative fabric, as in Yeats' image in his poem 'He Wishes For the Cloths of Heaven': 'Had I the heavens' embroidered cloths . . . and the dark cloths / Of night and light and the half-light.'

Our human 'cloth' is different from any heavenly weave. We cannot hear the music of spheres and stars, nor read what birds write on the dusk. It is all indecipherable, niver spoken or read in any language we've met, even in Jamie's supremely language-conscious poems. Not in Scottish poems, with their different-from-English vowels (niver for never, whustles for whistles), nor English-voice poems. Skeins of fate turn from us to their own hame, wherever that is. What is left is a soun on the wind's moan. The other world may print the wind with unreadable (though maybe human) signs. But in the end we have to treat it as deef and dumb.

Plus we can do a spot of signing ourselves. Just as the barbed wire makes a sign tae the wind, the poem is a sign to the unearthly world that, blind as we are in front of its strangeness ('closed in' by 'this muddy vesture of decay', as Shakespeare puts it), we are okay without understanding what it says. We can gesture towards the hidden mysterious things, and one way to do that is a poem. But our signs, our poems, are rooted in the human world, details and relationships: in our lovers, histories, senses; our connectedness. For connectedness is where we live. Our own skeins, that connect us to

119

each other, make up our territory. It is the other world, of fate and hidden meanings, that sounds so <u>bereft</u>.

As a sign-off for a major collection, whose other poems were full of dialogue, graffiti, contemporary Scottish lives and wild imaginative tie-ups between (for example) the Dalai Lama and the island of Skye, this poem made a wonderfully emptying ending. It is poetry announcing its belief in this world, and letting everything else ride away where it will, on the wind. We'll never know our future, nor all the meanings of the world around us, just as we never know all the meanings of a poem.

And that's okay. We can live with not understanding everything. We have to.

16. Les Murray

ON HOME BEACHES

Back, in my fifties, fatter than I was then,
I step on the sand, belch down slight horror to walk
a wincing pit edge, waiting for the pistol shot
laughter. Long greening waves cash themselves, foam change
sliding into Ocean's pocket. She turns: ridicule looks down,
strappy, with faces averted, or is glare and families.
The great hawk of the beach is outstretched, point to point,
quivering and hunting. Cars are the surf at its back.
You peer, at this age, but it's still there, ridicule,
the pistol that kills women, that gets them killed, crippling men
on the towel-spattered sand. Equality is dressed, neatly,
with mouth still shut. Bared body is not equal ever.
Some are smiled to each other. Many surf, swim, play ball:
like that red boy, holding his wet T shirt off his breasts.

(1996)

Murray is an internationally acclaimed Australian poet, born in 1938, who grew up on a farm in New South Wales. His poems fuse razor-sharp description with passionate belief in sacredness, poetry and art, and wonderful sudden images, slithering between tenderness (for human beings and the natural world) and rage. His books are dedicated 'to the glory of God'. Stubbornly, unglamorously, the poems identify with nature of all kinds, from landscape and animals to human nature, above all the 'poor white' underclass from which the poet comes. Uncompromising, beautifully crafted, deeply learned and felt, they find (and make) beauty in unexpected places. In dispossession, ungainliness and pain as well as in what surrounds all that: cities, dust, wild fauna. With great moral and poetic authority, his work holds intellectual, social, personal and religious elements all in play at once.

This poem is about the agony of being unclothed (on the beach, when you are fat), and so it clothes itself in classic shape: a SONNET, whose classic proportion of eight lines to six creates a 'waisted' shape. But Murray denies his SONNET a waist and opts for BLOCK FORM − for a poem about not having a waist, about the misery of your own block form.

The first eight lines are physical description with an emotional undertow. The first syllable ricochets through the OCTET: back, fatter, strappy, back. The OCTET's second and second-last lines are the only ones that don't have that short A. Instead they have short E: belch, outstretched. Short I echoes through fifties, wincing, pit, pistol, families; short O in shot and pocket. The OCTET is a sonic maze of pistol shot vowels whose aggression is underscored by sharp consonants like K, T, ST: back, fatter, step: pit edge, waiting, pistol shot, laughter; pocket; hawk, outstretched, point to point, cars, back.

The deliberately unattractive words (belch) lead to a deliberately unattractive commercial image: greening waves cashing themselves into foam like cheques turned into 'greenbacks'. The metaphor (bitter at the lucrative holiday business) is intellectual, but slides makes it physical too. The waves becoming foam are a promise (like a cheque) made real in cash: then the foam slithers back into sea. The change is double: both money and transformation (a 'sea change', as in Ariel's song from Shakespeare's *The Tempest*) from wave to foam and back.

The stop-start rhythm, breaking the line in different places, stresses emotionally key words: back, fifties, fatter; step, sand, horror; edge, pistol shot (two stresses, dragging the line over the line break), laughter. It gets the stop-start of waves, but also the poet's to and fro of action and feeling summed up in wincing.

Wincing is a TRANSFERRED EPITHET: it really should apply to the speaker, his flinching emotion and body as he approaches the sea, rather than the sea. It describes how he feels as he sees the sea's edge: it is the lip of a pit. Walking here, for him, is wincing. W connects them. Sea edge is pit edge. The beach which should be paradise is hell.

Ocean profits from this hell. The words She turns turn the spotlight from nature on to humanity. Ridicule and Ocean are personified. Ocean, a singular who keeps becoming plural (waves), parallels the ridicule which looks down in contempt: the singular idea turned into plural humanity (faces, families). The singular glare of sun and sea turns to a mocking sea of human eyes.

The poem's first free-flowing line gives an overview of the beach as a hawk's wingspan. Lovely, but in the next line this hawk continues the pursuit suggested in wincing: horror, pistol, averted, glare. The whole beach is hunting the poet.

To an English ear (and Australia too has 'point to points'), the wings' description suggests a race-meeting, adding to the sense of persecutory social gathering. The OCTET's last word rings back to its first. Front and back, the hunted poet is surrounded by surf. The ocean is persecutory commercial society, the beach a predator looking down on him, the sea of cars is more surf. The whole description breathes violence, pursuit and a savage sense of the outsider, a man marked down, marked out. The title bitterly points out that this is what home always was: alienation.

Different SONNETS move differently from OCTET to SESTET. In No. 8, the SESTET develops the OCTET, from sexual suggestiveness at home to sexual experience in a New World. Here, the SESTET is a move from description to reflection. Murray has described himself as a reflective rather than lyric poet, and his main intellectual point here is physical inequality; the way it hurts and how you survive it. But the move from describing to reflecting accompanies another shift: a shift of tone, from personal I to a universal you. Reflecting on where he came from (emotionally, geographically), the poet moves to other people, inviting readers to share the alienation his poem is describing.

New vowels, binding together the SESTET's first two lines, echo a persecuting word in the OCTET: peer, there, bared all pick up glare.

Short vowels echo the OCTET in more openly aggressive words: pistol and ridicule again, kills, killed, crippling. The softer consonants also lead to savagery: the I of still to ridicule, pistol, kills, killed, crippling, towel, still, smiled, play ball; P (peer) to pistol, crippling, play. Both P and L take us back to the OCTET's sharp ST: pistol, gets, spattered, dressed, neatly, still, shut, wet T shirt and (the climax) breasts.

The last three lines give the OCTET's persecution (by glare and hawk) more active menace. Clothed body is a shut mouth, so bared bodies presumably 'bare' their teeth. Relations with other bodies is where injustice bites. Happy bodies pair off as curved mouths smiled to each other (the only hint of sex in an archetypally sexual scene), but ridicule is a pistol, which separates women and men. Smiled recalls ridicule (from Latin *rideo*, I smile): paired bodies smiling superiorly at the fat.

Murray is working towards that lone red (both sunburnt and blushing) boy. When he tries to play ball (join in, join the system, the social gathering), wetness reveals what he cannot bear to bare. Though prepared for harmonically by dressed and wet, the last word breasts is a shock. Dressed or not, those awful breasts are exposed when *wet*. The inequality of bodies will out.

If the OCTET is a chase, the SESTET closes in for the kill (after killed, spattered implies blood), turning ridicule to murder, laughter to slaughter. The victim is both that miserable boy there now, and a revelation of the poet as he was. But the pain packed into these lines reaches out to other people: anybody (and any body) afraid of 'baring' themselves and their secrets, their breasts, to the outside world.

17. U. A. Fanthorpe

RISING DAMP

'A river can sometimes be diverted but is a very hard thing to lose altogether.'

Paper to the Auctioneers' Institute, 1907

At our feet they lie low,
The little fervent underground
Rivers of London

Effra, Graveney, Falcon, Quaggy,
Wandle, Walbrook, Tyburn, Fleet

Whose names are disfigured,
Frayed, effaced.

These are the Magogs that chewed the clay
To the basin that London nestles in.
These are the currents that chiselled the city,
That washed the clothes and turned the mills,
Where children drank and salmon swam
And wells were holy.

They have gone under.
Boxed, like the magician's assistant.
Buried alive in earth.
Forgotten, like the dead.

They return spectrally after heavy rain,
Confounding suburban gardens. They infiltrate
Chronic bronchitis statistics. A silken
Slur haunts dwellings by shrouded
Watercourses, and is taken
For the footing of the dead.

Being of our world, they will return
(Westbourne, caged at Sloane Square,
Will jack from his box),
Will deluge cellars, detonate manholes,

Plant effluent on our faces,
Sink the city.

Effra, Graveney, Falcon, Quaggy,
Wandle, Walbrook, Tyburn, Fleet

It is the other rivers that lie
Lower, that touch us only in dreams
That never surface. We feel their tug
As a dowser's rod bends to the surface below

Phlegethon, Acheron, Lethe, Styx.

(1982)

Born in 1929, Fanthorpe is a much-loved poet of very poised, debunking humour, sophisticated wit and sarky direct speech, but also enormous compassion, tenderness and profound historical reflection. She has worked both as a teacher and a hospital clerk, and her poems breathe a deeply English feel for countryside: for a modern pastoral of shopping centres, gardens, human gatherings, but also for the history underneath contemporary landscape and behaviour. In one poem, Arthurian knights' horses have dwindled away to become the shaggy ponies of the English moors. In another, the bad fairy at a christening dishes out a seedy, Jeffrey Barnard-like life forecast. 'Right,' says the baby concerned. 'That was roughly / What we had in mind.' In their delicate, insightful ruminations on history, myth and art, her poems draw on practical observation of vulnerable, anxious people swamped by brutally impersonal administration. They are on the side of the human – against pomposity, armoured rhetoric, bureaucracy, impersonality, any retreat from generosity.

Poetry has had its didactic moments in the past, but these days poems which explain too much don't feel right. The spirit of the age responds to poems better if they only reveal or suggest. Without putting us off, this poem has to provide information we might otherwise not know (the presence of these underground rivers under London), in order to get across its insight: what such rivers might mean imaginatively, or symbolise, about ourselves.

To do this undidactically, Fanthorpe mixes nursery rhyme, incantation, wit (starting with the title and epigram), different tonal registers and a central pun. Lie low in the first line (returning in the last stanza and last word, lie lower, below), and underground in the second, both draw on the language of criminals as well as rivers.

The rivers are first characterised by fervent, which prepares us for their eventual connection with deep emotion in the last STANZA, which brings to our attention (since the poem is about something rising from a hiding place) both the Greek mythic underworld and the underworld of our own psyches.

The poem starts personifying these rivers by giving us their names in songlike, craggy litany. Then it calls them Magogs, which puts a new spin on the criminality theme. For in the Book of Revelation, Gog and Magog are enemies of God, while in British legend they are bad giants: giants who have been defeated in the past but, like the Titan under Vesuvius in Greek myth, are not dead but only sleeping. They live on in the English landscape as hills.

As criminals, then, their past acts are characterised by aggressive verbs. They carved, chewed, chiselled the basin where the city nestles, so trustful, and still comparatively so young. Nature's violence made a cradle for civilisation, but it has not gone away. Like Titans and criminals, these rivers have gone to ground; gone under.

And, like ghosts, they return spectrally. Like spies, they infiltrate, causing illness (chronic bronchitis statistics, Fanthorpe's hospital vision of pain masked by bureaucratic-speak). They flood us (deluge, with apocalyptic overtones of Noah). They sink the city whose cradle they made. Criminals or rivers, the underground retains, though unseen most of the time, its power to destroy.

In this elastically structured poem, each STANZA is a new and separate addition to the thought. Repeated sound-shapes hold each STANZA together: basin, London, children, salmon; rain, surburban gardens, silken, taken; return, Westbourne, Sloane. All the geological information we have to know, to enter the poem fully, is made funny and childlike by the 'This is the House that Jack Built' rhythm and syntax (washed the clothes and turned the mills).

Then she pivots, in five syllables at the STANZA end, away from nursery-rhyme structures into a soberer tone. And wells were holy begins a new idea, hooking into the next verse and related to it by rhythm. They have gone under, another five syllables, mirrors the holy line but also darkens its thought. Going under can mean dying; being defeated, like Gog and Magog. Or, like the bronchitis sufferer, pulled down by the rising damp of the title.

But dying also gives you power: the power of the dead. What is under is sacred, but also dangerous. What is boxed (in a coffin, as well as the cement conduits runnelling the rivers) and shrouded is also magic.

Instead of unpacking this thought in explanation, she gets it across with witty human comparisons: magician's assistant, bronchitis statistics. And also with a lyricism (silken / Slur haunts dwellings) which euphemises the rising damp of the title. She puns on footing: you get the picture both of damp walls and of ghostly footsteps. And under (since this poem is so much about the underneath things) all the wit and verbal grace is the idea of the revenant, the dead and buried person who returns to haunt you (buried alive, they will return).

In the last STANZA, Fanthorpe places all these compacted links between the dead, criminals and underground rivers, on a yet deeper level. These rivers with their barbarous names – Effra, Quaggy and co. – become an image also for the unconscious, and what we traditionally imagine flowing inside that. In the Greek underworld, Phlegethon was river of Burning, Acheron was the river of Groaning, Lethe was the river of Forgetting and Styx (the river by which the gods swore, when they had to swear an oath) was the 'black ferry', the boundary that separated the living and the dead. The just-dead souls gather on its bank to cross over into whatever afterlife awaits, into death.

And ever since, this ancient underworld has also been an image for our own unconscious minds. Freud, says Auden in his elegy to him, worked with 'fauna of the night'. The 'dumb' creatures of the underworld, like Furies, sit in the dark of our unconscious, and Freud (says Auden's elegy) was the first to give them the attention they deserve. That's why they mourn him. Torrents of fire, grief, forgetting and mortality lie, says Fanthorpe's poem, under the surface of all our minds; and dreams, like a dowser's rod, connect us to them.

These underground unconscious forces touch us, pull us down. Bends in the penultimate line reverses the movement of rising in the title. The rivers may have gone under but they are always there.

128

They rise and threaten us, like the dragons under the foundations of the castle in Arthurian legend, against which Merlin warns the king.

We live with all this dangerous stuff buried within us, in our cities, lives and minds. At some point, these forces will jack from their box. They are giants, ghosts, spies, criminals, sinister forces: shaping our cities, shaping our souls. We feel their tug. Life is a struggle to keep them boxed in and under; to stop them flooding us. They will always return, for they underlie our journey towards death: which is also towards them.

And yet, says this rich, playful poem, we can have fun, take in profundity, comedy, myth, nursery rhyme and dream, we can laugh at pomposity and find holiness and magic as we live our fragile lives on a slender crust above these dragons, these underground powers.

The world, it is said, is richer for having a devil in it: as long as you keep his neck under your foot. As this poem keeps it, under the heel of its quietly, playfully serious tone.

18. Fred D'Aguiar

MAMA DOT WARNS AGAINST AN EASTER RISING

Doan raise no kite is good friday
but is out he went out an fly it
us thinkin maybe there wont be a breeze
strong enouf an widout any a we to hole it
fo him he'd neva manage to get it high-up
to de tree top ware de wind kissin
de ripess sweetess fruit we cawn reach
but he let out some string bit by bit
tuggin de face into de breeze
coaxin it up all de time takin a few steps back
an it did rise up bit by bit till de lang tail
din't touch de groun an we grip de palin
we head squeeze between to watch him
an trace its rise rise up up up in de sky
we all want to fly in like bird but can only kite
fly an he step back juss as we beginnin
to smile fo him envy him his easter risin
when bap he let out a scream leggo string
an de kite drop outta de sky like a bird
a sail down to de nex field an we runnin to him
fogettin de kite we uncle dem mek days ago
fram wood shave light as bird bone
paper tin like fedder an de tongue o kite
fo singin in de sky like a bird an de tail
fo balance string in de mout like it pullin
de longess worm an he a hole him foot
an he bawl we could see seven inch a greenhart
gone in at de heel running up him leg
a vein he groanin all de way to de haspital
on de cross-bar a bike ridden by a uncle
she not saying a word but we hearin her
fo de ress a dat day an evry year since

doan raise no kite is good friday
an de sky was a birdless kiteless wait fo her word

(1985)

Born in 1960, D'Aguiar grew up in Guyana and London, trained as a psychiatric nurse and now teaches in America. His voice shifts between Caribbean and Standard English, and his forms shift between BLANK VERSE and rhymed STANZAS. Equally, his historical reference points shift between different narratives: those of Western literature versus the history and textures of post-independence Guyana (greenhart, here, for instance, is a savage native thorn) and African-American experience.

The title alludes to Yeats' poems of the Easter Rising in Dublin, when the Irish 'rose' against the English in 1916: perhaps particularly to 'An Irish Airman Foresees his Death'. The first half of d'Aguiar's poem is all foreboding. The anxieties are partly practical: maybe there wont be a breeze / strong enouf. The collective voice, the we, is separate from the doomed kite-flier. We are concerned for this boy on his own, widout any a we to hole it / fo him. Can he fulfil his ambition alone or will he (the perennial masculine fear) neva manage to get it high-up?

Then we move to the achievement (he let out some string bit by bit / tuggin de face into de breeze / coaxin it up all de time takin a few steps back) and excitement (we grip de palin / we head squeeze between to watch him) of spectators who, unlike him, accept limits (de ripess sweetess fruit we cawn reach) and obey a knowing warning when they hear one.

This warning is based not on practicalities but superstitious or religious belief. 'Mama Dot' is an Obeah mother-figure throughout the collection from which this poem comes. She is also an allegory of slavery, the archetypal female figure who lives for childcare and the endurance of her people, seen through the eyes of first a boy, then a young man who leaves Guyana to work abroad. Mama Dot is angry but cares for people. Her motto is survival in the face of

131

injustice. 'With all the talk of nationality we still hungry', she says in another poem. Flouting her warning ('Doan raise no kite is good friday') is flouting her inherited magic, her knowledge of how to survive in a hostile world.

The timider watchers admire his achievement. He went out an fly it. He gets it to rise up up up in de sky (like the 'Irish airman'): this sky we all want to fly in like bird but can only kite / fly. They envy him his easter risin.

This line, echoing the title, marks the halfway point, before the fall. What the Irish airman foresees in Yeats' title, of course, is 'his death'.

The shape of the poem, lines smoothly snaking on, one from another, like a string going up into the sky, enacts the act it describes. Poems describing how to make or do something are often talking about making a poem, too. The most lyrical lines here are the ones about what the kite can do, reach the tree top ware de wind kissin / de ripess sweetess fruit, and how it was made: fram wood shave light as bird bone / paper tin like fedder an de tongue o kite / fo singin in de sky like a bird an de tail / fo balance string in de mout like it pullin / de longess worm. The poem is identifying with this other made thing, the kite, in its delicacy: in how it can rise, how high and how waywardly, beautifully, it can fly.

As with kite-flying, the form looks artless but is not. The scene is let out like the string, bit by bit, with no punctuation to hole it. Just like the kite-flyer, the poet is coaxin something up all de time takin a few steps back.

He keeps it going mainly by conjunctions. These are both verbal – the an ('and') which joins the verbs and keeps the narrative flowing (an it did rise up . . . an de kite drop outta de sky) – and social: the joining of the people and their three viewpoints. Sombre Mama Dot, disobedient kite-flyer, and the watching, admiring, then horrified we.

For the poem is about disaster too. The second half starts with bap he let out a scream leggo string. The kite-string shape continues, but the physical and emotional movements it enacts and describes, go down – except that terrible thorn which goes up, into his vein.

The six lines describing the kite's creation come just after it has dropped outta de sky like a bird and sailed down to de nex field. The poem does not say if the flyer is Mama Dot's grandson or some other relative, but these lines of making which now divide that

132

lovely delicate creation from its flyer (now himself being unmade, with a seven-inch thorn gone in at de heel) could well stand in for his own creation; and all his nurturers' hopes for him during his nurturing.

The watchers' reaction to his fate begins with communal male sympathy with his ambition, turns from smile fo him to envy, then to fear for him: we runnin to him. After the accident, the sky itself is bleached of male aspiration: a birdless kiteless wait fo her word. Male action, that sexy, potent, worldly and other-worldly dream of being bird, is for ever, now, a 'waiting' on women's word; blocked by that sad, traditional role women have to take on in a world that is politically or physically unsafe: of making the boys keep, quite literally, their heads down. To stop them, as long as possible, from rising into that sky where men are so keen to fly.

19. Fleur Adcock

A SURPRISE IN THE PENINSULA

When I came in that night I found
the skin of a dog stretched flat and
nailed upon my wall between the
two windows. It seemed freshly killed –
there was blood at the edges. Not
my dog: I have never owned one,
I rather dislike them. (Perhaps
whoever did it knew that.) It
was a light brown dog, with smooth hair;
no head, but the tail still remained.
On the flat surface of the pelt
was branded the outline of the
peninsula, singed in thick black
strokes into the fur: a coarse map.
The position of the town was
marked by a bullet-hole; it went
right through the wall. I placed my eye
to it, and could see the dark trees
outside the house, flecked with moonlight.
I locked the door then, and sat up
all night, drinking small cups of the
bitter local coffee. A dog
would have been useful, I thought, for
protection. But perhaps the one
I had been given performed that
function; for no one came that night,
nor for three more. On the fourth day
it was time to leave. The dog-skin
still hung on the wall, stiff and dry
by now, the flies and the smell gone.
Could it, I wondered, have been meant
not as a warning, but a gift?

And, scarcely shuddering, I drew
the nails out and took it with me.

(1971)

Adcock was born in New Zealand in 1934 and moved to Britain in
1963. Over many decades her sharp, reflective poems have ranged
from jewelly exoticism to detailed physical scenarios ('she sucks at
earlobe, penis, tongue / mouthing the tubes of flesh') and equally
detailed sinister ones. Or wry feminist reflection: no one else, to my
knowledge, has written a poem like Adcock's 'Against Coupling',
which goes (tongue, as it were, in cheek) into the reasons why
women might prefer masturbation to men.

The detached, sceptical-formal part of her voice has an amused
moral authority; underneath, the poems are charged with anger,
eroticism, danger. Reality or dream, what she describes always
means more than it seems. She is a poet of no solutions: of giving
you what's there then standing back and seeing what you make of
it. Here, we are in thriller territory: bad-dream-land, *film noir*. A
territory of not-knowing, of being surrounded by danger as a
peninsula is surrounded by water. A place where a dog-skin nailed
to your wall – the one you describe in your title by understatement
as 'a surprise', the one you spend four nights with but whose smell
you don't mention till the end – may be a warning, protection, or a
gift.

The voice through whom we see this world is as sinister as
anything outside. What does this 'I', so alone and objective, so
acquainted, apparently, with violence (freshly killed, bullet-hole . . .
right through the wall), and yet so in need of protection (which in
gangland has a specific technical meaning), get up to in the day?
What is 'I' doing here, what has this I achieved when it's time to
leave?

The apparently objective the's and that's in the title (the
peninsula), first line (that night), and throughout (the outline of
the / peninsula, the position of the town, the dark trees, the bitter

135

local coffee), suggest we should know the place and what has to be done there, while reminding us that we can't. The message is: you've got to look deeper if you want to understand but you have to put up with guesswork in the end anyway, because you never, ever get the whole picture.

This message applies implicitly to life in general; it is also the principle underlying the poem's technical procedure. That all-in-one block is held closely together soundwise but never at the end of lines. Nothing so obvious. You always have to look deeper, inside the lines – which are all eight syllables long.

Writing in SYLLABICS, i.e. arranging the line according to how many syllables it contains, was fashionable in the sixties: it is amazing the variation of cadence and accent eight syllables can offer. Musically, this is a close network of sound-relationships. Several sounds in the first line carry right through: that gives you the dominant sound of the first half, echoed in flat, perhaps, that, flat, black, map. It continues in sat, that, that, but the main vowel-sound to take over is the OR of coarse, continued in wall, small, thought, for, performed, for, nor for, more, fourth, wall, warning. In is answered by skin (the important word), windows, maybe seemed and remained, then comes back with warning, shuddering. Found is echoed in windows, owned, brown, strokes, town.

This resonant first line is answered by the last: we move from in (came in) to out (I drew out). The only actual glimpse outside we ever have is through that bullet-hole, yet the lines ending on and, not, it, the, was, the, that, for keep taking you out and away. To find where you are, you have to look further.

Most sentence-endings and closures come somewhere inside a line. Not all: remained, map, moonlight, gone and gift are sudden resting points in this confused sinister world which deprives you of that finding a pattern which rhyme represents. (Rhyme is traditionally paired with reason, but this poem is not going to hand you much of that.)

Moonlight is the turning point. After describing the skin, looking at dark trees through the bullet-hole, 'I' acts on the knowledge by locking up and staying awake. Flecked and locked wake the K of skin (the key word), which follows in drinking, cups, local coffee, protection, function, came, skin, could, took.

The whole closed system of sound-relationships matches this closing-in peninsular world where no one says what they are doing, where we never see the people all around, whose intentions towards

136

us, menacing or kind, we never know. 'I' takes the dog-skin with her, warning or gift; as we, when it's time to leave, take the poem with us as a coarse map whose insight into our surprised, unknowing state in this uncertain world might just help us to get through it.

20. Simon Armitage

THE FOX

Standing its ground on the hill, as if it could hide
in its own stars, low down in the west of the sky.
I could hit it from here with a stone, put the torch
in the far back of its eye. It's that close.

The next night, the dustbin sacked, the bin-bag
quartered for dog meat, biscuit and bone.
The night after that, six magpies lifting
from fox fur, smeared up ahead on the road.

(1996)

Born in Yorkshire in 1963, Armitage has something of the deep-smouldering double care for both landscape and the language which describes it or squares up to it, as Ted Hughes, another Yorkshire poet. But Armitage's landscapes are urban and suburban as well as rural. There is more focus on the human and the social world moving through them than in a lot of Hughes. His poems lock on to humanity's impress on the natural landscape, like (in one poem) the angel shape you make in the snow by 'flapping your arms'. His streetwise, witty, double-edged, often sinister language presses up to and into life's inconclusiveness, rather than (as in Hughes) its mythic force. From hitchhikers, police catching you with marijuana ('it's cut and dried'), or millennial bonfires, the poems often end in deadpan regret; and the nihilist part of his voice is bleakly alive to distances between people. But there are also quietly powerful love poems; and you notice the deep sparkle of craft, like vintage champagne, and of love for poetic tradition and the tricks and tools it contains, in everything he does.

In my column I did Armitage very early when we had to do short poems. Later, I might have chosen a longer poem which expanded into other subjects. But this one – a little masterpiece from a collection which focused mainly on the stars ('The Fox' is, first of all, a constellation) – demonstrates on its small scale the power both of his technique and his connection-making.

Rhythmically, the poem is a tiny battleground between the DACTYL and the SPONDEE: a battle which tracks the poem's tension between freedom and capture, wild life and violence.

It begins with DACTYLS: the first half of the first line is the same pattern as the first half-lines of Homer's *Iliad* or Virgil's *Aeneid*. The first word is standing, but these rhythms belie stillness. They run quick (as a brown fox, perhaps), like the animal, but slow down for a moment at the word hide, as if forced to lie low (in its own stars, the poem's first SPONDEES, followed by low down). Then they pick up again and run on: down in the west of the sky. The watcher, I, picks up their rhythm (hit it from here with a stone).

The human agent introduces the violence with which the poem will end. What do you do when you see a fox that close? Wonder if you can hit it, apparently. Anyway, this watcher does. In his second line, he matches the first SPONDEE (far back) in the same place as own stars from the fox's second line. But the mention of violence skews the run-on rhythm. This STANZA ends with another SPONDEE, that close, and the second STANZA (knitted to the first by that sharp syllable sacked, echoing back) has a different rhythmic feel.

In this STANZA, after the first line, the beats in a line dwindle from five to four, and brutal SPONDEES gather (next night, bin-bag, dog meat) until we know the fox is dead (fox fur). Then the SPONDEES release their hold. Their double hammer blows have done their work. They let the DACTYLS rip on to the end to describe the result (smeared up ahead on the road).

Aptly, for a poem about a secretive animal, the poem is held together by inner rhyme and vowel-echoes. Ground is followed by down but narrows into own, low, stone (mirrored in close), then bone and road, which rings you back to D on the first line-end, hide. The fortunes of this network of sounds track the fox's story: it runs from hide to road via its own, low attachments (ground, stone, bone), threatened en route by the equally hidden rhymes (if it, hit it, picked up later in biscuit).

The first STANZA is long vowels, a balance between visible end-words (hide, sky, bone) and their seesawing internal echoes (I, eye, stone), and internal echoes inside the lines (stars, far). The second STANZA's rat-tat-tat sounds speed things up with X, Q, K, T, B (quartered, biscuit, meat, bag, magpie, sacked), getting the fox's snapping appetite but also foreshadowing its comeuppance.

Among the MONOSYLLABLES, many very hard, the participles' softer endings speak to each other. Standing is partnered by lifting, which takes those magpies over the edge of the nearly last line, up from the fox who once, like them, inhabited sky.

For this is a poem about distance and secret violence. If it hadn't appeared in a run of poems about other constellations, you would hardly think this fox was a star fox at all. That's the project, to demythify the constellation, make it literally 'stand' its ground, go to ground, be star and fox both at once: then bring it at the end to a 'smear' on the road. The poem moves from seeing the fox, to thoughts of hurting it, to being raided by it, and its unseen death. It is about secret wildness: and addresses a paradox about the state of wild things or wildness in Britain, and ourselves, today. The non-human 'wild' was once threatening and savage. These days it is vulnerable, threatened itself. By our roads and vehicles; and by our own wildness, our destructive impulses: I could hit it from here with a stone.

But this poem, as delicate and sly as its subject, also gestures to another fox poem: 'The Thought-Fox' by Ted Hughes, Armitage's

140

Yorkshire-born poetic predecessor, the great poet of wildness both in animal and human nature. Hughes' poem too is set at night, with a watching 'I' and a fox. There is 'no star' in it, but the watcher spots the fox's 'eye' gleaming as it comes 'about its own business'. Hughes' fox approaches the watcher's house, not to raid his bin-bags but to leap into 'the dark hole of the head', leaving prints on 'the page'.

For Hughes' poem is very openly about writing poems, about inspiration. This one by Armitage is about many things. But 'about' is a big word; a poem is usually about many different things at once. I think this one resonates with Hughes' poem, and so in its own way evokes poetic inspiration as a wily living thing, which lives its own secret life both in the stars and on the ground. A predatory, opportunistic visitor, linked to violence, which creeps up on you, raids you, is both vulnerable and wild.

21. Elaine Feinstein

ROSEMARY IN PROVENCE

We stopped the Citroen at the turn of the lane,
because you wanted a sprig of blue rosemary
to take home, and your coat opened awkwardly

as you bent over. Any stranger would have
seen your frail shoulders, the illness
in your skin – our holiday on the Luberon

ending with salmonella –
but what hurt me, as you chose slowly,
was the delicacy of your gesture:

the curious child, loving blossom
and mosses, still eager
in your disguise as an old man.

(1997)

Born in Liverpool in 1930, Feinstein grew up in Leicester, studied at Cambridge, and originally planned to do law. One of Britain's few major Jewish poets, she was the first to translate Marina Tsvetaeva into English; she knows Eastern Europe, especially Russia, intimately. In the fifties she became interested in the American 'Black Mountain' experimental movement in poetry, and wrote to its leader Charles Olsen. Olsen wrote back (a document now known as his famous 'Letter to Mr Feinstein') setting out his poetic principles to this enterprising – therefore obviously male – young British poet. In her formative years, therefore, Feinstein combined cutting-edge influence from East and West, and the way her voice has developed reflects both; though Tsvetaeva, perhaps, is the presiding influence.

Feinstein's spare, wry, compassionate lyrics often spotlight a single poignant detail which gets across a whole person or life, implying a much larger narrative. (She is a well-known biographer and novelist too.) This poem's delicacy reflects the delicacy of the small gesture it describes, while its blue recalls Cézanne, painter of Provence, who can pack such emotional power into the face of a rock or a turn of the lane.

It is a poem about pausing before the end, not knowing what is round the next turn in that lane. 'There's rosemary, that's for remembrance', says Ophelia in Shakespeare's *Hamlet*. 'Pray, love, remember.' This sprig of blue rosemary is also chosen for remembrance. The man will take it home to whatever ending awaits. The poem is choosing and gathering the scene in the same spirit: for remembrance.

The first words are we stopped, and the stops or pauses in the mainly three-beat line say it all. Poetry's concern with line and pause is about tension. Line breaks pull against the rhythm as you speak it, and the tension brings out particular sounds, word-relationships, and thoughts. Here the changing pause-pattern charts the movement of thought from that wish to pick a herb, to disease, pain and ageing; a holiday ending with salmonella, a child who has become an old man. The first line runs smooth, pausing at its end. The next runs on, reflecting that eager impulse, to the strong pause after home in the third.

Now come pauses at new places in the line. In the second STANZA, the first line is cut halfway by the CAESURA, a full stop, but its end runs on in ENJAMBEMENT, curling over into the next line. An ENJAMBEMENT is especially bold when the line-end cuts two words

143

which need to be together, an adjective and its noun, or some pieces of a compound verb (as here would have / seen). ENJAMBEMENT, run-on, denies everything this poem fears: stopping (see we stopped, the poem's first words), ending (first word of the second half).

This poem clusters several runs of multi-syllabled words followed by a two-syllabled one (rosemary, awkwardly, slowly; Citroen, Luberon, blossom; over, stranger, shoulders, salmonella, gesture, eager). These are what has long (by male metrical analysts) been called FEMININE ENDINGS: soft-feeling, multi-rhythmed endings, words which have a stressed first syllable followed by one or more weaker syllables. As, here, holiday, salmonella, delicacy. The echoing long vowels (lane, stranger; over, shoulders, chose, old; child, disguise) underline the skilfully awkward, softly dragging effect.

You could take the FEMININE ENDINGS to reflect the poet's observing femininity, hurt on the man's behalf by his clumsily careful gestures. But, starting with that key word rosemary, the poem is also talking, in its 'gesturing' at pause and ending, about human ending: about survival; about human ENJAMBEMENT in the face of ageing, frailty, illness / in your skin.

So pausing is what the poem takes off from. And pauses (after three beats and one beat, shoulders and skin) lead to its central parenthesis (our holiday . . . salmonella). This cuts short the first line of the second half, and begins the poem's tapering sense, as it runs down from long words to smaller, sadder words.

It also marks a move from sight to feeling, outer to inner. Seen (as by that imagined outsider, or any stranger) contrasts with the private hurt, in the only line with two breaks. The third verse ends with a strong pause, a colon, before seeing the rosemary-picker as a curious child, in . . . disguise as an old man; whose love for soft things (blossom, mosses) parallels that of the poet for him.

The poet is not the subject of any verb. She stays back: you has all the action. We are the first subject, you wanted is the reason for the stop; even your coat and any stranger are subjects of verbs. But when the poet appears she is the object of a verb: hurt me.

Hurt me, introduced by a strong MONOSYLLABLE, resonates with a famous modernist poem with a similar note in it which (as it happens) I have heard Feinstein read aloud: a love letter poem in the voice of a Chinese girl by Ezra Pound (whose echoes of earlier poetry included troubadours from, as it also happens, Provence).

144

In Pound's poem 'The River-Merchant's Wife', the woman married very young. Now she 'grows older' and her husband is away. Looking at paired-off butterflies, she says simply, 'They hurt me'.

Here, absence is all to come. We are still together: the poem's first word. There is a smile in the final line's denial, as if the illness/ in your skin, frail shoulders, old man, are truly disguise: and the reality is youth, sprig, child, blossom, and rosemary which 'keeps' – as a happier, luckier Shakespearian flower-gatherer than Ophelia (Perdita, in *A Winter's Tale*) says – 'seeming and savour all the winter long'.

22. Derek Walcott

From OMEROS

Seven Seas rose in the half-dark to make coffee.
Sunrise was heating the ring of the horizon
and clouds were rising like loaves. By the heat of the

glowing iron rose he slid the saucepan's base onto the ring and anchored it there. The saucepan shook
from the weight of water in it, then it settled.

His kettle leaked. He groped for the tin chair and took
his place near the saucepan to hear when it bubbled.
It would boil but not scream like a bosun's whistle

to let him know it was ready. He heard the dog's
morning whine under the boards of the house, its tail
thudding to be let in, but he envied the pirogues

already miles out at sea. Then he heard the first breeze
washing the sea-almond's wares; last night there had been
a full moon white as his plate. He saw with his ears.

(1990)

Walcott was born in 1930 in the Caribbean, and now divides his time between St Lucia and America. He is also a playwright and painter, and his poems are very painterly. Through his many books, in many very varied forms, his lyrical, smooth-cadenced, reflective poems, full of the play of light, colour, shadow, have an iridescence like the patina on Roman glass.

His book-length epic *Omeros* uses Homer's *Odyssey* ('Omeros' is Homer in Greek) to explore themes of alienation through different St Lucian lives: Caribbean fishermen and lovers, British expatriates, the poet himself. The epic is in TERZA RIMA, the chain-rhymed three-line STANZA form of Dante's *Divine Comedy*, in which the end-word of the second line in each STANZA rhymes with the end-words in the first and third lines of the next. Shelley used TERZA RIMA for his 'Ode to the West Wind':

> O wild West Wind, thou breath of Autumn's being,
> Thou, from whose unseen presence the leaves dead
> Are driven, like ghosts from an enchanter fleeing,
>
> Yellow, and black, and pale, and hectic red,
> Pestilence-stricken multitudes: O thou,
> Who chariotest to their dark wintry bed
>
> The wingèd seeds, where they lie cold and low . . .

English poets have done TERZA RIMA in several metres, mainly IAMBIC PENTAMETER, but for his epic Walcott picked the twelve-syllable ALEXANDRINE, which is classically as central to French tradition, especially narrative and drama, as IAMBIC PENTAMETER is to English.

Walcott does not chain-link every line with rhyme, but enough to get a feel of through-linkage (horizon to on, first STANZA to second; shook to took and settled to bubbled, second to third; whistle to tail, third to fourth). He underpins this feel by internal echoes. In the first STANZA, Seas echoes in coffee, heating, heat; the O of rose and loaves comes back in the second STANZA with glowing. The OR of saucepan, anchored, saucepan, water in the second is repeated in saucepan in the third, while kettle echoes settled and leads to bubbled and whistle. The Ds of the fourth (ready, heard, dogs, boards, thudding, envied) lead on through the Ws of washing, wares, white and saw, to the crucial word heard in the fifth STANZA.

The whole movement through these STANZAS is a gradual progress towards the revelation that Seven Seas is blind. Saw is the first time seeing is actually mentioned; ears takes its meaning instantly away. The passage is full of intimations of blindness, where hearing and other senses stand in for seeing. Despite the half-dark, the poet gives us visual images (ring, of the horizon, clouds . . . rising like loaves), but Seven Seas himself finds his cooking ring by its heat, not glow. Groped, to hear when it bubbled, and let him know it was ready are further clues, but they could all suggest a pre-dawn dark. Ears is the final revelation. The STANZAS move from half-dark through sunrise and glowing to light (white). But the character cannot follow that move. He can only hear and infer the dog, pirogues, sea-almond's wares. The moon is as round and white as his plate, but by now we realise he cannot see it.

Greek tradition says Homer was blind: and the poet's blindness belongs in a web of ancient Greek associations to darkness and light. Many 'seers' were blind too: Greek drama and religion is full of the idea that people in the dark 'see' truths other people cannot. A singer-poet like Homer, whose vision in the outside world is limited, sees more clearly the inner truths of imagination or of the gods. This passage works by inner dark and outer light. The outdoors of the sea, the trees, the moon; the indoors of the house; the darker indoors of blindness.

The man's name has Seas in it. He is intimately linked to this outer sea-world. He rose with sunrise (and as sea also rises), with clouds . . . rising like loaves (which brings us back to the kitchen scenario again). The horizon is a ring like his glowing iron. There is heat on the horizon, and heat on his stove. The boiling water might (but doesn't) scream like a bosun's whistle. The dog whines to be let in, but the man's imagination is out at sea.

For the thrust is always away: to outside, to the sea. Anchored, weight of water, leaked, bosun and boards all speak of boats. When boats themselves appear, they are the object of his emotion rather than perception. This is the only thing we hear him feeling about. He envied the pirogues. Unlike Seven Seas, the boats go out beyond (already miles out): the rhythm underlines his feeling about them. Most lines are perfect ALEXANDRINES; the pirogues-and-breeze lines have thirteen syllables not twelve, suggesting extension, getting away from limit.

But the last STANZA, where the lines come clean about his blindness, works through seesaw rhymes, which either fall inside a line, sitting in its own interior (night/white), or spool between the inside of a line and its outside (wares/ears). Outer words are linked to inner ones, as the outer world mirrors the inner. Only by his ears can Seven Seas get away from his own indoors.

TERZA RIMA is an Italian form, the epic's theme is Greek, the ALEXANDRINE is French, and the language is English. Walcott grew up on St Lucia speaking English, but spoke French Creole patois with his older female relations. Creole is fading there, he has said, like the old music, under the influence of American TV stations. So St Lucia too is an evolving confluence of several European languages. He has written about how strange it was to learn to read and write European poetry in a world very different from the landscapes it traditionally painted. How do Wordsworth's daffodils come across to someone who has never seen a real one?

Every poet keeps wanting to make and pattern new things as well as possible. But Walcott's enterprise is also to colonise back European poetic tradition, in response to the direction of previous political (and current touristic) colonisation. His language and rhythms use Europe's poetic techniques, conventions, musical and literary imagination, to write about a physical and human world previously alien to those metres and languages. Technically, TERZA RIMA combines a powerful forward momentum with a continuous structure. By making this distilled blend of four European cultures to describe a non-European world which its inheritors once colonised, Walcott gives new momentum to European poetry while continuing its structures.

23. Gillian Allnutt

BARCLAYS BANK AND LAKE BAIKAL

The bank walks in at half past seven, dressed and unembarrassed
by its sponsorship of Beethoven, the best

of music, *Hammerklavier*, here in its own town
Darlington.

Demidenko, Nikolai, in concert, self-exiled,
walks out of another world

like one who's wandered, handkerchief in hand, into the town
to watch the hammer of the auctioneer come down

and then, instead, plays Beethoven
as if he were alone.

He looks like Silas Marner so intent upon his two thick leather
   bags of gold
he lost the world

we live in: cough, cold, cufflink and the ache and pain
of bone.

It looks as if the light, Siberian, is breaking slowly over Lake
   Baikal,
as if our ship of fools

and bankers, borne upon the waters
of a bare

adagio, may founder in a quite uncalled for and unsponsored
sea of solitude.

But not tonight, dour Demidenko, dealer in another world's
dear gold –

for Darlington's recalled. At ten to ten
the bank picks up its leather bag, walks out again.

(2001)

Born in London in 1949, Allnutt studied at Oxford and now lives
in County Durham. Her spare, meditative poems, rising from
religious and rhythmic intensity and quirky imagination, weave
mystic and biblical themes into detailed physical landscapes. These
landscapes are pastoral but also emanate a desultory urban
shabbiness: the 'blown plastic bags' of England today.

This poem is in rhymed COUPLETS and except for the last (which
seals and signs off the poem) these are CONSONANT RHYMES:
unembarrassed/best, gold/world, water/dare, Baikal/fools,
unsponsored/solitude. These unexpected rhymes (which often
yoke words of different stresses and syllables and very different
vowels) and unequal line-lengths underscore what the poem is
doing: relating two different worlds (one of the poem's talismanic
words, see another world, the world / we live in, another world's).
Not the worlds only, but also their different values, symbolised by
gold. One runs on money and sponsorship (Barclays Bank), the
other on art and light.

The relation between Darlington and light . . . breaking slowly
over Lake Baikal (which the pianist conjures up as he plays), pivots
on two things, the reference to George Eliot's *Silas Marner* and an
unspoken cliché: the idea of being 'transported' by music (as in
borne upon the waters / of a bare / *adagio*). Art 'transports you'
somewhere else: another place, where our ship of fools . . . may
founder. Not Lake Baikal but a sea which Barclays cannot sponsor:
solitude.

In *Silas Marner*, the hero's gold is changed to a different kind of
gold. In place of his stolen savings he finds a baby whom he brings
up as his own daughter, and she alchemises his miserliness into
generosity and love. In this poem the *Silas Marner* image, leather /

bags of gold, first belongs to the pianist. By the end it attaches itself to the bank as 'it' picks up its leather bag.

In the poem's first and last lines, the bank is personified in its own town / Darlington. This bank, which has the worldly power to sponsor Beethoven, is all dressed up, unembarrassed by the power it seems to possess over what is so much more truly powerful than itself. 'It' walks in, walks out of music that recreates a dawn landscape in another world. The self-exiled pianist, by contrast, is a dealer in yet another world's / dear gold. He looks like one who's wandered into this place, or any place, by accident. He plays as if he were alone, and had lost the world of ordinary ache and pain / of bone.

This full rhyme between the fifth and the seventh COUPLETS picks up those between town and Darlington, town and down, one of the two main echoes that hold the poem together. The other is world/ gold, recalled. Everything in this poem is about relating two things, whether they are lines, vowel-sounds, consonants, worlds, or different kinds of gold.

All these relatings work towards presenting and juxtaposing two men. One has a name, provenance, personal emotions, similes, the other has become a neuter, an it, an institution. The poem reveals them to us in the same place, joined for a while by their interest (emotional or financial) in the same music. It is a revelation of momentary contiguity: the unemphatic joining (see and in the title) between Barclays and Lake Baikal which the unemphatic CONSO- NANT RHYMES, of which it is made, reflect.

24. John Hartley Williams

JOHN BOSNIA

We have the biggest mushrooms in the world.
If you are lucky enough to collect a basketful,
Take them home & cook them.
Wait a year or so. If you're still alive
Buy some more & try again. Either way
The process is definitive.
Then we have Hercegovina, which means (roughly),
The Prince Who Drank (And Keeps Drinking) (And Is In A
    Perpetual State of Drinking)
The Wine. We call this the continual case
Which does not exist in yr language. Yet.
Climb our many mountains, you will see a shepherd descending.
For *dvije banke* he will sell you the body
Of his goat. We are hard people. We take our pleasure fiercely.
Someone told me to ask an Englishman
To write this down on paper for me. Is this word 'fiercely'
    correct?
It sounds funny.
I have been ejected from more restaurants in yr country than in
    any other.
Our waiters are not like yours. They are very male. They are not
    embarrassed to embrace you,
Press their moustaches against yr ear & tell you to leave,
Whilst holding yr waist in a tight grip.
It feels very unusual, but Englishmen think it more direct &
    honest
And grow to like it. And if you can
Wrestle the bloomers off the swarthy women of my country
You've had it, my friend, you're done for. When a Bosnian
    woman
Presses you to eat, you may not rise from the table
Until you are dead with exhaustion. You must experience
What it means to go beyond gratification.

Then you will understand. Ah, we are too patriotic, I know,
And when we kiss
Often it is kinder to put a knife in someone's ribs. But we are
   very gentle people.
We have the biggest mosquitoes.
Strangely, the nights here are vacant of whine. How do you
   sleep?
I was caught in a storm
Driving my melons to market. The old horse skipped a little
And then fell into the Drina, turning it red. All
The opened faces of the melons began to talk in prophecies.
   They said:
Stand up & go to London. Ask an Englishman to write this
   down:
'My name's John Bosnia. I have lost my cart & my crop,
And before you throw me out of this restaurant
I am going to read you this poem.'

(1993)

Williams, born in 1944, is a deeply sophisticated and original poet,
both emotionally searching and very funny. He has taught
linguistics in Africa, now teaches English in Berlin, and knows
former Yugoslavia intimately. His poems have explored sex, politics,
the Wild West and language in a fantastic range of styles and forms;
both formal lyrics and swashbuckling experimental FREE VERSE. In
layout, his mix of traditionalism (here, for example, capital letters
begin each line) and ignoring of convention (the ampersands, the
abbreviated yr) shake you into reading with fresh eyes and mind.
   This poem first appeared in *Klaonika*, an anthology which asked
poets to write poems expressing sympathy for Bosnia before Britain
withdrew its opposition to attacking Serbian bomb positions (which
finally ended the siege of Sarajevo). The poem is about ethnic
cleansing, about being trapped in a violent land gone mad, but also
about longing for outside, and specifically English, help. It

expresses all this mainly through three things: the tone, the relation between an I and a you, and symbols. Mushrooms and mosquitoes give you the flavour of the land itself, but also stand in for bombs and planes. The melons which fall into the river are also the innocent dead, whose opened faces begin to talk in prophecies.

The speaker moves from boastfully describing his country (We have the biggest mushrooms ... mountains ... biggest mosquitoes) to the moment when he himself, in a quasi-agricultural disaster, encountered the violence head-on (caught in a storm / Driving my melons to market). There is no open mention of ethnic cleansing and massacre: that is all in the old horse skipped a little / And then fell into the Drina, turning it red.

The tone gets the anxious pomposity of someone not quite sure of the language he is speaking, as in the nervous Latin derivations correct and ejected (which musically pick up that sinister yet, later echoed in direct as the speaker moves into more fluid gear, more confidingly intimate). This tone allows for the unexpected jumps of someone speaking a language not his own, but also someone in emotional trauma. Then we have Hercegovina: in this inconsequential way the speaker introduces the land and language where the violence came from which began the First World War.

The speaker's own language stands like a shadow language behind the poem's words. It contains some features, he says, which are not in yr language: like the continual case – suggesting continual conflict, perhaps. For the deep parallel in this poem (rising, perhaps, out of the poet's long experience in linguistics) is between land and language, as if language itself is a kind of landscape. Both languages and lands evolve. That sinister little word Yet, standing by itself, suggests that our own land, like our own language, may change; may become more like the Balkans, 'continually' violent. The formally described definitive process with which the poem opens is how the speakers of this language, like the inhabitants of this land, have learnt to deal with their environment, their predicament. Maybe the violence of that predicament will eventually radiate out to the rest of the world, to us: like the shot in Sarajevo in 1914.

Hints of continual hurt and menace are everywhere (if you're still alive, I have been ejected, you're done for; I have lost). And the word he says sounds funny, whose spelling he questions (is it correct?), is fiercely.

The speaker describes a world where nights are vacant of whine. Again you fill in a shadow language whose idiom this phrase might

155

translate, but you also suspect that you can't hear mosquitoes in a bombing raid. This is a world where you are 'ejected' from restaurants, whose waiters 'wait' to bounce you. The speaker assumes a permanent asylum-seeker life, and implicates the reader in it when he expects also to be 'thrown out' of the platform of appeal which the poem itself represents (*before you throw me out of this restaurant*). This place where the poem is read and heard, the place of communication where the reader meets the speaker's words, is a restaurant, a temporary 'rest' for the refugee, before he is shoved out yet again.

The tone is full of pride (biggest . . . in the world; very male; Englishmen think it more direct & honest; a Bosnian woman . . . then you will understand; ah, we are too patriotic, I know). But it also creates a wishful intimacy with the you the poem addresses. The figure from which the speaker distinguishes himself is an Englishman (see feels very unusual, but Englishmen . . . grow to like it): i.e. someone who had the accidental fortune (see if you are lucky enough) to be born in the one European country in the twentieth century that was not invaded, occupied and/or split by civil war, genocide, holocaust or racial violence; whose language does not possess the continual case. Yet underlines how fragile England's lucky immunity from large-scale violence may prove to be.

For the poem is also about universal experience, universal vulnerability: you must experience / What it means to go beyond gratification / Then you will understand. Questioning 'your' experience (how do you sleep?), the poem suggests the you and the I are really in the same boat, both of mortality and of maleness (*vis-à-vis* the women whose bloomers – hint of that word's other meaning, 'big mistake' – you may try to wrestle off). The direct you keeps looping the reader into John Bosnia's world: if you are lucky enough, if you're still alive, yr language, yr country, if you can . . . you've had it, my friend, you're done for (a note of jovial male camaraderie here), you are dead with exhaustion.

The you addressed by the speaker may be the reader, but is also the poet. As if John Hartley Williams is John Bosnia's version of an archetypal Englishman (as John Bosnia is a Bosnian Everyman) but also John Bosnia's amanuensis. Or as if the speaker is the poet's Bosnian alter ego, dictating the poem. Someone told me to ask an Englishman / To write this down on paper for me.

The whole thing is a clever, passionate, angry, self-referential and urgent appeal for responsible reading of this poem, or this situation, as one which concerns the whole world. This suffering is, or should be, or may one day be, our suffering. What is grown in John Bosnia's country must be 'taken' home: the disasters, violence and loss of which the poem speaks only by symbol and implication. (*I have lost my cart & my crop*.) The poem is a witness to suffering over the Drina to be read in London. It masks its tragedy with humour, just as its language implies it is masking another language we do not know, but whose features our own may acquire. You smile; but you know what it's doing.

25. Colette Bryce

BUSTER

Under a forty-watt bulb the plastic kettle bubbles
along to a scratched Patsy Cline. A swivel mirror
cranes its neck as if to catch the light, but finds
two redwebbed eyeballs, framed in a stubbled face.
Buster braves his throat to the wavering blade.

Shaved, he scuttles the stairs and out
then labours back three flights with a bagful
of jangling bottles, slots the chain to the lock.
Midnight, he shivers and thumps the fire,
whose single bar is growing dim, causing his jar

of 5p coins to suddenly shudder, suddenly ring.
Come two, he roars a toast to the coats that hang
to a human shape on the back of his door.
And he was hoovering come four, and weeping;
just cursing the way, the ups and downs of the floor.

(1999)

Bryce was born in Derry in 1970, twenty years after Muldoon: she is one of the new generation of Northern Irish poets. The poems of her first collection are musical vignettes of people and belief; little dramas that are both domestic (a woman queasily facing a raw Christmas turkey) and political (a Belfast woman flinging money back in the face of a British soldier who has sent a Catholic child for cigarettes).

Musically, this poem begins as a statement about the first two letters of its title, of the man's name: B and U. It sums up the sound of its first scene by a word in stressed position at the end of the first line, bubbles, underlining it by echoing both its letters (under, bulb, redwebbed eyeballs, stubbled, Buster, blade, bottles, thumps, bar, then suddenly, suddenly, come, come, just, ups, downs), and its shape (kettle, swivel, scuttles).

Accompanying this music is a close weave of vowels holding individual STANZAS together and linking one to the other. Short A runs from the first to the whole poem's halfway line (ending in lock, which itself echoes, in an end-of-Act-One closure, forty-watt, bottles, slots): plastic, scratched, Patsy, catch, back, bagful, jangling. As you say the poem, you take your first breath after the long I of Cline, which continues (light, finds, flights) to begin the poem's second half (midnight), widening out to the long A of cranes, framed, face, braves, blade, shaved, labours, chain.

The second half has a different music, as Buster, who shaved simply to go out and buy booze for his lonely night, begins getting drunk. Sonically, shivers and thumps grow out of swivel and those early Us, suggesting how his changing consciousness develops from the state he was in while shaving and drinking his tea (that plastic kettle). Things are altering soundwise too now: short I carries on through dim, ring, hoovering, cursing; the long wide I of fire widens further to bar, jar, causing, roars, door, four, floor. Floor is where the poem ends – and Buster probably will too. He has moved, or we have moved with him, from under to floor.

Within that move, a whole Pinteresque drama has taken place. Inanimate objects like kettle and mirror are the first active agents (bubbles, cranes . . . as if to catch, finds). Cinematically, it is the mirror that finds bits of Buster for us first (two redwebbed eyeballs). Then comes his first active verb, he 'shaves', but he is not really in control. It is more like being sacrificed: the blade seems more in command than he is, yet even that is wavering. By the time we get to his name, he is not just the passive object of verbs but a victim (he braves his throat to the wavering blade) in his own poem, own life. The slyly comic linguistic effects, making Buster a victim of the inanimate world around him, from that blade to the ringing jar / of 5p coins to the bumpy floor, avoid sentimentalising the pathetic life they conjure up.

Gradually, Buster takes something like charge of the poem's actions, but his verbs are those of an animal. An animal that is timid and overworked (scuttles, labours); also defensive, miserable and cross (slots the chain, shivers, thumps). Even at his merriest, he is an animal in its lair (roars). His conviviality plays itself out in a travesty of humanity (coats that hang / to a human shape). His humanity appears while he is doing human actions: either cleaning (shaving, hoovering), or expressing emotion at his defensively burrow-like life (weeping, cursing). Yet what he is angry at is again animistic: the ups and downs not of his life or mental state, but of his floor.

In the last two lines comes a change of tense (was). It is as if another voice comes in, someone who has overheard, or been imagining, this scene in the present tense. This saner voice moves into reportage. The scene is over and done with. Speaking from a perspective of more ordinary, more human experience than Buster can manage, it opens the poem to properly shared communication and also takes us on, out of the poem.

26. Tom Paulin

KLEE/CLOVER

Nightwatch after nightwatch
Paul Klee endured
'horribly boring guard duty'
at the gasoline cellar
and every morning
outside the Zeppelin hangar
there was drill then a speech
tacked with junk formulas
he varnished wings
and stencilled numbers
next to gothic insignia
a private first-class
with a lippy dislike
of their royal majesties
and *Flying School 5 (Bavaria)*

he wrote home to Lily
it's nice this spring weather
and now we've laid out a garden
between the second and third runways
the airfield's becoming
more and more beautiful
each time a plane crashed
– and that happened quite often
he cut squares of canvas
from the wings and fuselage
he never said why
but every smashed biplane
looked daft or ridiculous
halfjoky and untrue
– maybe the pilots annoyed him?
those unlovely aristos
who never knew they were flying

primed blank canvases
into his beautiful airfield

(1994)

Paulin, an Irish Protestant with close ties to Nationalism, was born
in Leeds in 1949, grew up in Belfast, and currently teaches English
at Oxford: a poet who is also a passionate and original critic and
political thinker. His work in every genre is deeply informed by
politics: in particular by historical, literary and philosophical
understanding of the roots of Protestant ethics. His very various
poems often fuse divergent worlds, exploring the way different
selves live in and deal with the demands of different landscapes, but
spinning off into issues of art, myth, history, language, love, society
and childhood memory.

As a young man in the First World War, the Swiss modernist Paul
Klee painted aircraft logos for the Kaiser. This image gives Paulin a
slanting, tender way into the ruthlessness with which art plunders
life, refuses hierarchies and other systems, turns instruments of
power into beauty: the way that creativity, in the end, outlasts
destruction.

It quotes Klee's own writings, not just his letters but his
reflections on art. Volume I of Klee's *Notebooks*, entitled *The
Thinking Eye*, came out in translation in 1961 and his ideas about
the plastic thinking that underpins an artist's distillation of formal
relations inspired painters of the sixties: in particular how, as Klee
put it, to 'take a line for a walk' (title of the collection from which
this poem comes). Klee wrote about how to make movement a
central aspect of thinking about form; how to explore what forms,
lines and colours can do when they don't have to describe anything.
'You discover their own character', said Klee.

Paulin's poem is implicitly also about poetic 'line': how you move
on from where you start in a poem, as well as on canvas. It begins
with an image of how the great painter himself started: as a lippy
private who turns crashed junk into blank canvases, the prerequisite

for his art. The poem takes the artist's side, the side of the personal (personal letters, personal vision), against unlovely aristos of every kind. Its own democratic avoidance of punctuation – no inequalities like capital letters – is a contrast to the gothic insignia of royal majesties and *Flying School*s, or the impersonal junk formulas (echoes of formal) in the speechifying drill.

Using the skills of layout and stencilled numbers which the airforce employs him for, the artist also creates *a garden / between the second and third runways*. He finds ways of making unofficial, unprogrammed beauty blossom between numbered runways and formalities of line. Klee keeps to geometry (he cuts canvas in squares), as he keeps to guard duty and varnish. But as a private, he has a private way of seeing those machines which are the reason for the *Flying School*'s existence. They start to look daft, ridiculous, halfjoky and untrue, while he slices bits from their wings which will acquire far deeper power and truth in the world, as art.

The first lines hold together musically round the OR of boring (watch, watch, endured, horribly, morning, formulas), the feminine ending of cellar (hangar, formulas, numbers, insignia, *Bavaria*, and on to *weather* in the second verse), and the rippling echo of gasoline and Zeppelin (picked up, perhaps, in wings). Most K sounds belong with the enemy, the hierarchic powers that be: tacked with junk, gothic, first-class, *School*; the squares and canvas belong to the opposition, the hierarchical closed-off way of seeing deployed by the military. The painter takes them over. For his own name also begins with K: Klee (which also means 'clover' in German). The raw material of art starts off in the enemy's camp. You use what the enemy produces, and make your own things out of it.

The longer lines of the second half are more relaxed: the poem is blossoming and softening like the airfield, *becoming / more and more beautiful*. But it is all still one long line: a line which the poem is, like Klee, 'taking for a walk'. No full stop, no dot to stop its flow. There are a few end-harmonies (garden, often) and internal rhymes (crashed, smashed meshing with canvas and ridiculous), but from each time onward the power increasingly shifts to the story, the mystery (he never said why) of what the man is doing.

Direct quotations from the artist ('horribly boring', *nice this spring weather*) underwrite the poem's own, casual, talkey voice (and that happened quite often). This tone lets the poet, or the voice of the poem, increasingly identify with the artist. The climax of this convergence is the last three lines. They smile, but they also point out the divergence of vision between pilots and painter. The pilots and their planes have all the negatives (*un*lovely, *un*true). For Klee, that negative becomes a useful blank. The artist or poet uses what other people do not see; they want to say the unsaid, paint the so-far-unseen.

So the last lines suggest the artist's inside-out way of seeing. The machines other men are proud of, handle and drive are to him (and they never knew) primed blank canvases on which he is ready to paint. They land on something else he has made, whose beauty he is proud of. Since Klee means 'clover', maybe the painter is 'in clover' here. Despite 'boring guard duty', this is the artist's Eden, a perpetual supply of blank canvases, of preparation for creation.

But he has *laid out a garden*, his woman's name is Lily; his own is 'clover'; he is tending an airfield. Art may serve war by stencilling on machines titles like *Flying School 5 (Bavaria)*, but is really on the side of organic growing things. The prerequisite for art is not the subject you paint, or the canvas you paint on, but the flowering of individual vision. By the way he sees, by the way he has unseen or re-seen how other people see, Klee has turned the whole place into a work of art where lines, not planes, take off into free air. His beautiful airfield.

27. Carol Ann Duffy

PRAYER

Some days, although we cannot pray, a prayer
utters itself. So, a woman will lift
her head from the sieve of her hands and stare
at the minims sung by a tree, a sudden gift.

Some nights, although we are faithless, the truth
enters our hearts, that small familiar pain;
then a man will stand stock-still, hearing his youth
in the distant Latin chanting of a train.

Pray for us now. Grade I piano scales
console the lodger looking out across
a Midlands town. Then dusk, and someone calls
a child's name as though they named their loss.

Darkness outside. Inside, the radio's prayer –
Rockall. Malin. Dogger. Finisterre.

(1993)

Queen of the eighties renaissance, whose poems combine scouring feminist wit, social anger, dramatic originality and steely intelligence with a clear, gentle lyricism, Duffy was born in 1955 in Glasgow, of Irish parents, and went to Liverpool University. She made her name with two sorts of poem: monologues which spotlit some abuse of power (a psychopathic killer, a bomber, the victim of police brutality, and, more recently, the wives of famous heroes), and love poems with a pure, Yeatsian lilt.

This SONNET ends a collection whose main dynamic is the guilt and loneliness of ending a relationship. It is a poem-prayer about sounds (utters, sung, hearing, chanting, calls). These sounds come into you from outside at a moment when you feel (through days, nights, dusk, darkness) there is nothing inside but desolation. These sounds become prayer in the first STANZA, truth and its pain (which enters our hearts) in the second, musical scales in the third, and the radio's final shipping forecast in the final COUPLET. But they all come over to you as the world's sudden gift, by the consoling power and courtesy of music.

Over the three QUATRAINS, several other people as well as you (which includes the poet's 'I' and the impersonal 'one') need this comfort. First, a woman whose crying is implied but not mentioned. She lifts her face from the sieve (suggesting both tears falling through the holes and the uselessness of tears) of her hands, to stare at minims – the most basic musical notes, with resonances of the bare 'minimum' you need (for, say, going on living after the loss of happiness). What she stares at turns from something seen to something heard: these minims in the tree are not drawn there, like a child's drawing of an apple tree, but sung.

The second person is a man who suddenly hears his youth. The truth of it enters his heart via distant Latin chanting, the poem's METAPHOR for the sound of a far-off train. Maybe he was raised Catholic, maybe he hears his school days. Despite being faithless now, some inner familiar thing, a truth he didn't feel contact with a moment before, is in him again, thanks to the sound of that train.

Thirdly, Grade I piano scales, the most basic steps of music (compare the 'minimum' behind minims), console some anonymous lodger. The word reminds us we all are temporary lodgers in the world, whatever property we own. Then, fourth and more ambiguous, someone calls and the call sounds – to the poet, to the poem, to any listener – like the naming of a loss.

They are all very slight things. The stress is on how little – the minimum, the basics – you need to console you. 'The place of salvation is very small', goes a Buddhist saying. 'Maybe even a window.' Their music is <u>small</u> and <u>distant</u> like the 'still small voice' of God in the Bible (1 Kings 19). There were tempests, wind, earthquake and fire, 'But the Lord was not in' any of them. Then 'after the fire a still small voice' – words Tennyson re-used in 'The Two Voices': 'A still small voice spoke unto me, / "Thou art so full of misery, / Were it not better not to be?"' When earthquake and fire pass through you, the only things your spirit can hold on to (rather than giving in to the temptation of 'Were it not better not to be?') may be tiny. This poem closed Duffy's collection, *Mean Time*. All these small sounds in it are, in a sense, <u>Grade I</u>: basic musical reminders, in a 'mean time', of first steps and childhood faith.

These little sounds culminate in the <u>radio's prayer</u>: that litany of <u>distant</u> place-names, <u>familiar</u> but never (by most people) seen, coming in from <u>darkness outside</u>. The midnight weather report, reaching out to risky little outposts like Dogger and Rockall, is an image of a lonely small voice, music to the ears of people emotionally at risk.

Because the consoling comes through voice, music and sound, the poem's own music and sound are all-important. The sound that cradles the entire poem is AY, implied in the title and first rhyme word: <u>prayer</u>. The first line stresses the sound with pauses after the first examples (<u>days</u>, <u>pray</u>). It plays a part in the rhymes of each STANZA and the last COUPLET: <u>pain</u>, <u>train</u>, <u>scales</u> (matched by <u>calls</u>); returns to <u>prayer</u> again, and ends with <u>Finisterre</u>. It hums inside the poem in <u>faithless</u>, <u>pray</u>, <u>grade</u>, <u>name</u>, <u>named</u>.

Other echoes set up their own lace-work of resonance. <u>Some</u>, the poem's first sound, echoed in <u>utters</u>, <u>sung</u>, <u>sudden</u>, <u>some</u>, <u>Grade I</u>, <u>someone</u>, narrowing en route into <u>town</u>. The long O of <u>although</u> is picked up in <u>so</u> (with a pause after it that gives it emphasis), <u>although</u>, narrows into <u>now</u>, and rings on to <u>piano</u>, <u>radio</u>.

At first the poem seems all hushed vowel. The opening consonants are muted, the first line ends in vowel, and when consonants start at line-ends it is with the soft F of <u>lift</u>, <u>gift</u>, followed through in <u>faithless</u>, whose related soft TH slides on into <u>truth</u>, <u>youth</u>. In the third QUATRAIN, S takes over: hissing gently at every line-end (<u>scales</u>, <u>across</u>, <u>calls</u>, <u>loss</u>) and the interior (<u>console</u>, <u>dusk</u>, <u>someone</u>), to spread itself over the COUPLET in <u>darkness</u>, <u>outside</u>, <u>inside</u>, <u>Finisterre</u>.

We cannot pray, says the poem. We are faithless. Both meanings of faithless – having no religious faith and (maybe) having betrayed or left a lover – underlie Pray for us now: which resonates with the prayer, 'Pray for us sinners now and at the hour of our death'.

The poem is about deep loss which is not 'named', only implied through other people's responses to sounds. It could be loss of faith, or of a much believed in relationship. Whatever, the poem, like the radio, is now reaching out away from it into darkness, trusting – like a child not knowing what will come – that the first steps out will lead somewhere good. Reaching all the way out to Finisterre, whose name means 'end of the earth'.

28. Seamus Heaney

THE SKUNK

Up, black, striped and damasked like the chasuble
At a funeral mass, the skunk's tail
Paraded the skunk. Night after night
I expected her like a visitor.

The refrigerator whinnied into silence.
My desk light softened beyond the veranda.
Small oranges loomed in the orange tree.
I began to be tense as a voyeur.

After eleven years I was composing
Love-letters again, broaching the word 'wife'
Like a stored cask, as if its slender vowel
Had mutated into the night earth and air

Of California. The beautiful, useless
Tang of eucalyptus spelt your absence.
The aftermath of a mouthful of wine
Was like inhaling you off a cold pillow.

And there she was, the intent and glamorous,
Ordinary, mysterious skunk,
Mythologized, demythologized,
Snuffing the boards five feet beyond me.

It all came back to me last night, stirred
By the sootfall of your things at bedtime,
Your head-down, tail-up hunt in a bottom drawer
For the black plunge-line nightdress.

(1979)

Heaney was born in Northern Ireland, on farmland outside Derry, in 1939; he later moved south to the Republic. He has taught in universities from Belfast to Harvard. His poems have immense intellectual and moral clarity. They are muscular, but the words shift through the lines like gold dust poured on a jeweller's scales, weighed and calibrated to the last milligram.

You need both craft and technique, he said long ago. Craft is what you learn; technique is not only the words but also your 'stance in life, your reality'. His power lies partly in his musical subtlety. You feel each word very physically in the line, moving alive against others like one rope among many holding a sail in wind. But the power also comes from his own 'stance or reality' which is always towards fusion. His words bring things into relation to each other at every level: formal, moral, political, linguistic, emotional. There is a passionate tension in them, too, between critical intelligence and sensuous feeling; and also a deep sense of moral responsibility.

Responsibility mainly to four things. To poetry, its literary tradition and sounds, its private and public roles. To words themselves, which in his hands become almost physical things. Both English and Irish words: their echoes, philological derivations, plays of meaning – and their history, whose echoes you can wake if you treat them right. Thirdly, to human history, especially in Ireland. The first poems he wrote, he said, 'were about the Northern sectarian problem', and his work is permeated by textures of the earth he comes from.

But finally, underneath all the other things, Heaney's work runs on the importance of generosity: of honouring individual feeling. In my column, I discussed his work on St Valentine's Day, so here is a love poem.

It is a letter to a woman, mediated through male poetic tradition. Just as Armitage's fox poem (No. 20) gestures back to an earlier fox poem by Ted Hughes, so this skunk poem bows to a skunk poem by Robert Lowell.

Lowell's poem 'Skunk Hour' is a cry of pain from a poet watching other people's 'love-cars', whose garbage is raided by a female skunk with an 'ostrich tail'. Heaney's poem turns that flouncy, dirty femaleness into a shyer, softer female sexuality. The animal, the female, is still a visiting alien (this is a male poet describing femaleness), but is <u>ordinary</u> as well as <u>mysterious</u>: like the 'ordinary swoon' of sex, in W.H. Auden's poem 'Lullaby', another male love poem by a master of poetic form.

Heaney's skunk sexiness is animal (snuffing picks up whinnied – even the fridge is animate), but also playfully theatrical. The stage resonances (boards) gesture to the curtain-dropping, striptease imagery of damasked, paraded, sootfall, plunge-line (see Lowell's 'ostrich tail'). The vowels and smells borrow epithets from easy language about glamorous actresses (slender, beautiful), as if the night visitor the poet expected were a woman to be 'broached'. The combination of dirt, distance and old-fashioned masculine fantasies of female theatricality turns wife into something whose reality is hidden, uncertain; a word where new life can be woken; a glamorous performer of whom the poet is voyeur; a stored cask whose contents (after eleven years) have mutated to something richer but upsettingly unknown; a lover to whom letters must – more carefully than you thought – be composed.

The night visitor, the wife she is an image of, and the poet are all intent on some hunt. The skunk for garbage (as in Lowell); the poet for the right word; the wife for a nightdress. All are tentative, tense, performing. But the poet's hunt is also a waiting game (night after night): an image of writing as waiting for the words, that might come from beyond the veranda where small oranges glow; from the darkness of night earth and air. An image of poetic inspiration which turns up silently, erotic and unexpected, at your veranda or desk light.

The poem's movement begins with up. The first word's vowel gives skunk in the first (and fifth) STANZA, hunt and plunge in the last – where up (as in sex) entails down (head-down, tail-up). The poem is an erotic arc, plunging down (bottom drawer, plunge-line). Its erotics of up and down are structured in unrhymed QUATRAINS. The first STANZA (going up) is all images of expectation. The second has images of waiting, presented one-foot-after-another in four end-stopped lines. The middle two STANZAS flow together (fusing the poem's centre) in a run from air to of California. They give the poet's erotic dilemma: first, anxiety about love-letters; then how to cope with that dilemma – love-rhetoric, which suggests that California's beautiful sensuality, along with its flouncy mysterious indigenous visitors, are useless without you.

You appear first through your absence. Smell, taste, wine all turn into this absence which is both spelt (like love-letters) and implicitly 'inhaled'. Sensuality has <u>mutated</u>, like the <u>vowel</u> in <u>wife</u> (is he a 'waif' without her?), into unbodied breath.

The fifth STANZA gets down to physicality, from <u>absence</u> to presence (<u>there she was</u>). This is the revelation of the body. Not yet the wife's: only in the last STANZA do we move from the skunk's nocturnal visits to the woman she stands for. Once <u>tense as a voyeur</u>, the poet is back (<u>it all came back</u>) with <u>you</u>.

And <u>stirred</u>. By what? <u>Sootfall</u>. The poem is also about sexual longing and this word hangs everything that the poem has built up – the striptease imagery, parading <u>damask</u>, reverential decoration of <u>chasuble</u>, black, odorous animal – on the intimate euphemism of <u>your things</u> at bedtime. We move from <u>black</u> in the first line to <u>black</u> (presumably lacy, fragrant, and soft) in the last. In their softly thudding rhythm, the multi-syllables with liquid (L, N, R) consonants – DACTYLS (<u>chasuble</u>, <u>funeral</u>, <u>visitor</u>, <u>beautiful</u>, <u>glamor-ous</u>), TRI-SYLLABLES accented in the middle (<u>veranda</u>, <u>eleven</u>) and BI-SYLLABLES which may be TROCHEES, SPONDEES or IAMBS (such as <u>slender</u>, <u>mouthful</u>, <u>voyeur</u>, <u>sootfall</u>) – suggest the tense and possibly (especially at night) smutty sensuality of that central word, <u>California</u>; which was nothing, absolutely nothing, without <u>you</u>.

29. Sarah Maguire

SPILT MILK

Two soluble aspirins spore in this glass, their mycelia
fruiting the water, which I twist into milkiness.
The whole world seems to slide into the drain by my window.

It has rained and rained since you left, the streets black
and muscled with water. Out of pain and exhaustion you came
into my mouth, covering my tongue with your good and bitter
   milk.

Now I find you have cashed that cheque. I imagine you
slipping the paper under steel and glass. I sit here in a circle
of lamplight, studying women of nine hundred years past.

My hand moves into darkness as I write. *The adulterous woman
lost her nose and ears; the man was fined.* I drain the glass.
I still want to return to that hotel room by the station

to hear all night the goods trains coming and leaving.

(1991)

Maguire is a British poet born in 1957. She has worked as a gardener and (as with Paulin) whatever else her poems are about there is usually a strong political dimension to them too somewhere. Her dark erotic poems explore themes of imprisonment, religion, trauma, love and healing in different landscapes from Mediterranean pastoral to inner-city brick.

The woman left behind by her lover has been a theme in men's poetry and song since Greek times. As Peggy Lee sings in 'Black Coffee', man is born to go a-loving, woman to weep and fret. She has to stay at home and drown regret in coffee and cigarettes. Women lyricists have used the theme in their own way: as in Carly Simon's pop song about male narcissism, 'You're So Vain', which anticipates the vain male's disappearance from her life, while the singer's dreams of him (who thinks, rightly, her song will be about him) become 'clouds in her coffee'.

In this poem, the clouds are swirls of aspirin; perhaps to douse the hangover left by love. Obviously there's pain – hence the aspirins – but it will be, like the aspirin, soluble. What everyone knows about spilt milk is there's no use crying over it. The first STANZA sees the whole world sliding into the drain. The last summing-up word says this is all about leaving.

But this is not going to be a 'cryin' over you' poem: it is precisely about *not* doing that crying. Anyway the whole world is doing it for her: It has rained and rained since you left.

The first line and a half sets up a tension between two sorts of language. The scientific register gestures towards the discipline this not-crying will involve. Pain is going to be soluble, trails in the water are mycelia, the white filamental tubes of a fungus or the spawn of a mushroom.

The poem seems to promise to describe everything with the same detached informed analysis, but a different register of tone pulls against this, coming from the unspoken word 'semen' (Latin for 'seed'); spores, fruiting, milkiness. This seed is both good and bitter. It came from the man's pain and exhaustion, covering the woman's tongue with milkiness as rain covers the streets, black and muscled, with water. The first two STANZAS are full of pain and solution; black muscle and cloudy white; scientific observation and sex; liquid (water, milkiness, water, milk) and fertilisation.

Fertilisation happens through the poem's resolution (see soluble) of feeling, rather than in the relationship. The poem twists the aftermath of sex into nourishment. Despite the bitter side of things, the poem is not crying: instead, in the third and fourth STANZAS it sets up a new tension between the outside commercial world (cashed that cheque, steel and glass) in which the man now moves, and the private lamplight where the woman explores nine-hundred-year-old writings that also suggest disparity between the lives of women and men.

The contrast between woman and man comes over in the textures of the physical things around each, and the words that describe them. Everything around the woman in the first two STANZAS is smooth and liquid (glass, water, rained, muscled with water). Vowel sounds set up here linger through the poem (glass picked up by past, drain by rained, pain, came, drain, trains).

The DACTYLIC rhythm of the first words, soluble aspirins, runs right through, binding the poem in a metre of closure (fruiting the water, drain by my window, muscled with water, slipping the paper, circle / of lamplight, *adulterous woman*, coming and leaving).

The man's act, and the sound of it, is a contrast to that DACTYLIC flow. Cashed that cheque, three long blows at the poem's centre, is a sudden shock of hardness. The woman's world after he left was black: the sharp A and K are a contrast to her long vowels (slide, drain, pain, mouth). We now find that that sharpness foreshadowed the man's act: the A and K of cashed that cheque.

What is hard, emotionally, is the fact that contact with him comes only through his absence. She knows what he's been doing only through money she gave him. This hardness is made aural in the sound of those Ks, and referential when his action of slipping the paper (which belongs, like sliding, with her own fluidness) brushes up against glass and steel.

The quotation's medieval shock is the only thing that makes explicit the injustice suggested in the verbal contrasts (rain versus steel, lamplight versus black, coming versus leaving). The woman sees and consoles the man's pain and exhaustion. But in the end, she loses. (Loses *nose and ears*; or in this case, needs aspirins, is depleted of money.) A man only gets *fined* (or in this case, cashes her cheque).

This calm poem, setting its face against complaint – the pain is stronger for being submerged – is itself something positive made from pain, and recreates what it speaks about: twists bitterness into milk.

30. Don Paterson

IMPERIAL

Is it normal to get this wet? Baby, I'm frightened –
I covered her mouth with my own;
she lay in my arms till the storm-window brightened
and stood at our heads like a stone

After months of jaw jaw, determined that neither
win ground, or be handed the edge,
we gave ourselves up, one to the other
like prisoners over a bridge

and no trade was ever so fair or so tender;
so where was the flaw in the plan,
the night we lay down on the flag of surrender
and woke on the flag of Japan

(1996)

Paterson, born in 1963, comes from Dundee: a folk-jazz musician who, like Muldoon, works brilliantly with rhyme and implication, has wonderful rhythmic control, enormous subtlety and originality, and deep intellectual curiosity. His seriously jokey, subtle, delicate poems may go anywhere in their allusions – into myth, Scottish emigration to England, love, Zen Buddhism. He has the sexual melody of Robert Burns, especially in poems of STANZA form like this, and his formal facility and strength communicate a questing sexiness which puts some women off as sexist but seems to turn others on. (He is the only poet I discussed in my column about whom young women wrote in to say, 'Can we have more by him?')

This is a man's response to a woman, and the poem's body plays back the sounds of her opening line. The OR of normal returns in storm, jaw jaw, flaw; the E of get and wet come in head, edge; the AY of Baby in lay, gave, trade, and another lay (as in Bob Dylan's song 'Lay Lady Lay' sometimes sung as 'Lay Baby Lay'); the sequence of M, N, and D in *I'm frightened* in storm-window, brightened, determined, ground, handed, tender, surrender, with the short IN of window flickering on into win ground, and widening into the key rhyme tender/surrender.

The running DACTYLS start off in PENTAMETER for the woman's words. The male poet using her words and their components to make his own poem cuts the five beats down to three. From then on we get a four-beat line (the first and third of each following STANZA), followed by a shorter one of three. For this poem, like the empire implied in its title, is about discipline and control of other people. It is about rules (what's thought to be *normal*, for instance) and also, formally, about challenging rules. It has the simplest of RHYME-SCHEMES, ABAB (own/stone, neither/other, edge/bridge), but challenges the protocol this form implies by not using the most basic formal tool of any writing: the full stop.

In the context of its collection, these formal procedures related this poem to a similar three-STANZA lyric five poems earlier, also about unfinished sexual business: 'Buggery'. Both poems make clear that they make the rules; they only play by other people's rules when it suits them. In buggery, empire or – what this poem seems to be about underneath its METAPHOR of empire – defloration, the poet is in charge, teasing and questioning the terms and the male attitudes underlying its own narrative.

Her words begin the poem, but are vulnerable in the way women are traditionally perceived to be. *Is it normal*: she is turning to his sexual experience to know about herself. *Baby* echoes blues, pop music: we are in love-song land, but *I'm frightened* takes this into danger, leading to the window which stood at their heads like a [grave] stone.

In the second line, he does what imperial patriarchy expects of its men, what male love poetry does to its muse: silences the woman. I covered her mouth with my own plays off the James Bond way of dealing with women: the strong male Hollywood cliché. We hear no more of her thoughts: the poet's mouth has covered hers.

The second STANZA underlines the idea of tussle and war implied in this silencing and 'covering' (win ground, the edge, prisoners, surrender). It echoes Winston Churchill's words, 'To jaw-jaw is always better than to war-war', to describe the lovers' previous argument – presumably about whether to have sex; making it more likely that she's a virgin. 'Now for sex' means 'Now for war', apparently. Before, there were two jaws against each other. Now one mouth has covered the other.

Both 'give themselves up'. Give up (to pleasure, to each other), suggests give in (to desire, to each other), as if the power they have is equal. But empire is about unequal power. A woman silenced after one line, a man expounding for eleven. Behind the giving is conquest and government. 'She is all states, and all princes I', says John Donne in a similar scenario.

The third STANZA shifts the METAPHOR from war to trade. The two most glamorous eras of male English poetry, when some of the most brilliant male love poems of all time were written, coincided with the two strongest eras of British imperialism and trade: Victorian and Elizabethan. Music (see the pop song echoes in *Baby*, and the poem's love song stance) is called the 'food of us that trade in love' in Shakespeare's *Anthony and Cleopatra*. No trade was ever so fair or so tender gives defloration the authority of Elizabethan-sounding quotation: the point is the appearance not just of authority but (as in 'imperial' trade negotiations) equality.

Control, whether poetic, sexual or imperial, implies unequal power, one force controlling another. In a love poem, the poet always has the whip hand over the loved person: control over what happens to them and how they appear in the poem.

Fair trade, was it? Fair as in 'equal'? Or 'lovely': in which case, from whose point of view? They lie down on a (presumably) white sheet, like the flag of surrender (back to Churchill and the war.) They wake on the flag of Japan, one of the last imperial flags, used loosely by Western film as an exotic emblem of a sexually unequal society and a ritualising male military tradition. (Also, of course, a country with which Churchill himself was at war; and which was, in the end, defeated.)

Visually, though, this flag is a white <u>ground</u> with a red spot. The rising sun (see <u>brightened</u>, <u>woke</u>) of conquest; or the O of a bloodstain, the aftermath of defloration.

All poets work with what they've got. The stronger they are, the more their poems question what they're working with and what their voice can do. In this poem, Paterson's voice confronts its own maleness in a strongly male genre, perfected by Elizabethan men: the sexual conquest love lyric. He is sending it up and taking it further, both at once; both using tradition and questioning it (<u>where was the flaw</u>) as if his maleness were 'at war' with itself; plumbing anxieties that spin off from the male desire for (and habit of) mastery. He is exploring sexual inequality from the 'imperial' perspective.

The collection from which this poem comes is called *God's Gift to Women*, and the book's cover shows a girl tied to the tracks in front of an oncoming train. One theme of the book is that 'God's gift to women', that phrase for a lady's man, one who fancies himself, may also seem (to a man) to be pain. Not that the poems do anything to stop this pain or train coming down on women. In a subtly self-mocking acceptance of supremacism, this one embodies it.

31. Helen Dunmore

THE SURGEON HUSBAND

Here at my worktop, foil-wrapping a silver salmon
– yes, a whole salmon – I'm thinking
of the many bodies of women
that my husband daily opens.

Here he lunges at me in wellingtons.
He is up to his armpits, a fisherman
tugging against the strength of the current.

I imagine the light for him, clean,
and a green robing of willow
and the fish hammering upstream.

I too tug at the flaps of the salmon
where its belly was, trying to straighten
the silver seams before they are sewn.
We are one in our dreams.

The epidural is patchy, his assistant's
handwriting is slipping. At eleven fifteen
they barb their patient to sleep, jot 'knife to skin',
and the nurse smiles over her mask at the surgeon.

But I am quietly dusting out the fish-kettle,
and I have the salmon clean as a baby
grinning at me from the table.

(1997)

180

Born in Yorkshire in 1952, Dunmore studied at Bristol University, taught in Finland for a while, and now lives in Bristol. She is a novelist too, and her poems – often in unshowy, gently cadenced FREE VERSE – turn story fragments into little lyric epiphanies. These are set in hiddenly sinister landscapes where men and women plunge into ambiguous and ambivalent relationships, watch babies get born, children grow up, young girls fall dangerously in love.

This is an elegantly disquieting poem about the inequalities of marriage. It compares a wife packaging a fish (we don't hear if she gutted it herself, but the belly is no longer there) to her husband, a surgeon, who is meanwhile opening women, removing something (uterus, baby, we don't know till epidural), and sewing them up.

From the first noun, worktop, the poem tackles the sexual politics of 'work'. What wives do is often not acknowledged as work, yet they operate (like a surgeon) at a worktop. Surgeons (especially gynaecologists and obstetricians who have such power over bodies of women – to remove things, and leave them with patchy scars) are mostly men. Their worktops are women's bodies. In his work the husband lunges, as his wife puts it, at me.

But another parallel is operating in this poem too. The woman writing this poem, imagining a wife, is like the wife at her worktop imagining her husband at his. The epidural (like the seams she straightens) is a handwriting. The command 'knife to skin' is a jot. The poem finds its own end as I (the wife or poet) has an end product looking back from the table. A baby, the end product of the husband's work; but also a completed poem, after you have worked hours at it and 'got it out'. Something that looks back at the person who has produced it, by an operation, by work: cooking, operating, writing.

The wife works for her husband (smiled at by that nurse, with all a mask's echoes of deception), both in preparing this gorgeous silver fish (yes, a whole salmon) and in imagining the light for him. The imaginative sympathy which people often mean when they say marriage needs 'working at' is archetypally attributed to women. This wife identifies with her husband's efforts (lunges, up to his armpits, tugging), and feels hers are so similar (I too tug) and they are one in our dreams. Her parallel is part of her 'work' of loving.

The poet helps her: partly by METAPHOR, giving the husband fish-language (fisherman, barb), turning her fish into a baby, but also by sound and rhythm. Vowel-harmonies echo between their respective

181

STANZAS (like flaps for her, patchy for him), and the key joining sound salmon flows through the poem gathering syllables as it goes like fish hammering upstream: salmon, women, opens, wellingtons, fisherman, salmon, straighten, surgeon; with its final N pinned down by clean, green, upstream, seams, sewn, dreams, eleven fifteen, clean, and spin-offs in hammering, skin, grinning.

More deeply, there is salmon's rhythmic shape, the TROCHEE, shape of both the title nouns and also of worktop, silver, husband, opens, lunges, armpits, tugging, current, robing, willow, upstream, belly, straighten, silver, patchy, slipping, patient, surgeon, dusting, table). This shape sews together all these STANZAS about sewing up women and fish; so closely that the wife's METAPHOR at the end completes the husband's work by delivering another TROCHEE, that all-important word baby.

Yet the poem also suggests imparities between husband and wife. The husband's violence (opens, lunges, tugging, barb) coupled with the nurse's smile over her mask; the fact that the wife's work is done for him while his is done (as he lunges) at her, via bodies of other women. Sympathy flows one-way: her to him.

But I marks a contrast, not a parallel. There is a further contrast at work between the imagining poet and the imagining wife. The wife works (cooking, imagining) for her husband; the poet writes the poem for herself (and us, to whom she intimates her scepticism about the parallel drawn by the wife). The wife wrapping her husband's fish in foil may also be his 'foil'. Her love (expressed in imagining and wrapping) may be 'foiled' by his lack of the same.

So an unspoken sadness glimmers from that green robing of willow, echoing traditional English 'green willow' songs of unrequited love. And yet, however unequal the husband–wife parallel, their relationship and the world they exist in, all three operations (preparing food, writing a poem, delivering a baby) depend in the end on the labour (see epidural, baby) of love.

32. Matthew Sweeney

THE HAT

A green hat is blowing through Harvard Square
and no one is trying to catch it.
Whoever has lost it has given up –
perhaps, because his wife was cheating,
he took it off and threw it like a frisbee,
trying to decapitate a statue
of a woman in her middle years
who doesn't look anything like his wife.
This wind wouldn't lift the hat alone,
and any man would be glad to keep it.
I can imagine – as it tumbles along,
gusting past cars, people, lampposts –
it sitting above a dark green suit.
The face between them would be bearded
and not unhealthy, yet. The eyes
would be green, too – an all green man
thinking of his wife in another bed,
these thoughts all through the green hat,
like garlic in the pores, and no one,
no one pouncing on the hat to put it on.

(1997)

Sweeney is a Catholic from Donegal in the Republic of Ireland, on the border with Northern Ireland. He was born in the Republic by accident, in 1952. His mother was booked into a nursing home in Derry, in the North, but happened to be playing cards on the other side of the border that night. Sweeney now lives in London but studied in Germany and is profoundly influenced by the deceptively simple 'fable' element of Eastern European writing. And also by cinema, as *noir* as possible.

His poems are existential Kafkaesque parables, tragi-comic, compassionate, surreal, irrepressibly curious, lonely as Giacometti sculptures, and full of sinister images (graveyards, priests, cacti, displaced or mutilated animals). They work simultaneously on a symbolic and realistic level: it is up to you how you take them.

Sweeney rarely uses METAPHOR: each poem is a METAPHOR itself. (Reviewers who miss what he is doing call his poems 'whimsical'.) His language is scrupulously plain because the place the whole poem exists in is imagination. Adding another layer of association, another imaginative departure point, would detract from the power of that effect. In shape, they are often BLOCK FORM, unrhymed, with vowel-harmonies and rhythm tying the lines together.

On the surface, this poem is straightforward, though fanciful: like one of those films that follow the fate of a lost object. Its power comes from tension between the transparently clear language and the bizarre, doors-into-other-worlds surprisingness of the imagination. It also hangs an increasingly sharp question mark over the observer's involvement. At one level it is description plus playful fantasy. At another, all anguished suspicion.

It is also about compassion, and the vehicle of this is the hat, on which the poem's sense of lonely lostness is projected. As a sound, it flickers through the first six lines (catch, perhaps, decapitate, statue), just as the thing itself flits through the square. The word returns at the end, as we hope the thing might return, one day, to its owner.

The sound-world has lots of little doubles (like the OR of thoughts and pores), but the sequences tend to tell a story of anxiety. Long O (blowing, alone) moans through (modulating sometimes to related vowels, as in along) to the strangely passionate repetition no one, no one. Short E moves through unhealthy, yet bearded, bed. But long EE is the dominant vowel. Starting with green, it echoes through cheating, frisbee, keep, people, growing through the poem in relation to other sounds; as in the combination AH-EE-OO (Harvard, cars, dark green suit, between, these . . . all through, green, too, garlic). Just as jealousy, whose colour is also green, grows on the mind in an obsessive combination of different worries.

Long I begins with that other key word wife, followed by eyes, and wife again, suggesting an unspoken sequence of thought: '*I have my eyes on my wife.*'

So the speaker is not the cool observer he seems. His I, or eye, has already been at work in that perhaps, imagining that James Bond type decapitation. He has already projected himself into the scene.

The sequence of tenses marks the moves by which the poet makes you accept the fantasy of the observing I: from is, is in the present to has, has, was, took, threw in the past; then back to the present in doesn't. After eight lines (as in a SONNET), a new grammatical mood begins with the subjunctive wouldn't.

Then, in I can imagine, the speaker comes clean. Those past tenses and subjunctives depend on his own, present-tense imagining, poured into the hat in its present-tense pouring along the ground (tumbles, gusting), which comes to rest (sitting) in an imaginary past before the hat got lost. Two more woulds flesh out the imaginary owner, introducing the visual climax all green man, whose resonances (the wild man of the woods, green jealousy) prompt the emotional climax: wife in another bed.

The sinister comedy of all this grows through the two absurdist metaphors. Like a frisbee decapitating an imaginary statue which does not resemble an imaginary wife; thoughts like garlic in pores, which leakily betray what you have taken in.

This is where Sweeney's plain language pays off. No 'poetic' vocabulary softens the hurt of another bed, underlined by the repeated no one over the line break. A man has given up here. Any man would be glad to keep what has been lost. But what he's lost had a volition of its own (this wind wouldn't lift the hat alone). He doesn't get it back. And what happens to one man may be happening to another. If the hat fits, wear it: compassion, even for an imaginary other, is the only antidote to uncertainty and isolation. We all wear hats, choose roles and lose them. The poem works outward, humorously, from the bouncing hat to the insight that we are all vulnerable to all kinds of loss.

If spotlighting anxious jealousy all through these fantasies seems overfanciful, if it seems I'm talking through my (or the poem's) hat: well, this is the poem's fancifulness at work. Fancifulness, or imagination, is what the poem is about, underneath a lost <u>hat</u>.

33. Vicki Feaver

JUDITH

Wondering how a good woman can murder
I enter the tent of Holofernes,
holding in one hand his long oiled hair
and in the other, raised above
his sleeping, wine-flushed face,
his falchion with its unsheathed
curved blade. And I feel a rush
of tenderness, a longing
to put down my weapon, to lie
sheltered and safe in a warrior's
fumy sweat, under the emerald stars
of his purple and gold canopy,
to melt like a sweet on his tongue
to nothing. And I remember the glare
of the barley field; my husband
pushing away the sponge I pressed
to his burning head; the stubble
puncturing my feet as I ran,
flinging myself on a body
that was already cooling
and stiffening; and the nights
when I lay on the roof – my emptiness
like the emptiness of a temple
with the doors kicked in; and the mornings
when I rolled in the ash of the fire
just to be touched and dirtied
by something. And I bring my blade
down on his neck – and it's easy
like slicing through fish.

And I bring it down again,
cleaving the bone.

(1994)

Born in 1943, Feaver teaches writing in Chichester; she refracts her warm, strong, very physical and sexy poems through myth, painting or fairytale, or domestic images of jam-making, female warmth, communality, fury, celebration or anguish. Feisty daughters christen a pink mix of emulsion paint 'Rubens' Bottom'; women burn sanitary towels; faithless lovers are drowned in a Gothic lily-pond.

This poems is on the theme of sexual revenge, concentrating its fury on a biblical scenario. Despite the vivid jewelled detail, its move from savage feeling to savage act is propelled very simply through five sentences which all (except the last) end in the same place in the line: the end of the first FOOT. The BLOCK FORM is structured in a sequence of sentences, each of which is progressively shorter as Judith takes her decision and brings herself to the act of murder. They are all, except the last, followed by And I.

The first sentence runs from Wondering how to curved blade. The second, from And I feel to nothing. The third, from And I remember to something. The fourth from And I bring my blade / down to slicing through fish. Then come the last two lines, the repeat blow like a coda, the only sentence beginning at the start of a line. These sentences, stages in a move towards murder, shift from one present participle to another, from thinking to acting: from wondering to cleaving the bone. Their sequence is an answer to the question asked indirectly by the first line: how can a good woman murder?

Within this forward drive, the medium is fierce female desire, which begins with a rush of longing for the warrior whom she describes in sexy pairs of adjectives: long and oiled, sleeping and wine-flushed, unsheathed and curved. She is holding his blade. In his fumy sweat (bringing back the F and S of wine-flushed face), she feels, for a moment, that she would be sheltered, safe. The royal embrace (see purple and gold) of a warrior would be an archaic haven, a canopy. She would see emerald stars, melt like a sweet, become a passive delicious nothing.

But the first main verb (I enter) tells us she is the opposite of passive. She is the subject of only active verbs. The first line flung us that paradox, a good woman can murder. The UR sounds of murder were instantly picked up in her victim's name: Holofernes. Murder and this man will belong together for ever: and it will be her doing. She is an active woman and this is her act.

The mood switch that explains how the moral transformation comes about is memory. After I feel comes I remember. She stops feeling desire for the man in front of her, and remembers the man he killed, her husband, who died in front of her. Soundwise, this second picture of her above another prone, unconscious man is linked to the first by glare at the end of the line, which echoes hair. Paintings of Judith tend to show her holding a man's head by the hair, over the glare of his dead eyes.

The next line translates this glare to a barley field, site of domestic harvest, traditional place in English pastoral for lovers and their lasses to lie down together. Here it becomes a field of death. The man's head is burning. As if crops were burning, and all that remained was stubble. What remains of her husband is a cooling corpse.

This scenario continues the sensuousness of the first: a woman looking longingly at a man's body. His body is stiffening; harsh stubble is puncturing her body; she pressed him, she is flinging herself on his body as, for a moment, she wanted to fling herself on Holofernes. The rest of this memory (joined by semi-colons not full stops, for it is all part of the same thing) is her emptiness.

This is the key word. It expresses her loss, explains her murder. It echoes pressed, then gets repeated. She wanted to be sheltered by the warrior, she threw herself on a stiffening body and now, without any man to touch her, she is empty as a temple / with the doors kicked in. Even her image for missing a man is savage invasion. The whole poem is an active female take on the violence of sexual touch, even when what happens is not sex but murder and death. She flings herself into ash, just to be touched.

And also to be dirtied. We are still in the magnetic field of that opening moral question, how does a good woman do murder? Answer: she gets dirtied. She had dirty thoughts about Holofernes; dirtied is the last adjective she uses of herself before she brings the blade (her blade now, not his as in the sixth line) down on his neck. She is touching a man at last, but it is like slicing through fish. Instead of cleaving to him in sex (as she imagined doing, 'melting' on his tongue) she is cleaving his bone.

34. James Lasdun

EVE

I like that room,
the warm one with the machines
where the woman folds her shed skins.

I hang in the broken ceiling, watching her,
barely distinguishable
from the cold water pipe
and the coiled power cable.

I watch her all winter:
her longlegged hands,
the glinting needles of fur at her nape,
her red warmness
drifting in mammaly billows.

And now I show myself;
Pour my flickering head
into her sac of air,
and slowly, willed against her own will,
her face rises like a rising moon,
opening palely to mine,

and in the wide O's of her eyes,
I see myself: my head like a big cut jewel,
the little watch-jewels of my eyes, yes,
my tongue the alive nerve of a rock,
and I feel her want,
a yearning almost,
as though for something already about to be lost,

and I offer myself.

(2001)

Lasdun was born in London but has taught poetry mainly in America; he currently lives in the Catskill mountains outside Woodstock in upstate New York. His deft, lyrical poems are classical in feel but often free in form; their wit, and felt intelligence, are both musical and sharply reflective.

This poem is from a collection which focuses on moving to the Catskills, and making new bonds with rural America after leaving a European life: a family that 'lopped / our branch off from the family tree: / anglophone Russian-German apostate Jews'. The poem is called 'Eve', but is really all about the male ego observing Eve. Intellectually and musically, the sinuous movement from I to myself leads to the revelation of who this watcher is. Every verse begins with I (I like, I hang, I watch; And now I show myself; and in . . . her eyes, / I see myself; I offer myself.)

So this is a poem about self-image; about how the archetypal woman, object of the male gaze, mirrors the male self. The poem builds up a picture of the watcher by describing the woman he's watching. He starts by seeing her in his own terms (shed skins). Then, from cold and coiled, describing things he identifies with and from which he is barely distinguishable, he moves to qualities in her that are the opposite of himself: longlegged hands, fur at her nape, red warmness, mammaly. He is seeing her in terms of other animals. Prey animals, presumably.

In the second half she becomes (as women so often are for men) his mirror. He describes himself enticingly in terms of things women traditionally desire: a big cut jewel; the little watch-jewels of my eyes (see the double meaning in watch). What he sees, or 'watches', in her is first of all a battle of wills, in which (so he feels) her face is willed, by him, against her own will, to rise and open to mine like natural objects so often used by male poetry as METAPHORS for women: moon and flower. Then he feels in her a want, / a yearning. That is when he makes his offer.

The whole thing, moving towards his offer like a snake rising to the charmer's pipe, works on three levels at once. It is the poet's amused way of describing a woman's shocked discovery that all winter a snake has been hibernating in the outhouse where she did the washing. It is also the voice of the devil, tempting Eve with, not an apple, but himself. Finally, at a more general level, it is the voice of male narcissism: man looking at and into woman for what is like himself, yet different enough that he can see in her a reflection of his self: and see it, moreover, as glitteringly attractive and powerful

192

(a big cut jewel, a tongue the alive nerve of a rock), forcing her to 'open' to his will. A vision of himself as desired by her.

Soundwise, this journey of self-revelation is parallelled by the journey the long O sound makes through the poem. You could call this poem the story of O and its permutations: from room (picked up in moon), to the OR of warm (echoed in water, all, warmness, pour), with the long OH of folds, broken, cold, billows, show, own, opening, O's, then echoed in the tentative almost, as though; plus the WUH sound of one, power, now.

All these plays on long O are literally brought up short when the snake makes his self-statement in the last STANZA, and the voice mutates to short O sounds with a sharp vowel to follow. Watch, rock, want, lost: these words tell their own story of a woman's Paradise about to be lost (at least in the snake's, or devil's mind).

The Story of O was the title of an erotic French novel of the sixties by Pauline Reage, about a young photographer's initiation into bondage by her master. Lasdun's is a brilliantly voiced poem, which plays with the way male lyric traditionally objectifies women – just as Reage's novel, modelled on the Marquis de Sade's *Justine*, played with the way male pornography objectified women. One shouldn't make too much of the parallel, but sexual enslavement is certainly one undertone on the agenda as this narcissistic reptile – also, presumably, a real-life inhabitant of the Catskill mountains – 'offers himself'.

35. Patience Agbabi

TRANSFORMATRIX

I'm slim as a silver stiletto, lit
by a fat, waxing moon and a seance
of candles dipped in oil of frankincense.
Salt peppers my lips as the door clicks shut.
A pen poised over a blank page, I wait
for madam's orders, her strict consonants
and the spaces between words, the silence.
She's given me a safe word, a red light
but I'm breaking the law, on a death wish,
ink throbbing my temples, each vertebra
straining for her fingers. She trusses up
words, lines, as a corset disciplines flesh.
Without her, I'm nothing but without me
she's tense, uptight, rigid as a full stop.

(2000)

Born in London in 1965, brought up both by her black Nigerian parents and white foster parents, Agbabi studied at Oxford and is now a performance poet. Transformation, things becoming something else, is an important theme in her work. Her formal variety reflects the way she unites different worlds: the genres of poetry (which should really be thought of as a spectrum) that are often kept separate, like oral performance poetry and literary poetry, communicated mainly on the page; black idioms like rap, and classic forms like the SESTINA.

This is a SONNET about sadomasochism. It is in BLOCK FORM, but broken syntactically at silence into equal seven-line halves. The first half sets out the scene: I is both a conduit of language, a pen, and (metaphorically) a stiletto, a dominatrix-type whore. In both roles she is raw material for madam's dressing-up, in a session where she will act as medium in a seance that is both literary (consonants, spaces between words, ink) and transgressively sexual (madam, strict, red light, throbbing, trusses, corset disciplines flesh). The session will be dangerous, but madam provides a safe word.

Safe word is the technical term for a word agreed beforehand so the passive partner in an S & M encounter can signal that they've *really* had enough: they really really must stop. But in this poem, paradoxically, the safe word is marked by the traditional emblem of danger, which is also the sign of a no-go area, the prostitute's district: red light. But introduces the reckless intention of the dressed-up I – both the corsetted whore, and raw language – to ignore that paradoxically dangerous safe word.

The first QUATRAIN, an ABBA RHYME-SCHEME followed through in the second (half-rhymes, lit/shut, seance/frankincense, echoed in wait/light, consonants/silence), sets going two short vowels: the I of slim, silver, stiletto, lit, dipped, lips, clicks, which leaks over into the second QUATRAIN (strict) and third (wish, disciplines, rigid), and the A of fat, waxing, candles, which runs on to blank, madam. The longer vowels of the third QUATRAIN (held together by wish/flesh) are introduced by safe (see breaking, straining) and light (see lines, uptight). Tense in the last line hauls back the B rhyme of the first eight lines (seance etc), 'trussing up' the poem in a corset of half-rhyme to stop, self-gesturingly, at stop.

The sentence and the scene setting end after seven lines, at silence. The eighth line carries on the scene but introduces the idea of the safe word. The SONNET's TURN comes on but.

I is breaking a safety law, but a law of SONNET form – that the

TURN comes after the OCTET – is also being, if not 'broken' (for poetry's 'rules' are not as rigid as all that), at least unsettled. The RHYME-SCHEME stands, despite the strong end at the seventh line rather than the eighth. But the increasing sense of danger that marks the last six lines has already begun in the eighth (She's given me).

These unsettlings of form slyly suggest the poem's under-image: the preparation for the sexual scene is also a preparation for writing the poem, for the 'transforming' relation between a poem's raw language and its form. The two characters I and she are also two sides of the writing self, or the poet and (if you think of that as female) muse. You have the paraphernalia of classic inspiration, the fire (lit, candles), romance (silver, moon), whiff of religious possession (oil of frankincense), and paradoxes (salt peppers my lips). But you also have the 'disciplining' technique. I is the body, each vertebra/straining: that reckless (see death wish) lunge out towards new things to think, new ways to say them, and new associations in which language (or the psyche where it wells from) becomes a medium for other-worldly messages. Form (madam) is 'disciplining': all orders, fingers imposing strict consonants, trussed-up words, and lines.

The last two lines sum up this tense relationship. Without her, I'm nothing, says raw sexy inspiration, dressed up by technique's orders. But without me / she's barren. Form by itself is brittle, rigid as a full stop. Inspiration flouts form's orders to the end, breaking another SONNET law. SONNETS classically take one of two forms: EIGHT AND SIX when each two of the six lines of the SESTET pair off in rhyme, or three QUATRAINS with a rhymed COUPLET at the end. What you do not normally have is a rhymed four at the end. In this poem's last line, stop echoes up as if the last four lines were a QUATRAIN.

So this wayward I, the transformatrix ('transform' plus 'matrix') which we call inspiration, both obeys and, on a death wish, remakes a few 'rules' for a SONNET whose surface speaks of dressing for violent sex, but which is also about transforming throbbing language into art: about breaking and re-making rules in writing a poem whose body and flesh is made of dangerous, not safe, words.

196

36. Michael Donaghy

LIVERPOOL

Ever been tattooed? It takes a whim of iron,
takes sweating in the antiseptic-stinking parlour,
nothing to read but motorcycle magazines
before the blood-sopped cotton and, of course, the needle,
all for – at best – some Chinese dragon.
But mostly they do hearts,

hearts skewered, blurry, spurting like the Sacred Heart
on the arms of bikers and sailors.
Even in prison they get by with biro ink and broken glass,
carving hearts into their arms and shoulders.
But women's are more intimate. They hide theirs,
under shirts and jeans, in order to bestow them.

Like Tracy, who confessed she'd had hers done
one legless weekend with her ex.
Heart. Arrow. Even the bastard's initials, R.J.L.,
somewhere where it hurt, she said,
and when I asked her where, snapped 'Liverpool'.

Wherever it was, she'd had it sliced away
leaving a scar, she said, pink and glassy,
but small, and better than having his mark on her

(that self-same mark of Valentinus,
who was flayed for love, but who never
– so the cardinals now say – existed.
Desanctified, apocryphal, like Christopher,
like the scar you never showed me, Trace,
your (   ), your ex, your 'Liverpool').

Still, when I unwrap the odd, anonymous note
I let myself believe that it's from you.

(1993)

Donaghy was born in America in 1954 from an Irish Catholic background, and now lives as a traditional Irish musician in London. His poems are glitteringly witty with a dark, off-beat erudition, intellectually complex but light-toned. Their polished forms are as varied as their subjects, which range from Byzantine empresses to Irish love-knots, from Caliban to Arctic explorers. He is a poet of ideas – of history, music, metaphysics, religion. The tragic quirks of past human lives rub shoulders in his work with contemporary relationships, all summoned up in a tone of confiding intimacy which hopes you'll find the world as metaphysically and entertainingly lunatic as he does.

This poem is about love. About 'telling your love'; about love's pain, badges and scars; about the <u>iron</u> behind a Valentine's pink satin; about the Valentine heart as <u>mark</u> of inner fantasy and outer pain. About the wish to display or announce love, wear it on your sleeve (or skin); about the way we <u>bestow</u> it and <u>hide</u> it; or deny it, till it is <u>desanctified</u>, <u>apopcryphal</u>.

The poem moves from masculine love to feminine, starting with <u>motorcycle magazines</u> in the tattooing <u>parlour</u> (that strangely genteel word for a <u>blood-sopped</u>, <u>sweating</u>, <u>stinking</u> place of pain) to another place of male desperation, <u>prison</u>. Pivoting on the hearts which prisoners <u>get by</u> with while they miss their lovers, it moves to the lovers they might miss: to women, who are <u>more intimate</u>; and so to Tracy's 'confession' (bringing out the Catholic motif announced in <u>Sacred Heart</u>, continued in saints <u>Valentinus</u> and <u>Christopher</u>, the <u>cardinals</u>, and the last line's <u>let myself believe</u>).

The theme of love's pain moves from <u>blood-sopped</u> through to the *double entendre* of <u>legless</u>, the split implied by <u>her ex</u>, the <u>arrows</u>, the label <u>bastard</u>, and <u>hurt</u>. But, says the poem, you cannot erase the 'trace' of love entirely. <u>Had it sliced away</u> sounds fine and easy; but you are left with the <u>pink</u> (as in the clichéd Valentine) and <u>glassy</u> scar.

Still, a <u>scar</u> is <u>better than having his mark on her</u>. The lines shorten as the poem moves into successful cut-off and retraction: desanctified saints, Tracy's refusal to say where on <u>her</u> the mark was, the bracketed blank which stands for the scar, the <u>odd anonymous note</u>.

Vowel-harmonies (<u>legless</u>/<u>ex</u>, <u>heart</u>/<u>bastard</u>/<u>hurt</u>, <u>dragon</u>/<u>iron</u>, <u>R.J.L.</u>/<u>small</u>/<u>apocryphal</u>/<u>Liverpool</u>) hold the lines together, and the poet pulls the IAMBIC PENTAMETER about like plasticene, lengthening it to show us something (the needle, the broken glass, the R.J.L), shortening it to four beats occasionally, sometimes for comic effect (somewhere where it hurt, she said), and then permanently when we get to the bracket and Valentinus. The second line lengthens to six beats as you wait in that grim parlour (where the four Ss, five Ts and three K sounds hold everything up). The fourth is lengthened for blood-sopped cotton and needle. The sixth line is three beats as the poem stops describing and moves on to the pain itself. Hearts are hurt; see skewered, blurry, spurting, blood, needle, broken glass (behind which stands the answering rhyme, 'broken hearts').

Men (bikers and sailors) wear their hearts on arms and shoulders. Women hide theirs – which leads into the STANZA which breaks the formal row of six-liners, and moves everything into the personal. To Tracy, who tried to obliterate all 'trace' of her love and never showed the poet the scar from her tattoo (as Viola's imaginary sister, in Shakespeare's *Twelfth Night*, 'never told her love'), and whose name the poet will shorten at the end to Trace. Even love you've got away from leaves some 'trace'.

Starting in a buttonholing, upfront way (Ever been tattooed?), and ending with a mock-regretful farewell, Donaghy scoops together disparate images to get across universal pain at the (potential) emptiness at the heart of love. Inside the brackets from self-same mark to 'Liverpool' are more brackets, enclosing a white blank, the '(   )' which stands (among other things) for the scar never shown, the anonymous note, the affair that didn't happen, the saints who have lost their 'St'. The aftermath of love is erasure, hiddenness.

But though the poem hints at the damage and hollowness of love, though the boyfriend becomes a sliced-away initial (her ex, or X), the last line closes on a note of hope. In love, you let yourself believe that something universally yearned for, a wrapped gift as invisible as sainthood, will come your way. Women hide their love, their mark of pain endured, in order to bestow it.

The idea of sharing love, of a universal code by which you tell your love, turns on the paradox that something miraculous is also ordinary (the 'ordinary swoon' of lovers, as Auden put it in a famous love poem). In love, something extraordinarily vulnerable and violent, a heart pierced by an arrow, gets sliced and skewered with everyday implements: biro ink, broken glass, on to a macho biceps or somewhere where it hurts on a woman's covered body.

The story of a flaying, someone peeling off a man's skin with a torture instrument (see <u>whim of iron</u>), which they <u>now say</u> never happened, has created a <u>whole culture's deepest, most clichéd <u>mark</u> of yearning. Everyone's little clung-to bit of salvation in loneliness was generated in that story of a martyrdom: of a destruction and a pain that turn out, in the end, not to have been true. A Valentine is about showing or telling your love: an <u>anonymous</u> 'trace' of love that may, later on, be denied.

Though hearts get hurt and <u>broken</u>, even the <u>skewered</u> and <u>spurting Heart</u> is <u>Sacred</u>, sanctified by human longing if not <u>the cardinals</u> of Rome. And so, says the poet in his self-mocking sign-off, he can still <u>let</u> himself fantasise about 'unwrapping' one, sometime. Not from under <u>shirts</u> or <u>jeans</u>: in the <u>odd note</u> he might just get from <u>Trace</u>, one day.

37. Jackie Kay

IN MY COUNTRY

walking by the waters
down where an honest river
shakes hands with the sea,
a woman passed round me
in a slow watchful circle,
as if I were a superstition;

or the worst dregs of her imagination,
so when she finally spoke
her words spliced into bars
of an old wheel. A segment of air.
Where do you come from?
'Here,' I said, 'Here. These parts.'

(1993)

A black Scottish poet born in 1961, Kay grew up in Glasgow adopted by white parents (her first collection powerfully addressed the adoption process from different perspectives). She now lives in Manchester and has also written children's poems, radio drama, a life of Bessie Smith, and fiction. Her poems address important social and political issues through the personal, and at first glance their power is often masked by their humour.

I chose this poem, like Simon Armitage's (No. 20), in the early days of my column, when the poems had to be as short as possible. Like Armitage, Kay also writes wonderful longer poems, often very funny – miniature dramas, soliloquies, encounters in a train, stand-offs in the kitchen – so this one does not represent the range of her voice in the fresh, laughing ways her poems are known for. A recent collection, for instance, tackled injustice, identity and racism through images of investigative dentistry.

But one motif in much of her work is alienation: being adopted, being a woman in a male-run society, being black in a white-run society. She often gets at alienation obliquely, through vivid dialogue and a smile. In one poem a child takes the classroom's pale hamster home for the weekend. It scampers up the chimney and she tries to wash it but when, shamefaced, she brings it back to school on Monday, the 'po-faced' little thing is still black.

'In My Country', however, approaches alienation through echoes of archaic song lyric (folksong, negro spiritual), and music is an important subject in her prose work too. The poem makes its political point first through punctuation. It has the formal line-symmetry of a song – two STANZAS, six and six – but is not going to play by all the formal rules and goes straight in with no hierarchic capital letter or polite introduction. The waters evokes a ballad world of alienated Babylon or Zion, protest rock, down by some river where you weep – for your people, for exile, for injustice.

In this songlike world, river and sea can be honest and shake hands, but humanity is estranged by superstition: the worst dregs of imagination. Sonically, the staring woman belongs with the superstition and imagination with which she looks at the speaker, while the speaker belongs with honest natural things that get on with each other. As water matches river, so sea rhymes with me.

Many of the vowel-echoes holding the STANZAS together are widenings out of, or variations on, the first OR of walking, picked up in waters. This is reharmonised in one direction by down and round; in others by the short O of honest, watchful, the OH of slow, so, old, the ER of circle, were, superstition, worst, her words, which slides into the culminating echoes of bars and parts, air and where, here and here. The central cohesive chime is over the STANZA divide: the 'shaking hands' between those two Latinate abstracts, two mental processes, imagination and superstition. A harder sound builds through the second STANZA, starting in the unpleasant dregs, attributed to the woman's imagination, echoed in segment – part of the prejudice driving that old wheel of xenophobic or intolerant imagination – and the poet's said, which answers the woman's spoke in words which challenge that prejudice, put a spoke in that old wheel.

But there may be more to the wheel, and the language around it, than that. As an image, it follows circle (the one the woman steered round the speaker). The words air and bars associated with it have extra meanings: both a musical one (country airs, bars of a song) appropriate to the song atmospherics (down by the waters, down by the riverside), and also a behavioural one – an air of, say, suspicion; and bars that fall, like the 'colour bar', between people who do not shake hands.

The song flows over the STANZAS, but the two figures are divided, and the punctuation marks their division. The woman's question has no quotation marks. *Where do you come from?* could be from an old song or fairytale. It is what you are asked in remote rural places all over the world. The poet's punctuation – modern, correct, direct – brings in up-to-date reality. No more lower-case balladry, no more singing in the wind or on the vacuum of a blank page. The poet is laying claim to capitals, quotation marks, her own identity (in this landscape, not in someone else's imagination); the right to these parts, an honest river, how things are done now – to a 'shaking' of hands.

Earlier, the woman passed round me as if I (the poem's first capital letter, but introduced in an 'as if' clause) were a superstition. Even the grammar is unclear between them. Syntactically, the woman, the subject of the main verb passed, must also be the subject of the participle. Though at first it feels as if the poet should be the one walking by the waters, grammatically this must be the woman. She has grammatical dominance: she is the subject of passed and spoke. Now I is the subject of the main verb, and shifts the tone into the modern world. Songs have changed, Scotland has changed. Here is 'my country' too.

And yet, says the poem, unjudgementally laying the STANZAS out

203

like two palms spread open, 'My country' includes this very alienation. In 'On Home Beaches' (No. 16), 'home' is the place you feel not at home, uncomfortably up against inequality. In this poem, the here where its I 'comes from' is a place where she is, sometimes, passed round, seen as a superstition, as worst dregs.

38. Paul Farley

KEITH CHEGWIN AS FLEANCE

The next rung up from extra and dogsbody
and all the clichés are true – days waiting for
enough light, learning card games, penny-ante,
while fog rolls off the sea, a camera
gets moisture in its gate, and Roman Polanski
curses the day he chose Snowdonia.

He picked you for your hair to play this role:
a look had reached Bootle from Altamont
that year. You wouldn't say you sold your soul
but learned your line inside a beating tent
by candlelight, the shingle dark as coal
behind each wave, and its slight restatement.

'A tale told by an idiot . . .' 'Not your turn,
but perhaps, with time and practice . . .' the Pole starts.
Who's to say, behind the accent and that grin,
what designs you had on playing a greater part?
The crew get ready while the stars go in.
You speak the words you'd written on your heart

just as the long-awaited sunrise fires
the sky a blueish pink. Who could have seen
the future in the late schedules, where I
can't sleep and watch your flight from the big screen;
on the other side of drink and wondering why,
the zany, household-name years in between?

(1997)

Born in Liverpool in 1965, Paul Farley studied at the Chelsea School of Art, and his poems crackle with spooky detritus like talking light bulbs, spud guns, treacle you pour 'into every orifice' to feel hardening over you. They have a poised, streetwise elegance, fuelled by bizarre imagination, subtle technique, changes of tone and quirky, innovative angles. 'Industry had a sex life once' begins one poem.

This one is about how you become the person you turn into; about what it does to you to wait, in the wings, for fame. Also about imagining what went into someone else's outer career, and inner journey, to make them what they are. It conjures up the image of life as 'A tale told by an idiot', in Macbeth's soliloquy when he hears his wife is dead. Life, he says, is 'but a walking shadow, a poor player, / That struts and frets his hour upon the stage, / And then is heard no more'. 'As' in the title speaks to the whole idea behind acting: presenting yourself, while representing someone else.

Many *Macbeth*-like resonances of bad luck colour the protagonist's media-drenched understanding of a world in which the image you present to others has, unluckily, a lasting effect on yourself. Farley wanted, he told me, to write a poem about someone it was impossible to feel compassion for, 'Who blew it, by turning up at work drunk, and was a secret alcoholic, who never got his act together, and was completely media-ed out.' Keith Chegwin began his career in a TV sitcom, which Farley watched as a child in Liverpool in the seventies; he later became a celebrity by appearing on a nude game show (zany, household-name years).

The *Macbeth* resonances mesh with the minor role which the youthful Chegwin played in Polanski's film *Macbeth*: Fleance, Banquo's son, who will – so the witches prophesy – beget a line of kings, while Macbeth himself will beget none. Fleance's career, therefore, is tipped to flow in the opposite direction from Keith's. His father is murdered, he only just escapes with his own life, but his line will, outside the play, stride to the top; whereas Chegwin is a bit-part actor who maybe once, secretly, aimed for the top, but eventually gets known for being something ridiculous (see Macbeth's word 'idiot').

The visual setting symbolises the yearning to arc on up into the limelight, and the darkening of that ambition (as in Macbeth's soliloquy, 'Out, out, brief candle'). It begins in darkness, waiting for enough light (see candlelight; stars go in – with a pun on film stars). In the end, you may get your long-awaited sunrise and blueish pink dawn but, for Keith at least, the night comes back (late schedules, can't sleep).

Making anything – a film, a poem, your own career, the integrity (or otherwise) of your own soul – involves hard choices; but also, for some people, a lot of frustrating waiting around for other people. The camera (which decides how you are seen) gets moisture in its gate, the director 'curses' (like the witches in *Macbeth*). Keith's beating tent evokes the hidden heart on which he 'writes' one sad line of script.

Presumably that heart is also beating with the ambition to play a greater part, maybe even Macbeth himself (who speaks the famous quote). The director, aware of Keith's ambition (and ambition is the theme of *Macbeth* too), flatters him (perhaps, with time and practice), but really chose him for his pop-star hairdo. That hairstyle was from Altamont – another *Macbeth*-like omen, for Altamont was the famous concert that ended in violence and death, a big media disaster for the Rolling Stones.

The formal approach is seemingly straightforward and classical, but plays and pulls at both rhythms and rhymes. The poem has a straightforward ABABAB RHYME-SCHEME, but with some very unstraightforward rhyme-relationships: dogsbody, penny-ante and Polanski, Altamont, beating tent and restatement. The basic line is IAMBIC PENTAMETER with enough straightforward examples to keep you feeling the beat. But Farley cuts back sometimes to four beats, or lengthens to seven, as in the third line – enough light, learning card games, penny-ante – for Keith's days of waiting and 'learning'. Now his career has plummeted (from next rung up to sold your soul; from hopes of a greater part, accompanied by that hopeful 'writing' on your heart) to the situation of the answering long line, the climax in the third last line: can't sleep and watch your flight from the big screen. Which shows the poet himself, confronting his anti-hero at last, imagining the inner impulses that went into the shaping of his career, and wondering why.

39. Moniza Alvi

MAP OF INDIA

If I stare at the country long enough
I can prise it off the paper,
lift it like a flap of skin.

Sometimes it's an advent calendar –
each city has a window
which I leave open
a little wider each time.

India is manageable – smaller than
my hand, the Mahanadi River
thinner than my lifeline.

(1993)

Alvi is half English, born in Lahore, Pakistan, in 1954, and came to England as a baby. She grew up in Hertfordshire; her first collection had a section called 'Presents from Pakistan', exploring the homeland she had never seen through the impressions and tokens it left on her English upbringing. Saris sent from aunts in Lahore 'didn't impress' her English schoolfriends; nor did her mother's cooking pans with their technicolor 'palette' of spices ('like powder-paints') and 'golden rivers' of ghee. In a later collection the poet returns to the subcontinent as an adult, trying 'to touch' its languages.

This double provenance is the departure point for Alvi's bold, colourful, surprising, often comically surreal imagination, which takes off in lavish visual detail from domestic objects, bodies and their clothes, or from unnoticed stones and small spots in a landscape, or in art. Her poem 'I Would Like to be a Dot in a Painting by Miró' asks, 'Would it be worthwhile / to roll myself towards the lemon stripe?' She tends to work in sequences of poems like a painter, mining a particular vein of absurdity for its graphically unfolding images. One sequence about pregnancy charts the biological changes in the wife through the voice of the watching husband ('My wife took to walking on all fours') who becomes pregnant himself. 'I'd ask my wife to place her pregnant ear / to my stomach and listen to the trauma of the sea, / throwing us up as driftwood on the beach.'

In this poem from her first book, a child looking at a map of the place she came from, which she does not remember but hears about all the time, becomes an image for the way all children learn the world. You, in your small body, are somehow related to this vast, important, unknowable thing, which magnetises all the adults around you, but which is outside and faraway. You know it needs effort, you have to respond, be adequate to it (enough), but can only comprehend it by reducing it to what you already know: your own skin and hand, the toys and small epiphanies (advent calendar) of your circumscribed life.

This is all on a tiny scale. It is miniature work, and about smallness; about a child's vision of what it does not understand, and a process of miniaturisation. In its own small body, the poem reduces what is immense and unknowable to comically manageable proportions.

It starts from a conditional, if I stare . . . long enough, which gives the child power over 'India'; power to prise it off the paper.

'India' is fragile, paper and skin, something stuck on, which you can remove. The speaker, the I, is grammatically in charge, the subject of the verbs. I can lift this country like a flap of skin. In the next STANZA, the map is the verb's subject – sometimes it's an advent calendar – and I is grammatically subservient, appearing in a relative clause introduced by which and dependent on the verb of which each city is the subject: has a window. In the third STANZA, the gradual process, over time, of staring long enough to be in charge of this enormous country, seems to have worked. It is now manageable (from the Latin *manus*, hand): see the chime of manageable, hand, than. This huge thing is smaller than / my hand, a frail, miniature India. The Mahanadi River, feeding the vast delta on the Bay of Bengal (whose flooding has caused untold deaths and disasters for centuries in Orissa, and still does), is thinner than my lifeline. Thanks to the process of time, which lifeline echoes.

But the grammatical movement tells a different story. Grammatically, India is taking control. It is now the subject of the main verb; I, the subject of the main verb in the first STANZA, has dwindled to my, my. As I reduces India to a manageable size, India is becoming more syntactically active – and I is also learning more of its details, from each city to the Mahanadi River. India is asserting its influence, insisting on being known while the I voice (and the overt thought), believes the balance of power is moving in the opposite direction: that given long enough, over time, it will grasp the country in the palm of her hand.

An advent calendar speaks of child life in Britain, not Pakistan, and the revelations of Christ's birth brought home through a sequence of lifted paper 'windows'. But Advent also means 'Coming'. This poem reverberates against another one in the same sequence, 'Arrival 1946', where someone coming to England for the first time (presumably from the subcontinent) 'stares' at this other country, as unknowable to him as India is to the child here. The boat docks in Liverpool. 'Tariq stared / at an unbroken line of washing / from the North West to Euston . . . These are strange people, he thought – / an Empire, and all this washing.'

In 'coming' to the other country, to an understanding of it, you start by 'staring' at the small things. You prise off a bit at a time, open now one window, now another. Understanding, says this small poem in a sequence of poems about coming to grips with another world you do not know but which belongs to you, where

210

you were born (see <u>my lifeline</u>), is a series of small revelations, a little wider each time.

40. Glyn Maxwell

THE BREAKAGE

Someone broke our beautiful
        All-coloured window. They were saints
He broke, or she or it broke. They were
        Colours you can't get now.

Nothing else was touched. Only our
        Treasured decoration, while it
Blackened in its calm last night, light
        Dead in it, like He is.

Now needles of all length and angle
        Jab at air. They frame a scene
Of frosty meadows, all our townsmen
        Bobbing here to mourn this,

To moan and wonder what would mount
        And ride so far to grieve us,
Yet do no more than wink and trash,
        Not climb down in here even.

Most eyes are on the woods, though,
        Minds on some known figures.
At least until they too turn up here,
        Sleep-white, without stories.

Things it could have done in here
        It hasn't done. It left it all
The way it was, in darkness first, now
        This, the dull light day has.

We kneel and start. And blood comes
        Like luck to the blue fingers
Of children thinking they can help,
        Quick as I can warn them.

(1998)

212

Born in 1962 of Welsh origin, brought up in Welwyn Garden City, Maxwell studied English at Oxford, poetry at Boston, and now teaches poetry in Massachussets. His astonishing technical facility can make syllables, vowels and consonants do absolutely anything. The restless, energetic voice riffs through evasively ordinary speech, exploring love, politics, comedy, war or quirky narratives (about, for example, being red-headed, or the middle son in a fairytale) in brilliantly elaborate syntax and forms. I once heard another poet say, 'Glyn is the most postmodern of the lot of us'; but he does it all through a voice whose main note is wide-eyed English boyishness.

This one is the first poem, and the title poem, of a collection which is an arc of Englishness. It moves from the First World War to English landscape, the English abroad, and then, more personally, on to love and a baby daughter. Breakage increasingly comes to stand for a 'break' with a communal past (a beautiful / all-coloured world, townsmen in a frosty scene like pre-war England), but also a personal past: the first STANZA's broke, broke, broke cocks an eyebrow at Tennyson's poem 'Break, Break, Break' which mourns the poet's dead friend and 'a day that is dead'.

In a collection, poems speak to each other like songs on an album, widening each one's individual resonances. In its arc, this whole collection suggests that making comes from breaking. A creativity set free by some initial 'breakage' is summed up in the poems about the new baby.

But each poem also has to work purely within its own terms. This one is a perfectly turned mystery box of threat (needles, jab, blood) to established comforting life-certainties, embodied in the familiar certainties of religion (saints, He, and the echo from the Lord's Prayer in Things it could have done . . . / it hasn't done; we kneel) and of genre literature like the cosy English village murder mystery, or fairytale (woods, known figures, stories).

The poem shows a moment when such certainties are shattered. What is broken is not just a window but a window on the world: a way of seeing and understanding it. This was a way of seeing people that was treasured as beautiful. It is now lost for ever (colours you can't get now), leaving uncertainty behind. Uncertainty about who is responsible (someone, he, or she or it, some . . . figures) depersonalises into what or it.

Uncertainty about why leads on to a 'warning'. If you haven't a clue why evil came (or why it only destroyed one thing), how do you know what it'll do next? In its collection, this poem is followed by a war poem so you feel, as you read this poem and then read on, that what it will bring next is war. The spoilt-Christmas aura (decoration, frosty scene) comes over in the tones of a child who up to now has always been confident of what he's been told, whether that was grammar (he broke, or she or it broke) or religion (dead, like He is). All this foreshadows a later poem in the collection which describes London gathering for war in August 1914, seen through the eyes of a boy whose seaside outing has been spoiled by the call-up.

Yet this poem also moves, ambivalently, towards self-discovery and growing up. Colours are lost, blackened; darkness is first; light dead. But light, though dull, returns. So do colours, sufferingly, in blood, luck, blue. I emerges from communal our, us, we, distinguished from children, the subject of its own verb.

In atmosphere, tone and content, the poem is about uncertainty, spoiling, lack of control. But the technique laughs at all that. Little sudden energetic images (bobbing, sleep-white) are the linguistic tip of a whole iceberg of cunning architecture. Technically, this is all about the opposite of uncertainty: control of syllable, breakage of line. The first QUATRAIN sets a syllable-count for each line of seven, eight, nine, six; the pattern repeats (give or take a few lengthenings and shortenings) throughout.

There are dozens of ancient Welsh, Irish and French SYLLABIC forms like this. Most have extra game rules too – about, say, cross-rhymes (see window/now, it/it, mount/down, was/has), and strict metrical patterns governing line-ends (see the SPONDAIC or TROCHAIC end of each STANZA, get now, He is, warn them). Maxwell's form brilliantly conveys his poem's emotional paradox – that new things come from losing old ones, making comes from breakage – by enacting uncertainty and damage through flawless metric certainty, and making something new from ancient (and, paradoxically again for such an English voice, Celtic) formal rules.

41. Sharon Olds

I GO BACK TO MAY 1937

I see them standing at the formal gates of their colleges,
I see my father strolling out
under the ochre sandstone arch, the
red tiles glinting like bent
plates of blood behind his head, I
see my mother with a few light books at her hip
standing at the pillar made of tiny bricks with the
wrought-iron gate still open behind her, its
sword-tips black in the May air,
they are about to graduate, they are about to get married,
they are kids, they are dumb, all they know is they are
innocent, they would never hurt anybody.
I want to go up to them and say Stop,
don't do it – she's the wrong woman,
he's the wrong man, you are going to do things
you cannot imagine you would ever do,
you are going to do bad things to children,
you are going to suffer in ways you never heard of,
you are going to want to die. I want to go
up to them there in the late May sunlight and say it,
her hungry pretty blank face turning to me,
her pitiful beautiful untouched body,
his arrogant handsome blind face turning to me,
his pitiful beautiful untouched body,
but I don't do it. I want to live. I
take them up like the male and female
paper dolls and bang them together
at the hips like chips of flint as if to
strike sparks from them, I say
Do what you are going to do, and I will tell about it.

(1985)

Olds is an American poet born in San Francisco in 1942; her poems seem to well up out of sensation and perception like a burst water main. They are full of risky line breaks like the line-ends here on the, its, if to; the ENJAMBEMENT is so daring that any ordinary, orderly idea of line-ending throws up its hands in horror. This is not carelessness and laxity but honed technique, rising from the way Olds has developed her voice. It gives the poems a feeling of no-holds-barred frankness. It looks artless but is not, as would-be imitators discover.

The power of her poems lies also in the precise, vivid sensual detail, their moral clarity, and a strong movement of thought. She may not seem it, but she is always in control of the tone and where it is heading. One collection, *The Father*, was about her father's abuse of her as a child.

At first glance, this seems to be a poem about a photograph. But there is no photo: the boy and girl are separate, each at different formal gates of their opening adult lives. The poem also seems like instant confessionalism, but is structured in two groups of twelve, followed by six lines which contain the poet's decision: what she does about the scenario she has described. You can track the structure by the verbs attached to I. It starts with I see: with seeing the parents' 'former' selves (implicated in formal) at the gates of their colleges: that place where you are supposed to complete your education, though the real learning is about to begin. It moves to I want, a section which hints at what that learning involves, and on to I don't do it: a negative act which is also (for the reader who has followed this learning curve) a moral choice. The verbs pass from watching to acting, I 'taking' control of her parents' futures so that she, in the future, will tell.

The opening vision presents the May of two lives which 'may' still (line eight) be happy. They are about to graduate, they are about to get married. They are in classic male and female pose: the man in motion (strolling out under a wedding-like arch), the girl static, by tiny bricks like little stitches. You get the feel of a wedding photo without the reality. They are linked only by the poet's perception: I see them.

This vision sees the violence behind both. Glinting blood, for him; for her, wrought-iron, black sword-tips, and a still open gate. She could still go back or escape, but these first twelve lines are all seeming innocence. Innocent is the centre of their self-vision: the word sums up this May idyll in this section's last line.

216

Some of the echoes which hold together these first lines resonate with the rites and life-expectations of all American kids: gates leads to colleges, plates, gate, graduate, to head, married, kids. But hip (which will come violently back in the plural at the end), moves first into bricks, then sword-tips; red and bent lead on to head (which also leans towards blood) for the man; balanced by the long I of light, tiny, iron, behind for the girl (underpinned by I and my, for the poet is already implicated in this: the poem's first word is I).

Innocent sums up the non-existent photo, the picture of two (as it were) dumb kids. The are unaware of the swords, of blood to come. Then we hear the phrase which seals this vision, with all its tiny presages of menace. Speaking it, you could place the stresses on two different sequences of words: innocent, never and hurt, or innocent, hurt and anybody. But either way the main stress falls on the words innocent and hurt. An opposition which the poem deeply explores. Who is to blame for all the hurt to come?

The second twelve lines expand the possibilities of both words, and intimate both the hurt to come, and their innocence: they cannot imagine it. The first sentence begins and ends on the ring of I, die; the second moves from I to body – which picks up anybody at the end of the first twelve lines. This chaos of innocence and hurt is all about 'bodies'.

The cohering vowels of this chunk begin with want: stop, wrong, wrong, want, want. The nasal ring of want reappears in wrong, things, imagine, going, going, woman, man, children, going, going, before moving on again to want. There is a more optimistic vowel: up flickers on to stop and a sympathetic view of each parent as hungry or untouched. It introduces the way to stop the hurt. Yet this is the vowel that brings hurt out into the open (suffer), and stops the poet stopping them. But will introduce the last six lines that force them on.

The middle section, of this poem structured by the movements of I, shows I in imagined action, talking. The direct speech (don't do it) leads to incantatory lists which pick up the accented words of the first section. The doom of do (don't do it, do things, ever do, do bad things) echoes the repeated you, you, you, you, you, you. As the line lengthens from four beats to five, the accented heard (the future incest and abuse all un-heard) echoes hurt from the previous section. The four lines beginning you are, listing what the couple will do in the future, are balanced by four lines beginning her, her, his, his, listing their then untouchedness, their blankness of mind and body.

Since bodies are the medium here of innocence and hurt, banging them together is the poet's response: a bang that will engender her own body, and eventually that of this poem. For the poem's moves and structure are all those of its speaker, I (the poem's first word), who chooses her own existence at its end. We find both untouched parents-to-be turning to me as if the whole thing – whether they become monsters through tragic unsuitability or not – is up to her.

In the last six lines, the speaker chooses their corruption and suffering: because I want to live. What she told them in the second section, don't do it, is now what she says about herself. They are going to want to die, but too bad: she herself wants to live. It is her or them, and she chooses her own life.

But it is a violent choice. It accepts bad things done to children, and 'takes up' the whole Adam and Eve burden of male and female, and the knowledge of evil engendered between them (see, by contrast those pathetically innocent colleges).

As she makes her decision, the language gets lippy and sparky. She 'takes up' their figures as paper dolls, but when she bangs them together they are chips of flint. Before that last line come the sharp and hissing double consonants of hips, chips, flint, strike, sparks. The 'telling' that her poetry will do will come at a cost; with violence.

This seems a classic 'parents' poem, like Larkin's 'They fuck you up, your mum and dad'. It gets extra weight if you know Olds' collection *The Father*, but doesn't need it: by the end you are pretty sure that whatever went on was terrible. But it goes further than just forgiving the parents, as Larkin does in his line 'They may not mean to, but they do'. It takes responsibility for the parents' crimes. The poem recreates a moment at which the poet is able to stop them, and doesn't. She chooses it all, including the bad. As long – here the writing of poems comes in – as she can tell about it.

42. Paul Durcan

SELF-PORTRAIT, NUDE WITH STEERING WHEEL

I am forty-five and do not
Know how to drive a car
– And you tell me I am cultured.

Forty-five years creeping and crawling about the earth,
Going up and down the world,
And I do not know the difference between a carburettor and a
    gasket
– And you tell me I am a Homo sapiens.

Forty-five years sitting in the back seat giving directions
– And you say that I am not an egotist.

Forty-five years sitting in the passenger seat
With my hands folded primly in my lap
– And you think I am liberated.

Forty-five years getting in and out of cars
And I do not know where the dipstick is
– And you tell me that I am a superb lover.

Forty-five years grovelling behind a windscreen
– And you talk of my pride and courage and self-reliance.

Forty-five years of not knowing the meaning of words
Like transmission, clutch, choke, battery, leads
– And you say that I am articulate.

Forty-five years bumming lifts off other people –
And you tell me I am an independent, solitary, romantic spirit.

So it is that you find me tonight
Loitering here outside your front door
Having paid off a taxi in three ten-pound notes,
Nude, with a steering wheel in my hands.

(1990)

Born in Dublin in 1944, Durcan has crafted a unique, manically confidential voice which puts a surreal (or maybe super-real) imagination to work through self-deprecating tragi-comic narrative and social observation which shows us every detail in a bizarre and surreal light. He brings out the madness of what everyone takes for normal.

Sometimes the everyday reality of his poems is that of Russia, where Durcan has often travelled; but mainly their focus is the Irish Republic. In the years he developed his voice, that nation went through a process of extraordinary social change, and Durcan became the laureate of that change, charting the way the Catholic Church dominated everyone's imagination as new motorways and shopping centres sprang up around them and changed their lives. His poems sell out in Ireland as soon as they reach the bookshops – craftily candid poems, a wonderful blend of intimacy and formality, taking off from anything: sex, Catholicism, newspaper headlines, shop names, relationships, fatherhood, painting, curtain material in a department store, or the woes of masculinity.

This poem has three main ingredients: visual (seeing yourself as a painting), incantatory (the Mass-like repetition of forty-five years . . . and you tell me), and symbolic – the comically acute sequence of metaphorical connections whose centrepiece is the sexual symbolism of dipstick (which presages tonight, outside your front door, nude and in my hands).

As a piece of carefully structured self-refuting self-description, a 'self-portrait', it moves comically from know how and cultured, to up and down the world and Homo sapiens; to giving directions and egotist, to sitting, primly and liberated; to in and out of cars, dipstick and superb lover; to grovelling behind, pride and courage; to not knowing the meaning of words and articulate, to bumming lifts off other and independent, solitary romantic. This is the build-up to the four last lines, which sum up the male poet's archetypal situation of feeling shut out (in relation to both you and 'driving' a car): with a nod to the ancient genre known from Alexandrian poetry as the *paraklausithuron*, the 'song sung outside the beloved's shut front door', which begs her to open it, and herself, to him.

Nude, he is both naked Homo sapiens, an existentially helpless, stripped self-vision, but also a guy who has invested thirty quid in a taxi to get to a woman's door, loitering – as with intent – like a lover ready for action. Hoping (without saying so) to learn to drive. Hoping the front door opens. Here I am: you find me tonight.

The poem works through contrasting registers of language. The words that strip the persona are idiomatic, vivid and funny dramatic participles: creeping and crawling, grovelling, bumming, loitering. The praise words have an utterly different tone. They are full of grand empty abstracts: liberated, superb, pride, courage, self-reliance, articulate, independent, romantic. Their distance from ordinary life is underlined in the Latin Homo sapiens. These words skitter off the surface of day-to-day life where intelligence, independence, all the important things in life – culture, insight, freedom, sexuality, language – are summed up (the poem suggests) in driving a car.

The words that really matter, says the poem, are concrete and physical, and it enjoys their physical weight in its own body: carburettor and a gasket; transmission, clutch, choke, battery, leads. The poem mocks by self-mocking: laughing down the idea of being awed by the romantic image of the poet. Here is a figure who ought, if anyone, to know the meaning of words, but knows nothing of the steely, oily, generative reality and physical distinctions behind these critical words.

By the end of the poem, the poet presents himself holding the instrument that turns a car (and everything a car stands for in traditional, very much non-self-deprecating male self-imagery) around. But he possesses none of the power or knowledge that makes this all-important entity actually go. He has the external token of control, its symbolic handle, but not the thing itself.

Is this the poem's image for poetry, you wonder. This nude statement of helpless dependence on taxis, other people, and you – who has showered the poet with grandiose labels he (at least partly) doesn't believe in? This creature with no real knowledge of machinery or words, who is steering precisely nothing?

It laughs at itself, this poem: it questions the delusory status of archetypally romantic, independent, articulate poets who are also pathetically passive, primly helpless there in the back seat. It is a poem about not-knowing-how-to-take-control. But it also contradicts this message all through. It 'drives' flawlessly on to its own end, steering its own mad course in perfect control of every nuance.

43. Lavinia Greenlaw

INVENTION

My six-year-old mechanic, you are up half the night
inventing a pipe made from jars, a *ski-ing car*
for flat icy roads and a *timer-catapult*
involving a palm tree, candles and rope.

You could barely stand when I once found you,
having loosened the bars from the cot
and stepped out so simply you shocked yourself.
Today I am tearful, infatuated with bad ideas,

the same song, over and over. You take charge,
up-end chairs, pull cushions under the table,
lay in chewing-gum and juice
rip newspaper into snow on the roof.

(1997)

Born in 1963, Greenlaw grew up in Essex in the punk generation; her poems are profoundly involved in the project of reseeing, and remapping, the physical world. She used to be labelled a science-interest poet, but her comparatively few science poems are part of a much broader exploration of perception in every sphere.

Robert Frost said poetry should be 'a fresh look and a fresh listen'. Greenlaw has a wonderful ear and her poems have strong, subtle music, but their themes often concentrate on the fresh look. They may go into their subject through art, or technological discoveries like the disclosures of photography; or by imagining alien ways of seeing in another historical age, or by human encounters and relationships. But they are always probing fresh ways of seeing.

This poem describes a child making something new by putting familiar things together in imaginative ways; which is precisely what poems do. Again (see poems by D'Aguiar, Paulin, Dunmore and Lasdun, Nos 18, 26, 31 and 34) the poem gives another activity, especially a creative activity, extra depth and resonance by using it implicitly as an image of its own making. (How to make a poem, how you can do it newly, is what a poet is always thinking about underneath everything else.) This poem is the parent's 'invention': what she made from the child's creation.

The poem moves from the sound of I (My, echoed in night, pipe, icy, I, I) to the increasingly stronger sound you: you, you, loosened, you, you, pull cushions, you, chewing-gum, juice, newspaper, roof. It sets out a relationship in which the balance of looking after, between parent and child, momentarily shifts. When I am tearful, then you take charge. This is the only sentence which starts halfway through a line, and it underlines the child's initiative. The poem ends with this child, who once stepped out from one domestic structure and shocked itself, up-ending other ones to make a safe structure, a house with a protective roof.

In the soundworld through which this shift takes place, the important vowel-echoes come in clusters at different places in the STANZAS, but continue through the poem to make it all one coherent sonic world: AR (are, half, jars, car, palm, bars, charge), AY (made, today, infatuated, take, table, lay, newspaper), short A (mechanic, flat, candles, stand, am, infatuated, bad). The first STANZA, spiky with plosive, plashy consonants (P, L, T, K – mechanic, *ski-ing car*, flat, *timer-catapult*, palm tree, rope), also begins little explosions of short O or U with a sharp consonant after

223

(*catapult*, cot, which continues into shocked), and modulates into that phrase which 'invention' is all about: stepped out.

The second STANZA increasingly picks up on the gentler ND of candles (stand/found/loosened) which tips on into the third (up-end/under), giving a feel of continuous growth through this poem which is partly about the child's growing emotional strength and understanding.

The rhythm is four beats lengthening to five, with a DACTYLIC undertow held firmly in check, as if disciplining the DACTYLS is part of the process of holding the child safe in its adventurousness, its 'stepping out'. The second line of the second STANZA, for instance, couldn't be more different from, or have a more different rhythmic relation to the rest of its verse than, the second line of the last STANZA in Paterson's poem (No. 30), though it has the same pattern: a three-QUATRAIN lyric. Greenlaw checks the DACTYLIC flow with the SPONDEE stepped out, and lengthens that line to PENTAMETER for the child walking out of its cot (as lines lengthened by an extra syllable describe something else moving out in Walcott's poem, No. 22).

The first STANZA was sealed off from the rest; the sentence ended with the STANZA. The first three lines of the second describe the mother's moment of being the strong one, when the child is so young it can barely stand. In the fourth line, she is the weak one (the EAR of tearful/ideas, the A of infatuated/bad), and the feel of these tears and ideas spills across the STANZA break to over and over, opening the third STANZA with the fact that it is now the mother that needs help.

The child supplies it, replacing this unexplained grown-up complexity (infatuated) with strong simple verbs: take charge, up-end, pull ... under, lay in, rip. The complicated adult world (newspapers) is shredded to become stuff in the outside world against which the child has provided a roof.

'Up-ending' the structures of grown-up life, 'pulling' cushions into new places, 'laying in' things parents use to comfort children with (chewing-gum, juice), the child responds to the need, when its mother is tearful, for it to take charge against a siege (see *timer-catapult*) of bad ideas. Need, or necessity, is traditionally the 'mother' of invention. This 'invention' shows a child, of necessity, playing mother to mother.

224

44. Peter Redgrove

THE VISIBLE BABY

A large transparent baby like a skeleton in a red tree,
Like a little skeleton in the rootlet-pattern;
He is not of glass, this baby, his flesh is see-through,
Otherwise he is quite the same as any other baby.

I can see the white caterpillar of his milk looping through him,
I can see the pearl-bubble of his wind and stroke it out of him,
I can see his little lungs breathing like pink parks of trees,
I can see his little brain in its glass case like a budding rose;

There are his teeth in his transparent gums like a budding hawthorn
    twig
His eyes like open poppies follow the light,
His tongue is like a crest of his thumping blood,
His heart like two squirrels, one scarlet, one purple
Mating in the canopy of a blood-tree;

His spine like a necklace, all silvery-strung with cartilages,
His handbones like a working-party of white insects,
His nerves like a tree of ice with sunlight shooting through it,

What a closed book bound in wrinkled illustrations his father is to
    him!

(1979)

Born in 1932, a contemporary of Ted Hughes at Cambridge, Redgrove lives in Cornwall and his work shares with that of Hughes a profound mythological and sensuous engagement with both the rural natural world, and the nature of human psyches and bodies. But he goes about it a very different way. His poems give the lie to any idea that waves of apparently wayward METAPHOR are specifically a female thing (see No. 11). As with other poets who make METAPHOR one of their main organising principles, Redgrove's METAPHORS, glittery, exhilarating, exotic and extraordinary as they are, knit pliantly together and always move the poem forward. They have a sexy surface glamour but are not there just for decoration: they are organic to their poem, the basis of its structure; how the poem grows.

This is a playful love poem to the baby, offering it its own bright images and spell-like repetitions like a coloured mobile. It begins by comparing the baby to organic things. First the most inside thing, the skeleton. Then outwardly flowering growing things: a tree and its growing parts, rootlet, budding hawthorn twig; then flowers and animals, rose, poppies, squirrels. It moves on to harder, deader objects: jewels (necklace, silvery-strung – picking up pearl-bubble). When live things return they come not with the tender loony exuberance of the first STANZAS but a tone of comic bureaucratic-speak: working-party.

The poem is working towards the human world, and the things that have made wrinkled come about in the last line. 'Work', formality, working-party, coldness. All this is a contrast to the ecstatic glorying love of looping through him, stroke it out of him, pink parks; or brain in its glass case like a budding rose. The white of these insects leads to another hard thing, ice, which glosses tree when that too returns as a comparison.

These little pointers of hardness, coldness, the grown-up human world, prepare for the turnaround in the last line, when the poem imagines the baby looking back at its father (presumably the poet) to see him not as a growing thing, but man-made: an artefact, whose function is communication. But this one is closed. A closed book, the big cliché for what you cannot understand. In the line before, the tree of ice has sunlight shooting through it. Yet the word illustrations comes from 'light'. As sunbeams 'illustrate' the moon, so illustrations should illuminate – literally en-lighten – the reader. But these wrinkled ones are an oxymoron: they cannot enlighten the baby, explain to him what his father is all about.

The 'visible baby' himself is all about light and colour. He is transparent, see-through, 'pearly', white and glass, with transparent gums and eyes like open poppies that follow the light. He is red, pink, scarlet, purple, silvery. He is all openness. The I of the speaker looks in him and can see, can see, can see, can see. But the leathery wrinkled father is bound. The paean of praise begins with the baby's transparency and ends with the poet's opacity.

Soundwise, K, T and L (large, transparent, like, little, rootlet-pattern, glass, flesh, quite) prepare for the repeated can: they flicker through the poem in caterpillar, milk, pearl-bubble, stroke, little lungs, like pink parks, little, glass, light, crest, blood, like two squirrels, scarlet, purple, canopy, blood, necklace, silvery, cartilages, working, insects, closed, wrinkled.

They are also the main consonants of two key words. First skeleton, repeated in the first two lines, which tells us this poem is a vision of innerness: about suddenly seeing into the depth of life – that mad clarity which hits you when you have a baby or fall in love. And secondly, like: the word for comparison, this poem's mode of operation. Like is how the poem approaches this baby, the way his flesh is see-through, the way his skeleton is seen.

The poem is about both life and like: the bare bones of life (what is inside us), plus the way we see it through the mysteries of METAPHOR. As George Eliot put it, that 'we cannot say what something is, except by saying what it is not'.

Halfway through the second STANZA his and him gradually encroach on I can; from the opening of the third, I has disappeared. Grammatically, there are governs all the second half except the exclamation in the last line. Musically, his becomes increasingly important. Its Z begins in trees and rose, we get his teeth and his transparent gums in the next line, then poppies, handbones, nerves (while soft S swishes through insects, ice, sunlight, shooting) and the last line's closed and illustrations leading up to his father is, where the poet hands the climax over to the baby in another sound: not his but him.

The work of handing over to the baby's vision, instead of the father's, is done mainly by verbs. Apart from is at the end, the only verbs that belong to the father (or poet) are can see and stroke. The baby has loads of exciting verbs: all those active participles looping, breathing, budding, thumping, mating, working, shooting. The baby's verbs are ongoing, all grow and go: they prefigure his life as

227

his eyes follow the light. The father's verbs are receptive and static. His self is closed; the baby's waits on the touchline.

The tone is all play and tenderness (little, stroke it out of him), switching from the wildly imaginative (pink parks of trees, a crest of . . . blood) to the playfully solemn (quite the same as any other, a working-party of white insects), reminding you that imagination, surreality and METAPHOR are things we often use with and for children, when they are learning their own and other people's bodies. One character in the series of books begun by *The Wizard of Oz* is a Glass Cat who keeps boasting that you can see her insides working. But this baby is not of glass, he is flesh and blood.

METAPHOR is a key way of seeing the world at play, with children (the way we enjoy them learning the world), as well as a way in to writing poems. But even METAPHOR is working here to hand over the business of life and like from father to baby. The laughing tenderness is dad's, but freshness and surprise belong to the baby. The father's illustrations (or the METAPHORS by which his poem illuminates the baby) are wrinkled; the baby is visible all in himself. You could say the poem pits the poet's artifice, his like, against the baby's surprising, active, natural verbs, and what he is. In the end, the baby has all the cards. He is transparent and large and this poem is about him. All his father is doing, en-closed and bound in the book of his own self, is writing it.

45. Anne Carson

From HERO

I can tell by the way my mother chews her toast
whether she has had a good night
and is about to say a happy thing
or not.

Not.
She puts her toast down on the side of her plate.
You know you can pull the drapes in that room, she begins.

This is a coded reference to one of our oldest arguments,
from what I call the Rules of Life series.
My mother always closes her bedroom drapes tight before going to
    bed at night.

I open mine as wide as possible.
I like to see everything, I say.
What's there to see?

Moon. Air. Sunrise.
All that light on your face in the morning. Wakes you up.
I like to wake up.

At this point the drapes argument has reached a delta
and may advance along one of three channels.
There is the What You Need Is A Good Night's Sleep channel,

the Stubborn As Your Father channel
and random channel.
More toast? I interpose strongly, pushing back my chair.

These women! says my mother with an exasperated rasp.
Mother has chosen random channel.
Women?

Complaining about rape all the time –
I see she is tapping one furious finger on yesterday's newspaper
lying beside the grape jam.

The front page has a small feature
about a rally for International Women's Day –
have you had a look at the Sears Summer Catalogue?

Nope.
Why, it's a disgrace! Those bathing suits –
cut way up to here! (she points) No wonder!

You're saying women deserve to get raped
because Sears bathing suit ads
have high-cut legs? Ma, are you serious?

Well, someone has to be responsible.
Why should women be responsible for male desire? My voice is
    high.
Oh I see you're one of Them.

One of Whom? My voice is very high. Mother vaults it.
And whatever did you do with that little tank suit you had last year
    the green one?
It looked so smart on you.

The frail fact drops on me from a great height
that my mother is afraid.
She will be eighty years old this summer.

Her tiny sharp shoulders hunched in the blue bathrobe
make me think of Emily Brontë's little merlin hawk Hero
that she fed bits of bacon at the kitchen table when Charlotte
    wasn't around.

So Ma, we'll go – I pop up the toaster
and toss a hot slice of pumpernickel lightly across onto her plate –
visit Dad today? She eyes the kitchen clock with hostility.

(1995)

Poignant, funny, sensuous, daringly original, combining dry wit, erudition and compassion, Carson is a Canadian professor of Greek with a unique gift for turning human precariousness, and the deep wounds and rifts between people which suddenly open up in conversation, into startling lyric. The first woman to win the T.S. Eliot Prize, she has a knack of relating madly different worlds beautifully convincingly. One book reworks an ancient Greek story of a monster, Geryon, killed by Hercules, into a series of poems about a young gay American photographer whose encounter with 'Hercules' is not mortal combat but a love affair. He is wounded by a callous flirt.

What we have here is only half a poem, which is itself part of a sequence with three main subjects. One is grief for the end of an affair. The second is an identificatory obsession with Emily Brontë – her life, her understanding of pain, and her character Heathcliff who (like the poet) loses his love. The third is a visit to the poet's mother, in whose fridge cowers a yoghurt container 'beneath a wily arrangement of leftover blocks of Christmas cake'. The mother, who did not approve of the ex-lover, shoots questions like 'That psychotherapy's not doing you much good is it? You're not getting over him.'

In this passage, the blend between sceptical affection, sparring tenderness and defensive irritation prepares the ground for the poem's second half, when mother and daughter visit father, an ex-pilot in a home for Alzheimer's patients.

Musically, this poem begins by contrasting rhythms. Flowing sentences like the first STANZA (or the tenth, with that Summer Catalogue) are brought up short by bare single words (Not. Moon. Air. Sunrise. Women? Nope.) This contrast of registers and rhythms gets across in sound the poem's main conceptual contrast between the inside – the spirit, what people privately think and feel – and the ritualised, external outside of life: domestic chat and someone chewing toast.

The poem implies that the different Rules of Life operated by mother and daughter correspond to different sides of the spirit–body divide. Short, bare words belong to the poet, prosy flowing rhythms belong to the mother, or describe her. The poet, the I, sleeps with curtains open as wide as possible, likes to wake up, identifies with Emily Brontë who fed wild birds at her plate and loved the open moor. The mother has toast, not a hawk, by her plate. Her exasperated voice and furious finger say she is against high-cut bathing suits, International Women's Day, any exposure: light on your face, sun on bare legs. She prefers tight curtains, closed surfaces, keeping things in; so in the second half her gentle behaviour when she faces the glaring tragedy in her own life, the husband with Alzheimer's, is a heroic and moving surprise.

From the first line, working out by the way [she] chews her toast if she's had a good night, is about to say a happy thing, the poem is really about concern for the mother's inner feelings. These STANZAS are a choreography of intuition about the mother's feelings, from ridicule (Ma, are you serious – echoing furious) to appalled sympathy: my mother is afraid. Soundwise, afraid has been prepared for by the word of the overt argument, drapes, followed by rape, grape, Women's Day, disgrace, raped, into frail, afraid, and the reason for being afraid: eighty. The AY sound belongs with things Ma feels threatened by, including a Day for women who lay grievances bare (about being raped) and swimsuits for women who deserve to get raped. These are the things she pulls drapes against, doesn't want to wake up to.

Both arguments, over drapes and rape, bear on the poet's sexual grief explored in previous poems in the sequence, especially one remembering the sex. Rape? The poet wants to see light, understand – hence open curtains and psychotherapy. Her mother is all for covering up, hence her hostility to therapy and drapes.

From here, the AY sound moves on to plate, and – the climax of this passage which will move the poem on to its second half – today. Ma's hostility, a natural follow-on to one of our oldest arguments, is transferred to the kitchen clock. In family kitchens, hostility, fear and pain routinely happen in disguise. Emotions get displaced on to objects, drapes close over feelings. But the clock also reminds you of the passage of time: those eighty years in another guise.

My mother is afraid. Explaining something in a poem is often disastrous. You lose the tone. The reader follows some taut movement of words and then Clunk! – gets explained to. Carson avoids the clunk by making the explanation 'drop on' the poet, too. We have a hawk's act, dropping from a great height, before the hawk itself: which sits at another kitchen table, caught between two other women bound by affection but separated by opposing Rules of Life. Charlotte Brontë wouldn't let her sister Emily feed Hero at the table.

The soft Fs (frail, fact, from, afraid) separate this STANZA off from the rest. In this domestic maze of scepticism, indignation and old

232

arguments seen in terms of a computer menu, it is a window into soft, clear, inner feeling. The TRANSFERRED EPITHET frail (it's not the fact that's frail but Ma; and also the poet, when she sees how frail her mother really is) leads into visual details: tiny sharp shoulders, hunched, blue bathrobe, little merlin hawk. The explanation introduces the image for the poem's central concept: Hero-ism.

Carson could have called this poem anything. 'Random Channel', 'Slicing the Pumpernickel' or 'Visiting Dad'. This visit occupies the rest of the poem and knits the themes together: the poet mourning her lost love, Ma calming the unrecognising shell of her own lost love, the war pilot; and body versus spirit – for where is spirit, in an Alzheimer's-gripped body?

But by naming the poem after this strange Hero, a hawk at the kitchen table, Carson draws several strands of unlikely heroism together. The wild creature in the kitchen speaks to both mother and father. The mother, with her frailty that keeps going, makes 'wily arrangements' in the fridge and refuses to look at all that light, faces tragedy steadily. The father, a wreck of a man, once free to soar on wings like the hawk, is tied and tilting in a chronic care ward. Hero fits the spirit of them all.

Carson humorises the details: bits of bacon, when Charlotte wasn't around, hot slice of pumpernickel. She makes fun of her own efforts at dealing with all this, giving the toast an insouciant toss, sending up her own narrative with I interpose strongly. Like Ma, she uses external things to symbolise what she is doing. These details are the poem's own 'wily arrangements' for dealing with grief for everyone: for the father, the lover, the mother of eighty, Emily, and the poet herself.

46. Michael Hofmann

CHELTENHAM

The nouveau oil building
spoils the old water town, spook town, old folks' town.
My old parents, like something out of Le Carré,
shuffle round the double Georgian square

tracing figures of eight, endless figures of eight,
defected ice-dance trainers or frozen old spooks,
patinage, badinage,
reminiscence with silences.

Then a family event if ever there was one:
my mother reads my translation of my father,
who hasn't read aloud since his 'event'.
Darkness falls outside. Inside too.

Ted Hughes is in the small audience,
and afterwards asks my father
whether he ever, like an Inuit,
dreamed of his own defeat and death.

My father, who's heard some questions, but never anything
like this, doesn't know Ted Hughes,
perhaps hears 'idiot', gives an indignant no
in his miraculously clear English.

More laps of the marred green,
the pink sky silts down, a November afternoon
by the clock, his last in England.
The days brutally short; a grumpy early night.

(1998)

Born in Germany in 1957, Hofmann came to England at the age of four; he lives in London but also teaches part-time in Florida. His poems combine formal precision and bare language studded with sophisticated, often foreign, words, evoking a wryly ironic tableau in which flatly observed informal details of modern living (like Factor 25 sunblock) surround a self living at an awkward angle to a dry-lit, alienated world: an urban moonscape.

This poem is about coldness and doubles, surface and silence, and is speakingly silent about the pain underneath a <u>family</u>. Hofmann's collection *Acrimony* turned on conflicted relations with the poet's woundingly self-absorbed German novelist father. The collection from which this poem comes revisits that territory with rueful pity, after the father's death. The background people here are all cold – <u>defected ice-dance trainers</u>, <u>frozen</u> spies (<u>spooks</u>, i.e. ghosts), and <u>Inuit</u> Esquimaux – which underpins the chilliness surrounding the father and <u>family</u> at the centre.

Musically, doubleness is everywhere at first: from vowel-sounds to repeated words. The first STANZA starts off with <u>oil</u>, <u>spoils</u>, and <u>shuffle</u>, <u>double</u>; the second has <u>patinage</u>, <u>badinage</u> and <u>reminis-cence</u>, <u>silences</u>. You could draw a figure of eight around the first line of the second STANZA's two <u>figures of eight</u>. Its twin circles would be a sign for all the other doubles: the suggestion of double agents (where ruthlessness is surfaced over by <u>frozen</u> politesse), opposed worlds (Germany and England, East and West, <u>old</u> and nouveau), and the emotional doublet of <u>outside</u> and <u>inside</u>.

The backdrop is <u>Cheltenham</u>, an <u>old town</u> of <u>Georgian</u> façades but also Bonn's counterpart, the provincial HQ of spydom, redolent of <u>Le Carré</u>'s Cold War. The METAPHORS for what the <u>family</u> does as the three of them walk round the <u>double Georgian square</u> are two cold arts, skating and spying. <u>Patinage</u>, related to '*patin*' ('skate') and 'patina', suggests the art of surface manage-ment: espionage. (<u>Family</u> is the real Le Carré's word for his circle of spies.) What comes up instead is <u>badinage</u>: the art of speaking on the surface, of saying things whose meaning does not matter.

In this context of patina, <u>badinage</u> and <u>miraculously clear English</u> (which in thriller tradition is suspicious and gives away the German spy) overlie silent, unexplained inner chaos; maybe even that word the father will come up against later, <u>defeat</u>.

The third STANZA no longer 'circles' the subject but gets into it: it focuses on communication, reading <u>aloud</u>. It ought to tell us most, this STANZA, about what's going on underneath. All the ricocheting inner relationships of the family should open up.

There are two sorts of communication at work in this family event. Translation, comes from the Latin *translatio*, and literally means the process by which something is carried (*latum*) across (*trans*). It is itself a translation: of the Greek word *metaphora*, which means the same thing, and from which we get METAPHOR. In this poem, reading aloud carries words, and their meanings, across to the audience.

My mother reads my translation of my father is an extraordinary line, dense with possibilities of intimate family communication. But the poem puts closed-door quotation marks round the father's 'event' which has stopped him, himself, reading aloud. (In the terminology of a literary festival such as Cheltenham, a reading tends to be called an 'event'.) This double, the event, 'event', has us baffled, keeps us out. What was his 'event' – a euphemism for a stroke? A public trauma or defeat? We end this STANZA in the dark. Darkness . . . outside. Inside too. More doubles.

Halfway through the poem, we move to the audience. The pattern of doubled vowel-sounds picks up again in small, audience; afterwards, asks; father, whether; Inuit, defeat; then this, English; know, no; then marred, last; brutally, grumpy.

So far each STANZA, like each member of this family, has kept its soundworld to itself. Long O dominated the first (nouveau, old, old, old) with variations in OW (town, town, round) and OR (water, Georgian). The second married AY (eight, eight, trainers) with the skate-hiss of skates and ice (endless, ice-dance, spooks, reminiscence, silences). In the third, the OW of outside picked up aloud, the I of inside echoed my, my. In the communication STANZA, a bleed-over began, STANZA to STANZA, world to world. Event, 'event' echoes reminiscence, silences in the second. Now small picks up falls, and OO echoes too in the name of the double to the father himself, Ted Hughes. Two fathers are meeting, the poet's German father and the paterfamilias (till 1999) of British poetry.

But they do not touch (doesn't know Ted Hughes). The father's frozen apartness will never melt. The next STANZA replaces the exotic Inuit by English in the same place in the line. When father does finally speak aloud it is refusal: an indignant no. It is done in a droll way, but perhaps underlines how impenetrable the father's

236

thoughts are, like a spy's. Did he think the question an insult? No one knows: family relations here, as in Le Carré, run on silences.

This STANZA's sounds balance ISS (this, English), EAR (hears, clear), and short A (perhaps, miraculously), which the last STANZA picks up in laps. The formalities of clear Englishness are somehow, for this German writer, an endless treadmill with no emotional resolution. Back to the shuffle round that double square. Colours, like the humour of the confrontation, flare out here on this November afternoon but are marred; recalling the poem's first verb, spoils. As the event was marred: partly by that question of defeat and death which the father did not understand, maybe did not hear properly, and whose famous questioner he did not know.

The final colours behave like mud (silts) and move down. Day ends, and the poem ends (as, the poem implies, the father's life will end) on a fussy, grumpy note: of not really having heard, despite miraculous linguistic control, the voice of creative interest.

47. Pascale Petit

AS IF I WERE WINTER ITSELF

When I enter the hospital where my mother is lying

I will bring a flask of water collected from Lethe
and a flask from the Mnemosyne.

I will sip from each.
This will feel like swallowing shafts of sunlight.

I'll take deep breaths, hungry for canyon air.

A porter will rub fox-fire on my face
for the ride in the luminous lift.

Corridor walls will be translucent,
I'll see the trees imprisoned inside –

blue branches with old wounds as leaves,
red trees with raptor-roots.

Are you ready for the truth?

Ward Sister will ask, releasing
lemon-yellow and saffron butterflies.

They are the first flurry of winter
I'll reply, addressing

Mother's forgetting eye
and her remembering eye.

Then I'll say everything I always wanted to say to her.

The butterflies will mass on her bed,
rays streaming through the window
will wash us both.

Her hands will shake but that won't stop me.

(1998)

238

Born in Paris in 1953, Petit grew up in France, and trained first as a sculptor. Her poems are glittery, concentrated magic realism, exploring faraway landscapes like the Amazon and Tibet. They go into these landscapes for their own sake (she has travelled in the Venezuelan Amazon), but also as METAPHORS for relationships, both in childhood and with lovers.

This poem is about breaking through the constricting walls (see canyon, corridor) of the poet's relationship with a sick mother, by turning a hospital visit into shamanic ritual. Preparations for it include fox-fire rubbed on my face by a porter, a figure which in many myths is the archetypal janitor to some other world. The ritual question is asked by the Ward Sister, another everyday title. But the atmosphere of Jungian myth transforms this figure into the warden-guardian who tests the shaman on his journey.

The rite's purpose is a search for cathartic light: for letting light into the poet (fox-fire, swallowing shafts of sunlight); for seeing through things: luminous lift, walls . . . translucent. The yellow butterflies, the first free things, released after the test question, are the embodiment of light, or of enlightenment. The poet's answer is her password to the new realm; it transforms the butterflies into autumn leaves, like Shelley's leaves in his 'Ode to the West Wind' (quoted above, p. 147).

But these leaves, *the first flurry of winter*, come (presumbly) from the trees growing out of raptor-roots, whose leaves are old wounds. We are talking family trees, the unknowable roots of family trauma. Fox-fire, the phosphorescent glow given off by decaying timber, sums up the underlying connections between light, testing and a diseased tree.

These butterflies, the colour of light, become the sign of change, of approaching winter. Hence the title: As If I Were Winter Itself. When I enter the hospital, the poet writes, she enters on a transformative journey into *the truth*. In doing so, she becomes *winter*, and makes the leaves fall. Echoing Shelley, the blowing leaves are a sign of the mother's coming death.

Trees, leaves, rivers and death as crossing a river by a tree? The earliest Western records of journeys into death are tiny fifth-century BC gold plaques from southern Italy inscribed with Orphic poems, which tell the traveller to pass a tree en route to a river. Falling leaves have been used as an image for the dying in the Greek tradition since Homer; reworked by Sophocles, who lyrically evoked the Thebans' deaths from plague in *Oedipus Rex*, a passage brilliantly reused by Milton as well as Shelley. That image can also be an image of renewal as well of ending. Leaves fall, to make room for next year's leaves. Virgil reworked Sophocles' image in *Aeneid* Book 6, where dead souls mass on the banks of the Styx, desperate to cross to Elysium, like autumn leaves blowing over a river. Virgil used it in the context of not only death but a whole cycle of death and rebirth. As, in Shelley, the 'wingèd seeds' lie 'cold and low' in their 'dark wintry bed' until the spring.

Here, the leaves are only one stage on the image's journey. Butterflies are the main vehicle of all this transformation, and now they are transformed again: massing on her bed as rays streaming through the window.

The word 'window' was once the 'wind's eye', *le vent œil*. This window is the poem's first glimpse of any way in or out: for light, for looking, or for mutual understanding. We began in claustrophobia, with the poet hungry for canyon air. After luminous lift, the walls became translucent: the poet sees what was imprisoned inside. Now there is a window, maybe at last the poet and her mother can see each other, see out of the constrictions of the past. She can say everything I always wanted to say to her; the rays will wash us both. The sought light becomes a healing bath.

But it is a pretty astringent one. Her hands will shake but that won't stop me. The visit is an image of hope for a journey that will change, at the last minute, how mother and daughter see each other: for the rays of that primal relationship. A wish that resonates with anyone who has ever wanted to transform her relationship with a parent while they are still alive. But the process is not all sweetness and light. The poet is *winter*, not spring. *Are you ready for the truth?* suggests imminent mortality as well as a ritual bath. The poet's gift is water from Lethe, river of Forgetting (see Fanthorpe's poem, No. 17), and Mnemosyne, which is both the river of Memory and the personified goddess of Memory, mother of the Muses therefore of art, song and poetry.

For the poem is a gift, too. It is both the remembering and the forgetting of mutual pain; an act of facing up to Mother's forgetting eye / and her remembering eye. But it is all in the future: will is the operative word. Before any healing rapprochement, mother and daughter will both have to both remember and forget.

240

48. Neil Rollinson

GIANT PUFFBALLS

Can I make it home, or do I shit
in the woods? I squat above the moss,
breathing its pheromones, my scrotum
shrunk like a walnut in the cold breeze.
I push quietly in case the dogs
on their morning walks come sniffing.
It drops on the leaves
with a muffled thud, and the smell
is like marzipan, not offensive
as it is against the clinical spruce
of the ordinary bathroom. It steams
in the dirt; the undigested sweetcorn
bright as stones in a brooch.
Coconut milk, rice from Shanghai,
spice from Afghanistan,
all remaking itself; feeding the trees.
I clean myself on a sycamore leaf,
smooth as a grocer's handkerchief.
And then I see them: pregnant
as fish bowls, weird as a hedgeful
of skulls. I pull one out of its hole
gentle as a midwife, palping the domed
head in my hands; I carry it home
on the bus; it sits in my lap
like a baby, plump, bald as an arse,
smelling of milk and cinnamon.

(1995)

Born in Yorkshire in 1960, Rollinson lives in London and his first collection, *A Spillage of Mercury*, caused ripples and raised eyebrows with its focus on bodily fluids and body chemistry. 'Spillage' in the title (followed up in his second, *Spanish Fly*, whose title poem focuses on the chemical formula for an ancient aphrodisiac), points to the theme of sexual chemistry in many of his poems. But what crackles off Rollinson's pages is not obscenity but delight in language: in revelatory ways of seeing the world. He writes amused, rueful, gentle poems, profound, humane, direct and brilliantly imaginative under all the sexy physicality. The poet's overall theme, underneath the body imagery, is the richness and strangeness of the world about him.

The word 'poet' comes from the Greek *poieo*, I make, and you don't need to be a psychoanalyst to remember that shitting is a primal image of making. As Heaney says in an essay, one of the pleasures in life is when I show you my mudpies and you show me yours. No subject matter is 'poetic' in itself: what matters is what you make of it, and you can make poems out of anything. *The Penguin Book of Wine-Making* says you can make wine out of tea leaves or old bootleather. This poem rewrites the nature poem but is also, as its first verb tells you, about the discovery of making and 'remaking'.

It was a risky project. The tone could have turned arch or giggly, or come over as a boringly deliberate effort to shock. Instead it tells you about gentle surprise when the world is stranger and kinder than you expect; about how context changes things (not offensive / as it is against the clinical spruce / of the ordinary bathroom); about bringing home the riches you meet in the world outside.

'Exotic' is how you see, not what. The poet is looking at shit lying on dead leaves in an English copse but, in this English pastoral, the undigested sweetcorn in it glints, with imports from Shanghai and the spice route (last night's curry, presumably), bright as stones in a brooch. Treasure, like puffballs (or babies), turns up when you least expect it, changing your life as poetry changes your vision of the ordinary world.

Rollinson negotiates his way between his subject and the wide-eyed wonder of his theme, through his command of music and image. The sound that resonates all through is the O of home. Between the first home and the last, comes pheromones, scrotum, cold, stones, brooch, coconut, grocer's, bowls, hole, domed. Then back (with extra harmonics from marzipan, bathroom, sweetcorn,

Afghanistan) to <u>home</u>. It is replayed in the last word, <u>cinnamon</u>. The sound holds the poem together like the keynote repeated through a song.

Another dominant vowel, the EE begun by <u>breathing</u>, echoes on in <u>breeze</u>, <u>leaves</u>, <u>steams</u>, <u>feeding</u>, <u>trees</u>, <u>clean</u>, <u>leaf</u>, <u>handkerchief</u>. But it belongs only to the first twenty lines, and stops the minute the puffballs of the title appear: the <u>then</u> I <u>see them</u> moment when the poem moves into a new soundworld. The vowel-chimes round the key word <u>smell</u> (<u>clinical</u>, <u>bowls</u>, <u>hedgeful</u>, <u>skull</u>, <u>pull</u>, <u>gentle</u>) modulate into <u>hole</u> and <u>bowl</u>. Runs of three consonants or vowels are another way the poem holds its lines together: F (<u>sniffing</u>, <u>muffled</u>, <u>offensive</u>), T (<u>shit</u>, <u>squat</u>, <u>walnut</u>); I (<u>bright</u>, <u>rice</u>, <u>spice</u>), short O (<u>moss</u>, <u>dogs</u>, <u>drops</u>).

As the vowels create a particular sonic world for a 'quiet' early morning moment <u>in the woods</u>, so the METAPHORS make a cunningly interwoven image-world. Everything is related imagistically just as (the poem says) everything is related biologically. The puffball at the end is <u>bald as an arse</u>; as the poet's bare arse at the beginning. He pulled a <u>pregnant</u> fungus <u>from its hole</u> like a midwife, reminding you how he himself <u>squatted</u>.

These images 'remake' (see the sixteenth line) opposites into each other, turning human waste to birth and food. The smells of turds and <u>puffballs</u> are <u>marzipan</u>, <u>milk</u>, <u>cinnamon</u>. This is no bathroom reeking of artificial <u>spruce</u> (with its double meaning, both the fir tree and 'cleaned up'), but a real wood; yet its leaf is <u>smooth</u> as a human artefact, <u>a grocer's handkerchief</u>.

Why a <u>grocer's</u> and not, say, a bus conductor's? Because (apart from the long O which knits it into the O sequence) grocers mean food, wrapping up, preparation. All these images talk of taking care: rice 'feeds' <u>the trees</u>, he holds the fungus sitting on his lap <u>like a baby</u>, pushes <u>quietly</u> in case dogs turn up on their <u>morning walks</u>. Dogs, babies, food: all is taken care of, creating a pulse of physical tenderness through the poem.

Paradoxically, he gets this effect by METAPHOR, which remakes things by seeing them as something else. But his METAPHORS have a strange ricochet about them. Puffballs <u>pregnant/as fish bowls</u>? Fish bowls don't get pregnant; but a pregnant tummy is as round as one. You can look into both (via ultrasound scan) and see live things inside. The image sets up a triple relation of puffball, bowl and tummy which underlines the pregnancy motif (tummy, <u>domed head</u>). It reflects back on the startling appearance of the objects in the title – which are themselves oblique visual echoes of the turds the speaker produces along the way. This is the multiple image, these innocent and <u>not offensive</u> puffballs, turds, domes, or babies, which like the poet on the bus you carry <u>home</u> with you: or carry away with you, out of the poem.

49. Liz Lochhead

SORTING THROUGH

The moment she died, my mother's dancedresses
turned from the colours they really were
to the colours I imagine them to be.
I can feel the weight of bumptoed silver shoes
swinging from their anklestraps as she swaggers
up the path towards *her* Dad, light-headed
from airman's kisses. Here, at what I'll have to learn
to call *my father's house*, yes every duster prints her
even more vivid than an Ilford snapshot on some seafront
in a white cardigan and that exact frock.
Old lipsticks. Liquid stockings.
Labels like *Harella, Gor-ray, Berketex*.
And, as I manhandle whole outfits into binbags for Oxfam,
every mote in my eye is a utility mark
and this is useful:
the sadness of dispossessed dresses,
the decency of good coats roundshouldered
in the darkness of wardrobes,
the gravitas of lapels,
the invisible danders of skin fizzing off from them
with all that life that will not neatly end.

(1991)

A popular Scottish poet born in 1947, Lochhead studied at Glasgow School of Art and also writes plays. In all the comedy and straight talk, the themes of politics, love, sex and the sex war, monstrosity, childhood and memory, you feel both drama and art in her work: the swift movement, directness, challenge-and-answer of theatre, the sharp placing and framing of visual detail.

The poem is in two halves. The first sets the scene physically and emotionally: everything in it is still attached to mother. Real, detaching sorting through doesn't begin till the second half, when we see the actual detritus: old lipsticks. The whole thing is a 'sorting through' of emotion as well as things, and the tone is a balancing act between detachment and attachment, dry-eyed practicality and open acceptance of grief.

The first half has three sentences, and each gives a little more of the bereaved poet's emotion. The first begins dramatically (the moment she died, my mother), then instantly focuses on clothes and belongings, not people. Like stage lighting, or opening shots in a film, this poem choreographs human events by concentrating on objects. The first three-line sentence ends with activity in the poet's mind (I imagine them to be); the next (three and a half lines) starts there but moves to her mother's feelings as the poet imagines her, a teenager in the war, light-headed from meeting boyfriends (I can feel to airman's kisses).

The next sentence is that much longer, four and a half lines. It moves from the poet accepting future change (I'll have to learn), to that boundary (seafront) which often stands, in dreams or novels, for the boundary between here and the unknown, between life and death. These lines notch up the emotional register (yes), and yoke the objects of the title activity – domestic paraphernalia which the poet shared with her mother (duster) – with places her mother visited before she was born. Some distances the poet from mother, pulling away from that impulse of identification where the poem began (I imagine, I can feel).

But the poem is marking here what it is mainly about: separation, on several levels, including imagination. Reseeing mother after she dies means separating reality and imagination (see the stress words of the second and third lines, really and imagine), or separating mother as she was, from mother as she is in memory. Even her clothes are turning from how they really were to how the poet imagines them.

This is a post-funeral poem and, though the word colours runs through the early lines, the only colours that appear in it are silver and white, set against a litany of dark abstracts made concrete by clothes in the wardrobe: sadness, decency, darkness, gravitas. If this poem were a photo it would be black and white. It is about coping with the separation of all sorting.

Musically, the halves pivot on the OCK of stockings and frock. The sharp K and short A at the end of the first half, that exact frock, pick up anklestraps, kisses, snapshot, cardigan: sounds that support the dry-eyed tone and toughly practical end of the emotional scale. The second half follows that sharpness with K (lipsticks, liquid, stockings, Berketex) but begins the more fluent L of old, lipsticks, liquid, labels, like, Harella, manhandle, whole, which feeds into labels, invisible, all, life, will, neatly. The S of dancedresses in the first line now becomes the swish of sadness, dispossessed dresses, decency, coats, roundshouldered, darkness, gravitas, lapels, skin, as the poem moves into softer, darker tones, nodding to the Bible and the Latin of church services (mote, gravitas), and then hardens to Z (invisible, fizzing) as the poem moves off, like the mother's life, into air. The first half ends at seafront; the last half ends neatly at the word end while denying the end is ever neat.

Poetry gets its energy from tension between the human imperfections, untidiness and limits it starts from, and its own struggle for formal perfection, for music and cadence. The what versus the how. Physically and emotionally, what's left is untidy: danders of skin, detritus of clothes and emotion. But fizzing off reminds you that the motes of feeling and skin, of a life and personality you loved, are still there, a ganglion of energy, radiating out into the future after darkness and dispossession.

50. David Dabydeen

EL DORADO

Juncha slowly dying of jaundice
Or yellow fever or blight or jumbie or neighbour's spite,
No one knows why he turns the colour of cane.

Small boys come to peep, wondering
At the hush of the death-hut
Until their mothers bawl them out.

Skin flaking like goldleaf
Casts a halo round his bed.
He goes out in a puff of gold dust.

Bathed like a newborn child by the women.
Laid out in his hammock in the yard.
Put out to feel the last sun.

They bury him like treasure,
The coolie who worked two shillings all day
But kept his value from the overseer.

(1988)

Born in Guyana in 1955, Dabydeen studied in Cambridge and London and now teaches at Warwick University. He writes both in Guyanese Creole and Standard English. His first collection, *Slave Song*, had fierce, painful poems about coolie cane-cutters; *Coolie Odyssey* explored East Indian experience in London and the Caribbean.

This poem comes from a collection which revolves round J.M.W. Turner's painting 'The Slave Ship', and voices the stories of the slaves whom Turner painted thrown overboard into the waves, on an unexpectedly stormy voyage. The collection also includes poems in Creole (with translations): the swing between two forms of English creates a dramatic double perspective on two sides of colonial experience.

This one is about the value of an individual life, but that word is held back till the last line where it resonates against the title. Like the dream of gold in 'El Dorado', the value of an individual is kept from the overseer whose exploitative prejudice stops him 'seeing' this man's worth. The poem makes the coolie the one who hides his true value, and so turns that value into a rich secret: kept, like buried treasure, by the community who peep and wonder at Juncha, who bathe, lay out, put out, and finally bury him. In their care for him, they demonstrate the value of valuing; something the overseer (someone who 'sees' only what is 'over', i.e. on the surface) will never know.

The point of El Dorado is not only the dream of gold but the value of dream. Its treasure is an image of a hope that we'll find something surpassingly precious in our lives. And the deepest humanity is finding that in other people. This dream begins with childhood wondering at other people's lives, including the hush of their death. These mothers instil that wondering in their children; the overseer cannot see it.

The gold imagery moves from colour (yellow fever, colour of cane) to goldleaf and gold dust which link gold to life (last sun) and sacredness (a halo round him like the gold balloon around saints' heads on icons). With a whiff of rebirth (newborn child), Juncha is becoming a saint, while the overseer's cash currency (two shillings, what a coolie is 'worth' per day) rings hollow against the reverence and generosity (treasure stored up biblically in heaven or buried in earth) which the poem sets up as its gold standard of valuing a person.

Vowelwise, the poem is held together by short U (Juncha,

249

jumbie, one, colour, come, wondering, hush, hut, mothers, puff, dust, sun); which is echoed in the second syllable of a whole wave of two-syllabled words. From first to last word, one man to another, we hear Juncha, fever, neighbour's, colour, wonder[ing], mothers, treasure, overseer. The first STANZA, which sets the scene (and lays out, as it were, the dying man), is a close cell of private sounds. Long I (dying, blight, spite, why), the J of Juncha, jaundice, jumbie. But it also sets up sounds that resonate through the rest of the poem, just as its images of dying and yellowness move on too, to be transformed into death, community and gold. The T of spite is picked up in hut and out, a word which becomes increasingly important through the poem (goes out, laid out, put out).

The death – this 'going out' – happens in the central STANZA. The gentle L of slowly, yellow, blight and colour carries on to small, until, bawl, flaking like goldleaf, halo, gold, child, laid, feel, last, shillings, all and value. The long A of cane echoes through flaking, halo, bathed and day: Juncha turns the colour of the stuff he worked with all day, which the overseer gets money for producing. He ended as yellow as cane, as gold, yet his real worth was hidden: overseen and overlooked.

But I suspect there's other treasure buried in here too. I'd say that behind Put out to feel the last sun stands Wilfred Owen on an English soldier dying in a foreign field: 'Move him into the sun./ Always it woke him, even in France'. Behind the gold imagery for the undervalued man may shine Gerard Manley Hopkins' image of the 'grandeur of God', which 'will flame out' from the ordinary world 'like shining from shook foil'.

Even if I'm only imagining the presence here of these particular nuggets from the body of earlier English poetry – what Keats and a famous anthology called 'realms of gold' and a 'golden treasury' – the poem's politics entail using 'English' poetry, its diction, techniques and voice, to point up the emptiness in the values of those to whom it nominally or originally belonged (compare Walcott's poem, No. 22) – the values of those who 'oversee', overlook what is really valuable; those who turned both cane and human lives into money, i.e. gold. Not into poems, which radiate out from individual sensibility into compassion for other people.

51. Susan Wicks

ON BEING EATEN BY A SNAKE

Knowing they are not poisonous,
I kneel on the path to watch it
between poppies, by a crown of nasturtiums,
the grey-stripe body almost half as long
as my own body, the formless black head
rearing, swaying, the wide black lips seeming
to smile at me. And I see
that the head is not a head,
the slit I have seen as mouth
is not a mouth, the frilled black under-lips
not lips, but another creature dying; I see
how the snake's own head is narrow and delicate,
how it slides its mouth up and then back
with love, stretched to this shapelessness
as if with love, the sun stroking
the slug's wet skin as it hangs
in the light, resting, so that even the victim
must surely feel pleasure, the dark ripple
of neck that is not neck lovely
as the slug is sucked backwards
to the belly that is not belly, the head
that is merely head
shrinking to nameable proportions.

(1994)

Born in 1947, Wicks grew up in Kent and studied French; she has written powerfully, in several genres, on the body, childhood, domestic relationships, sex, illness and death, in a visionary style that combines silkily woven word-textures with oddly astringent transitions between thought and image.

This poem, from a collection called *Open Diagnosis* whose cover showed a 'magnetic resonance image' of the poet's own brain, ended a sequence of poems which charted a nightmare diagnosis of multiple sclerosis and the poet's response to this. Earlier poems in the sequence speak of the poet's 'flora and fauna', her own body cells and chemicals, in terms of poison ('cholinesterase, multiple sclerosis, poison oak'), and imagine the blindness and disability to come in titles like 'When I Am Blind I Shall', and 'A Disabled Toilet Is'. But where this poem is in the collection, things come suddenly okay. This poem is reprieve. She can resee the future free of threat. She is looking at a snake that she knows is <u>not</u>, after all, <u>poisonous</u>. The poem ends on an image of a snake's head <u>shrinking</u> like her own destiny <u>to nameable proportions</u>.

The poem displaces illness and death on to <u>another creature dying</u>. The poet is no longer the object of X-ray and diagnosis, but observes a death, and reinterprets not only what she is looking at but the way she sees herself in the world. She kneels, not as a <u>victim</u>, but to <u>watch</u>, <u>see</u>, and rediagnose what she is seeing. <u>I see / that the head is not a head, / the slit I have seen as mouth / is not a mouth</u>. The poem celebrates escape from danger with the <u>sun stroking / the slug's wet skin as it hangs / in the light</u>, resting, so that even the <u>victim / must surely feel pleasure</u>. Death is someone else's sliding reversal of birth, a slug <u>sucked backwards / to the belly that is not belly</u>.

The point is the <u>not</u>: that things are <u>not</u> as you have seen them. From the seventh line to the end we hear a long denial of danger: <u>not</u>, <u>not</u>, <u>not</u>, <u>no</u>, <u>no</u>. Something that could be horrible happens in a setting of pain-killing or triumphal flowers (<u>between poppies, by a crown of nasturtiums</u>), in sensuous words filled with liquid consonants (<u>frilled</u>, <u>narrow</u>, <u>delicate</u>, <u>dark ripple</u>) and slow-motion present participles (<u>knowing</u>, <u>rearing</u>, <u>swaying</u>, <u>seeming</u>, <u>dying</u>, <u>stroking</u>, <u>resting</u>) that turn carnivorous death into a dreamy caress. There are subcutaneously Christian images too. A <u>crown of nasturtiums</u> rather than thorns; death as a mouth sliding <u>up and then back / with love</u>, stretched . . . / <u>as if with love</u>; a sacrificial <u>victim</u> who <u>hangs / in the light</u>.

252

The ambiguous relation between the slug-and-snake drama and the poet's persona begins with the title and is underlined early on by the mention of her <u>body</u> which <u>the grey-stripe body</u> is <u>almost half as long</u> as. This <u>body</u> of hers is the body shown under threat in the picture on the collection's cover, and in the twenty-seven poems that precede this one, whose titles image a future of multiple sclerosis: 'How to Become Invisible', 'Walking too Far Into the Island', 'Growing Cold'. The title of this one, 'On Being Eaten By a Snake', with its seventeenth-century echoes (like Richard Love-lace's 'To Lucasta: On Going to the Wars' in which it is in fact the poet himself, not Lucasta, who is 'going' away to war), sneakily makes you think this poem is the culmination of her progress into death. But she is very precisely <u>not</u> being eaten. 'On being eaten' in fact means 'On something other than me – a slug – being eaten'; or 'On not being eaten'. For the poet, this is deliverance, not death. There is <u>another creature dying</u>, and the poem is turning the spectacle of that death into relief, into <u>pleasure</u>.

Soundwise, the EE of the title verb <u>eaten</u> reels through the poem in <u>kneel</u>, <u>between</u>, <u>seeming</u>, <u>me</u>, <u>see</u>, <u>seen</u>, <u>creature</u>, <u>see</u>, <u>even</u>, <u>feel</u>. But mainly this poem works by movement. The first seven lines with their balancing vowels (<u>knowing/own</u>, <u>path/half</u>, <u>wide/smile</u>) are complete to themselves. We still think the poet is doomed. She is kneeling <u>on the path</u> like Christ as He stumbled, smiled at by <u>wide black lips</u>.

The turnaround, the release from threat, comes at the CAESURA, the pause in the seventh line: <u>to smile at me. [STOP] And I see</u>. From here on the tension unravels. The next five lines, ending in <u>dying</u>, give the possibility of rediagnosis; then the truth of things comes snaking down the lines smoothly without a break. And all through, the danger word, <u>snake</u>, only mentioned in the title, is never heard.

52. Thom Gunn

STILL LIFE

I shall not soon forget
The greyish-yellow skin
To which the face had set:
Lids tight: nothing of his,
No tremor from within,
Played on the surfaces.

He still found breath, and yet
It was an obscure knack.
I shall not soon forget
The angle of his head,
Arrested and reared back
On the crisp field of bed,

Back from what he could neither
Accept, as one opposed,
Nor, as a life-long breather,
Consentingly let go,
The tube his mouth enclosed
In an astonished O.

(1992)

Gunn, born in 1929, is a major figure in twentieth-century poetry. His magical formal skill is balanced by profound responsible emotion and supple, dark, sexy intelligence with a gently wry smile at the bottom. He used to be paired with Ted Hughes (they overlapped at Cambridge) but he followed a more unconventional route and moved to California in 1954.

There are not many well-known gay male British poets: there are more gay women. Being gay was an important factor in Gunn's move to California before homosexuality was decriminalised in Britain. In the thirties, Auden wrote love poems which readers could interpret as heterosexual. By the fifties, society and what it wanted poetry to do had changed. Currently in the UK (unlike the US), high-profile male gay writing seems to run more to prose. Apart from Gunn's collection *The Man with Night Sweats*, from which this poem comes, the other big prize-winning AIDS-related collection published in Britain (Mark Doty's *My Alexandria*) is American. Gunn is a major star; as a homosexual poet he was also a trailblazing star, and is one of the most dignified, lyrical, intelligent, moving, musical voices we have.

Rhythmically, this poem is all about stopping: about where and how you do it. It has a short, three-beat line. The first three are ENJAMBED: the run-ons set up an expectation of flow, but then lids tight followed by a deafening CAESURA, and the new rhythm of nothing of his (stressing noth- and his), bring you up short. This is all about flow which is stopped. To make the point, the next lines are end-stopped. For this poem's rhythm is also its message: start-stop for a poem about breath stopping until there is nothing.

The poem opens with I, echoed by tight. I is kept out from contact with the inside by these lids – and yet there is an I on the inside, too: in tight. I faces a skin and a face introduced by the, not his; as if the dying man is already an object, a still life. But the man they belong to is both still and (as in the title) still alive, inside. There is nothing on the surfaces: but in the second STANZA he is there in that central act, of 'finding' breath.

Immediately you get a check (that comma); then the effect of stopping is cancelled by ENJAMBEMENT after the qualification and yet. Paradoxically, what runs on into the next line is a denial of continued breath. Obscure knack makes you think of breathing as a skill, something that can be acquired and lost. Then you start again (as the breathing starts and stops) with the repeated first line and a flow of lines lightly end-stopped with commas. The head arrested and reared back (like a reined-in horse, still subtly around in the next line's <u>field</u>) ends with the word repeated at the start of the last verse (and echoed in the first syllable of <u>accept</u>). <u>He</u> is going <u>back</u>, in lines whose rhythm is start and stop, with breaks at <u>accept</u>, <u>opposed</u>, <u>nor</u>, <u>breather</u>.

This jerky-breath effect lasts until the words <u>consentingly let go</u>. Only after that concept has been aired do you regain the easy ENJAMBEMENT flow, describing the object (<u>the tube</u>) which <u>what</u> (in the last STANZA's first line) referred to. This <u>tube</u> is his last to-and-fro-channel to the world. <u>O</u>, the shape of his lips, comes over as the sound of his final sigh, but also resolves the tube into another channel of communication.

This O is the last letter of fellatio, too. The idea of dying as sex, orgasm as death, goes back to Elizabethan love poetry (where 'I die' is a double entendre for 'I'm coming') and the Romantics: as in the *Liebestod* duo of Wagner's *Tristan*.

The poem's title has a double meaning. There is <u>still life</u> here, just; but <u>still life</u> painting is called *nature morte* in French. Like Holocaust narratives, AIDS poems have a foreknown end. It is just a question of how. By presenting the dying man as <u>a life-long</u> <u>breather</u> who finds it hard to give up this <u>obscure knack</u>, the poem keeps emotionally as still as any <u>still life</u>. The short lines say this is not about rousing emotion but reining it in: like that invisible horse and difficult breath.

In Gunn's *Collected Poems* this poem faces another in which the friend has died and returns in a dream to console the poet. 'I'm all right now', he says. 'How like you to be kind', thinks the poet; but then, since the dream is his own imagining: 'And, yes, how like my mind / To make itself secure.' That poem is partly about the way his mind comforts itself. This follow-on poem in its own way does that too: in its music, the stable relating of rhyme (each STANZA follows the same pattern ABACBC), and the way it shares the watching and living of death.

Iris Murdoch argued that Art should not 'console', but, whether you are making it or responding to it, art is one of the few things which can help us find a shape for pain so we bear it better. In the quietly <u>arrested</u> relationship here, in the movement from <u>I</u> (the poem's first letter) to <u>O</u> (its last letter and his friend's last sigh), Gunn creates a shareable form for the last <u>astonished</u> communication between one person and a dying other.

GLOSSARY OF
POETIC TERMS

ALEXANDRINE: A line of twelve syllables (standard metre in French poetry from the sixteenth century as the IAMBIC PENTAMETER is for English poetry), which in English is felt as six IAMBIC FEET: it becomes an IAMBIC HEXAMETER.

ANAPAEST: A unit of three syllables: *short short long* (like the word 'anapaest' itself), if you are working in terms of syllable-length as in GREEK VERSE, or two unstressed followed by a stressed syllable if you are talking in terms of stress. No one knows what the word originally referred to but it meant something like 'beaten back': because the DACTYL was the main thing, an ANAPAEST was a DACTYL backwards.

BI-SYLLABLE: A word of two syllables.

BLANK VERSE: Technically, this could mean any unrhymed verse that has (unlike FREE VERSE) a metre. But it's nearly always used to mean unrhymed IAMBIC PENTAMETER, see pp. 14–15.

BLOCK; BLOCK FORM: A poem without STANZAS.

CAESURA: A rhythmic 'pause' in a line: the word derives from the Latin for 'cut'. You make it by the way you pattern the metre, by phrasing, or by punctuation.

CONSONANT RHYMES: Rhymes in which the last consonant is the only thing that rhymes; the vowels don't. Strictly, this consonant should be at the end of the last stressed syllable. If the rhyme is FEMININE, the unaccentuated syllables should be identical (as in 'ready/study', 'little/scuttle', 'dizzy/easy'). You can vary the technique to create imperfect CONSONANT RHYME, as in 'tendrils/smile'. See No. 23, and p. 16–17.

COUPLET: A pair of lines that belong together in some way. They may be a two-line STANZA; or a 'rhyming COUPLET' which may or may not be set off as a separate part of its poem.

DACTYL: A metric unit of three syllables: *long short short*, or stressed syllable followed by two unstressed (as in 'asteroid'; 'unctuous'). This is extant Western poetry's first metre, from the time (eighth century BC) when the Homeric epics were put together. It was called *dactulos*, finger, a Greek word which is itself a DACTYL, because it referred to the finger's three bones counting upwards from your hand: *long short short*. In the transition from classical Latin poetry (which followed Greek rules) to modern European languages, the DACTYL lost its position as reigning unit to the more vernacular-feeling IAMB: especially in English, which has been called a naturally IAMBIC language.

DACTYLIC: A line or rhythm dominated by DACTYLS.

EIGHT AND SIX: The classic proportion of (one form of) a SONNET, an OCTET of eight lines followed by a SESTET of six. (The other main form is three QUATRAINS followed by a COUPLET.)

END-RHYME: A word at the end of a line that rhymes with one or more other line-endings.

ENJAMBEMENT; ENJAMBED: The carry-over of a phrase into the next line; a line or compound word carried over.

FEMININE ENDING; FEMININE RHYME: Technically, a word of two syllables whose last syllable is unstressed ('early', 'gremlin', 'learning'), and the rhyme between such words (relating those words to, for example, 'burly', 'Kremlin', 'turning'). I use it more widely (p. 144), to refer to words of three or four syllables, in which the last two syllables (if not the last three) are unstressed (as in 'feminine' itself); and a rhyme between such words ('fawningly/yawningly'; 'derogative/prerogative'; 'friary/diary').

FOOT; FEET: The basic metric unit, see pp. 14–15. Like music, poetry is all about movement (see the 'running' and 'pouring' derivations for the words TROCHEE and SPONDEE), so its units of movement are FEET. They work like musical bars, one BEAT in each, so a five-FOOT line is also a five-BEAT line, an IAMBIC PENTAMETER. As if you touched your own foot on the ground of it five times, as you ran or danced it through. A FOOT may be made of any rhythmic unit, DACTYL, ANAPAEST, SPONDEE, TROCHEE or IAMB, but only has one stressed syllable.

FREE VERSE: Verse that does not depend on a system of END-RHYMES (though it may rhyme as much as it likes, in any place in the line), and does not necessarily stick to any one metre. Not the same as BLANK VERSE, which is in metre.

GREEK VERSE: Of the verse that has survived, the first written poems are the two epics of Homer (who used DACTYLIC HEXAM-ETERS), the *Iliad* and *Odyssey*. After epic came sung lyrics (e.g. by Sappho): highly complex, brilliantly worked-out in metrical pat-terns, but vivid, direct and personal in subject and tone. In classical times (fifth century BC) the Greek tragic poets used mainly IAMBIC HEXAMETERS for dialogue and complex lyric metres for the choral songs. Amazingly, our own system of referring to syllable-pattern, beat, FEET, derives from the classification worked out by later but still ancient Greek scholars to analyse the metrics of these writers: the DACTYLS and TROCHEES of Nos 12 or 31 in poems addressing today's pubs and marital relations put us directly in touch with Homer and Sophocles.

260

HEROIC COUPLET: A rhyming pair of IAMBIC PENTAMETERS.

HEXAMETER: A six-FOOT line in any metre.

IAMB: A metric unit of two syllables: *short long*, or unstressed syllable followed by a stressed, as in 'again'. In Greek, the 'i' of IAMBOS is short like the 'i' of 'in', so the English word IAMB should sound like the rhythm it refers to. In GREEK VERSE, the IAMB was felt to be closer to ordinary speech than DACTYLS, TROCHEES and ANAPAESTS; and it is felt to be the natural unit of English verse.

IAMBIC; IAMBIC FOOT, FEET: A line or sequence of lines which uses IAMBS (or their metrical equivalents) as the basic unit of its FEET.

IAMBIC PENTAMETER: the five-beat line that has dominated English poetry since the sixteenth century. It is often hard not to think in it even in prose. But it does not have only IAMBS in it: there may be no actual IAMBS in any given line of IAMBIC PENTAMETER at all. Just as you can vary the pattern within each four-crotchet bar (say, semi-quavers, dotted crotchet and quaver, mimins, or a rest), so an IAMBIC FOOT can be made of other units (a DACTYL, ANAPAEST, TROCHEE or SPONDEE) instead. IAMBIC PENTAMETER is an astonishingly flexible thing: so flexible some people have argued it does not exist. Why call a line with no IAMBS, an IAMBIC PENTAMETER? What it comes down to in the end is feel: how we feel the turns and hesitations, checks and flow, of the PENTAMETER. IAMBIC PENTAMETER is in our bones, and affects how we feel our language.

MASCULINE ENDING; MASCULINE RHYME: A word ending in a single stressed syllable ('cat', 'along'); a rhyme between two such syllables ('mat', 'strong').

METAPHOR: A word or phrase which describes an object different in kind from that referred to by the word it describes, which therefore colours that word with the resonances of the METAPHOR word. In the phrase 'the curtain of night', the METAPHOR 'curtain' comes from a different world and brings all its potential associations (hiddenness, softness, theatricality, etc) to bear upon the other idea, 'night'. Also the principle of joining two words in such an application. METAPHOR comes from the Greek verb *metapherein*: to carry across, transport something from one place to another. The Latin word *translatio* (see No. 46) is an exact translation of the Greek word *metaphora*; at one level, translation and METAPHOR do the same thing: connect two worlds. See Nos 9, 11 and 44.

METONYMY: Using one word to stand for another, usually larger, more general thing: 'fond of the bottle' for fond of drink; 'fur and feathers' for animals and birds.

MONOSYLLABLE: A word made of a single syllable.

OCTET: A STANZA or group of eight lines; also called an octave.

PENTAMETER: A five-FOOT line in any metre (but in English normally IAMBIC).

QUATRAIN: STANZA of four lines, the commonest and most basic STANZA form in European poetry.

RHYME-SEQUENCE; RHYMING-SCHEME, RHYME-SCHEME: A regular pattern for END-RHYMES. One way of representing such a pattern is by letters, each standing for one rhyme position. So ABCABC represents six lines: the first end-word rhymes with the fourth, the second with the fifth, the third with the sixth. If not all end-words rhyme, you mark the ones that don't with X. So XAXB XAXB stands for two four-line STANZAS whose second and fourth lines rhyme with each other across the space between, but the first and third don't. (See p. 84 for an example.)

SESTET: A STANZA or poem of six lines.

SESTINA: An unrhymed BLANK VERSE form (six six-line STANZAS plus a three-liner at the end), invented by a thirteenth-century troubadour, which has come back in modern times. Heaney, for instance, has done wonders with it. Instead of END-RHYMES you repeat the end-words from each line of the first STANZA in a different order in subsequent STANZAS.

SONNET: Traditionally, any fourteen-line poem written in rhymed IAMBIC PENTAMETER, rhymed either as an OCTET and SESTET, or four QUATRAINS with a COUPLET at the end. Most SONNETS changed emotional or intellectual direction after eight lines in what is sometimes called the TURN. Modern SONNETS have played with and challenged all these 'rules'. They do not necessarily rhyme, use IAMBIC PENTAMETER, keep to fourteen lines, or have a TURN at all; or they put their TURN in other places. What they keep is the feel or spirit of the SONNET as a kind of concentratedly reflective poetic box. (See pp. 62–63, 91–93, 194–196.)

SPONDAIC: A line or rhythm made of or dominated by SPONDEES.

SPONDEE: A unit of two syllables: *long long* (from the Greek verb 'to pour', suggesting something 'poured out' for libation) or if you think in terms of accent, two stressed syllables.

STANZA: A group of lines (sometimes called a 'verse') that belong together, set off from other similar units within a poem by spacing.

The word is Italian for 'room': it suggests an image of the poem as a house with several rooms.

SYLLABICS, SYLLABIC VERSE: Verse in which you count the number of actual syllables in a line (whereas in metred verse what matters is how many stressed syllables, i.e. beats, there are in the line). There may be any number of stresses in it. (See pp. 136, 214.)

TERZA RIMA: An Italian form in interlocking three-line STANZAS. The first and third lines rhyme, the second rhymes with the first and third lines of the next STANZA, and so on.

TRANSFERRED EPITHET: An adjective that really describes one noun in the passage, which used to qualify another, e.g. 'frail' in No. 45 and 'wincing' in No. 16.

TRI-SYLLABLE: A word of three syllables.

TROCHAIC: A line or rhythm made of or dominated by TROCHEES.

TROCHEE: A unit of two syllables, *long short* or stressed syllable followed by unstressed (as in 'softly'). The word means 'running', or 'belonging to the dance', and the unit was an important element in archaic GREEK VERSE, especially lyric (which was usually danced as well as sung). In the Renaissance, when classically educated poets were turning quantitative Greek metres loose on stress-loving English, Philip Sidney pioneered TROCHAIC SONNETS. Till then, TROCHAIC rhythms had mainly appeared in English in popular verse, songs, or nursery rhymes.

TURN: The point where a SONNET changes direction of thought, atmosphere, or feeling. This often happens after the OCTET, but not always; and some SONNETS do not have one anyway.

ZEUGMA: A 'yoking' device, which brings together, often comically, disparate things, and often exploits a verb's power of being used in very different contexts (like 'have on', in the sentence 'Madonna had on the radio and a Gucci bra').

PERMISSIONS

Ruth Padel and Chatto & Windus would like to thank the poets and publishers for permission to reprint the following. Unless stated otherwise, permission is granted by the publisher in brackets:

FLEUR ADCOCK 'A Surprise in the Peninsula': from *Poems 1960–2000* (2000) (Bloodaxe Books); PATIENCE AGBABI 'Transformatrix': from *Transformatrix* (2000) (Payback Press, an imprint of Canongate Books); GILLIAN ALLNUTT 'Barclays Bank and Lake Baikal': from *Lintel* (2001) (Bloodaxe Books); MONIZA ALVI 'Map of India': from *Carrying My Wife* (2000) (Bloodaxe Books); SIMON ARMITAGE 'The Fox': from *Selected Poems* (1997) (Faber & Faber); COLETTE BRYCE 'Buster': from *The Heel of Bernadette* (2000) (Picador, an imprint of Macmillan); ANNE CARSON 'Hero' (forty-five-line excerpt): from *Glass, Irony, and God* (1995) (New Directions Publishing); EILEAN NÍ CHUILLEANÁIN 'Swineherd': from *The Second Voyage* (1986) (Gallery Press); DAVID DABYDEEN 'El Dorado': from *Turner, New and Selected Poems* (1994) (Jonathan Cape, an imprint of the Random House Group); FRED D'AGUIAR 'Mama Dot Warns Against An Easter Rising': from *Mama Dot* (1985) (Chatto & Windus, an imprint of the Random House Group); NUALA NÍ DHOMHNAILL 'Ceist na Teangan' ('The Language Issue'), translated by Paul Muldoon: from *Pharaoh's Daughter* (1990) (Gallery Press); MICHAEL DONAGHY 'Liverpool': from *Dances Learned Last Night: Poems 1975–1995* (2000) (Picador, an imprint of Macmillan); MAURA DOOLEY '1847': from *Kissing a Bone* (1996) (Bloodaxe Books); CAROL ANN DUFFY 'Prayer': from *Mean Time* (1993) (Anvil Press); HELEN DUNMORE 'The Surgeon Husband': from *Bestiary* (1997) (Bloodaxe Books); PAUL DURCAN 'Self-Portrait, Nude With Steering Wheel': from *A Snail in My Prime* (1993) (Harvill Press); U.A. FANTHORPE 'Rising Damp': from *Standing To* (1982) (Peterloo Poets); PAUL FARLEY 'Keith Chegwin as Fleance': from *The Boy From the Chemist Is Here to See You* (1999) (Picador, an imprint of Macmillan); VICKI FEAVER 'Judith': from *The Handless Maiden* (1994) (Jonathan Cape, an imprint of the Random House Group); ELAINE FEINSTEIN 'Rosemary in Provence': from *Daylight* (1997) (Carcanet Press); LAVINIA GREENLAW 'Invention': from *A World Where News Travelled Slowly* (1997) (Faber &

Faber); **THOM GUNN** 'Still Life': from *Collected Poems* (1993) (Faber & Faber); **SEAMUS HEANEY** 'The Skunk': from *New Selected Poems* (1990) (Faber & Faber); **RITA ANN HIGGINS** 'Some People': from *Sunny Side Plucked: New and Selected Poems* (1996) (Bloodaxe Books); **SELIMA HILL** 'The World's Entire Wasp Population': *Violet* (1997) (Bloodaxe Books); **MICHAEL HOFMANN** 'Cheltenham': from *Approximately Nowhere* (1999) (Faber & Faber); **KATHLEEN JAMIE** 'Skeins o Geese': from *The Queen of Sheba* (1994) (Bloodaxe Books); **JACKIE KAY** 'In My Country': from *Other Lovers* (1993) (Bloodaxe Books); **JAMES LASDUN** 'Eve': from *Landscape with Chainsaw* (2001) (Jonathan Cape, an imprint of the Random House Group); **LIZ LOCH-HEAD** 'Sorting Through': from *Penguin Modern Poets Vol. 4* (1995) (Reproduced by permisson of the Rod Hall Agency); **MICHAEL LONGLEY** 'Ceasefire': from *Selected Poems* (1998) (Jonathan Cape, an imprint of the Random House Group); **SARAH MAGUIRE** 'Spilt Milk': from *Spilt Milk* (1991) (Secker & Warburg) (Reproduced by permission of Sarah Maguire); **DEREK MAHON** 'Courtyards in Delft': from *Collected Poems* (1999) (Gallery Press); **GLYN MAXWELL** 'The Breakage': from *The Breakage* (1998) (Faber & Faber); **MEDBH MCGUCKIAN** 'The Butterfly Farm': from *The Flower Master and Other Poems* (1993) (Gallery Press); **PAUL MULDOON** 'Quoof': from *Collected Poems* (1989) (Faber & Faber); **LES MURRAY** 'On Home Beaches': from *Learning Human: New Selected Poems* (2001) (Carcanet Press); **SEAN O'BRIEN** 'Rain': from *Selected Poems 1977–2001* (2002) (Picador) (Reproduced by permission of Sean O'Brien); **SHARON OLDS** 'I Go Back to May 1937': from *The Sign of Saturn* (1991) (Secker & Warburg, an imprint of the Random House Group); **DON PATERSON** 'Imperial': from *God's Gift to Women* (1997) (Faber & Faber); **TOM PAULIN** 'Klee/Clover': from *Walking a Line* (1994) (Faber & Faber); **PASCALE PETIT** 'As If I Were Winter Itself': from *Heart of a Deer* (1998) (Enitharmon Press); **PETER REDGROVE** 'The Visible Baby': from *The Moon Disposes, Poems 1954–1987* (1987) (Secker & Warburg) (Reproduced by permission of David Higham Associates); **CHRISTOPHER REID** 'Tin Lily': from *Katerina Brac* (1985) (Faber & Faber); **NEIL ROLLINSON** 'Giant Puffballs': from *A Spillage of Mercury* (1996) (Jonathan Cape, an imprint of the Random House Group); **JO SHAPCOTT** 'Mrs Noah: Taken After the Flood': from *Her Book* (1999) (Faber &

Faber); **CHARLES SIMIC** 'Two Dogs': from *Frightening Toys* (1995) (Faber & Faber); **MATTHEW SWEENEY** 'The Hat': from *The Bridal Suite* (1997) (Jonathan Cape, an imprint of the Random House Group); **DEREK WALCOTT** 'Omeros' (fifteen-line excerpt): from *Omeros* (1990) (Faber & Faber); **SUSAN WICKS** 'On Being Eaten By a Snake': from *Open Diagnosis* (1994) (Faber & Faber); **C.K. WILLIAMS** 'Harm': from *New and Selected Poems* (1995) (Bloodaxe Books); **JOHN HARTLEY WILLIAMS** 'John Bosnia': from *Double* (1994) (Bloodaxe Books) (Reproduced by permission of John Hartley Williams).

INDEX OF POETS